The pop art and psychedelic movements of the late '60s were embodied in this ad for 1969 Javelins, offered in the eye-popping colors of Big Bad Blue, Big Bad Green, and Big Bad Orange. The glamorous Pucci outfits were not included.

▶ This 1957 Oldsmobile ad illustrates how midcentury cars were marketed as lifestyle extensions and status symbols. The elegantly casual woman, clad in the latest fashion, admires her new Ninety-Eight from a scoop chair, through a floor-to-ceiling glass wall, as the headline proclaims "Lucky you!" The perfect embodiment of modernist upward mobility.

Color, Fashion, Style and the Midcentury Automobile

JEFF STORK & TOM DOLLE

Foreword by
SUSAN SKARSGARD

SCHIFFER
PUBLISHING

4880 Lower Valley Road • Atglen, PA 19310

▶ This ad for the 1955 Dodge features an incredible surrealist Salvador Dalí–inspired mural, admired by a young couple of discriminating good taste. In the foreground, a model sports the latest fashion—a tweed suit with pencil skirt, introduced in 1954 by Christian Dior.

This book is dedicated to **Modernism Week Palm Springs**, *for becoming the perfect forum to relive the glamour of midcentury modernism. And to* **Great Autos**, *Southern California's largest LGBTQ car club, for the connection to other enthusiasts who share our love of the glamour, style, and fashion of the midcentury automobile. And, last, to the many unsung designers, engineers, artists, stylists, and marketing professionals who created these glamorous machines that still cast a spell so many years later.*

Other Schiffer Books on Related Subjects:
Damsels in Design, Constance Smith, ISBN 978-0-7643-5435-9
Luxury Design for Living, Steve Huyton, ISBN 978-0-7643-5421-2
Auto-tecture, Andreas K. Vetter, ISBN 978-0-7643-4848-8

Copyright © 2022 by Jeff Stork and Tom Dolle

Library of Congress Control Number: 2021942738

All rights reserved. No part of this work may be reproduced or used in any form or by any means—graphic, electronic, or mechanical, including photocopying or information storage and retrieval systems—without written permission from the publisher.

The scanning, uploading, and distribution of this book or any part thereof via the Internet or any other means without the permission of the publisher is illegal and punishable by law. Please purchase only authorized editions and do not participate in or encourage the electronic piracy of copyrighted materials.

"Schiffer," "Schiffer Publishing, Ltd.," and the pen and inkwell logo are registered trademarks of Schiffer Publishing, Ltd.

Edited by Karla Rosenbusch
Designed by Tom Dolle
Type set in Sentinel
ISBN: 978-0-7643-6390-0
Printed in India

Published by Schiffer Publishing, Ltd.
4880 Lower Valley Road
Atglen, PA 19310
Phone: (610) 593-1777; Fax: (610) 593-2002
E-mail: Info@schifferbooks.com
Web: www.schifferbooks.com

For our complete selection of fine books on this and related subjects, please visit our website at www.schifferbooks.com. You may also write for a free catalog. Schiffer Publishing's titles are available at special discounts for bulk purchases for sales promotions or premiums. Special editions, including personalized covers, corporate imprints, and excerpts, can be created in large quantities for special needs. For more information, contact the publisher.

We are always looking for people to write books on new and related subjects. If you have an idea for a book, please contact us at proposals@schifferbooks.com.

Contents

◀ *Glamorous couple is reflected in the freestanding pod headlights of the Virgil Exner–designed 1961 Imperial, from a Chrysler Corporation brochure.*

Endpaper Pattern: *Sample from the General Motors Archive of Berkshire cloth for a 1960 Buick Invicta four-door sedan. The fabric was offered in six color combinations. Photo from the Buick brochure, above.*

FOREWORD *by Susan Skarsgard* 9

INTRODUCTION 10

CHAPTER 1   **DRIVING TOWARD TOMORROW** 14
                         Postwar America Undergoes a Major Social Realignment

CHAPTER 2   **KAISER-FRAZER LEADS THE WAY** 28
                         Fashion and Styling Help a Struggling Company Get Noticed

CHAPTER 3   **MODERN LIVING** 48
                         Lincoln Is Inspired by a Pivotal 1949 Design Show in Detroit

CHAPTER 4   **DIAMONDS ARE A GIRL'S BEST FRIEND** 72
                         Cadillac Doubles Down on Traditional American Luxury

CHAPTER 5   **THE IMPERIAL COLLECTION** 94
                         Fashion Brand Comarketing Connects to the Female Market

CHAPTER 6   **READY TO WEAR** 112
                         Popular-Priced Cars Use Color and Fashion to Boost Sales

CHAPTER 7   **A WOMAN'S PLACE** 148
                         The Industry Struggles to Adapt to Women's Needs

CHAPTER 8   **DESIGNING WOMEN** 162
                         The Glass Ceiling Cracks as Women Become a Voice in the Industry

CHAPTER 9   **STRIKE A POSE** 178
                         New Technologies Lead to Widespread Use of Photography

CHAPTER 10   **BIKINIS & BUCKET SEATS** 190
                         The Youth Market of the 1960s Changes Everything

CHAPTER 11   **BUICK GOES ALL OUT** 210
                         "The Magazine for the In Crowd" Blows Minds—and Budgets

CHAPTER 12   **TURN, TURN, TURN** 234
                         Mary Wells, Pop Art, Op Art, and Psychedelia End the Sixties

ACKNOWLEDGMENTS 254

NOTES 254

BIBLIOGRAPHY 255

If you want the best dressed cars on the road, rely on a woman's touch.

Fisher Body does.

The beautiful interior of your 1969 General Motors car reflects good taste and good sense. One of the key reasons is that Joan Gatewood, Kathy Denek, Sue Vanderbilt, Margaret Schroeder and Bernadette Mate have worked their special magic.

They are among the GM Styling experts Fisher Body calls upon when it comes to interior design details best left to the deft feminine touch. A touch that results in car seats just the right height for a woman to enter and exit with ease. A touch that combines safety with beauty in this year's mini-buckle seat belt. And it's a touch that considers a woman's world of high-fashion heels and nylons in the design of carpeting, seat tailoring, steering wheels and controls.

GM's designing females are just five more reasons why so much of the buy is in the body. And Body by Fisher makes GM cars a better buy. Chevrolet. Pontiac. Oldsmobile. Buick. Cadillac.

Body by Fisher

▲ *This Body by Fisher ad from 1969 featured five women from the styling department at General Motors, including Sue Vanderbilt (front). Sue was one of the original "Damsels of Design" referred to in chapter 8.*

8 | GLAMOUR ROAD

FOREWORD BY SUSAN SKARSGARD

The day I stepped onto the General Motors Technical Center (GMTC) campus in 1994 was the beginning of my awareness of midcentury wonderfulness. This was when I began my job as a designer at GM, at this most iconic and important site, which was architect Eero Saarinen's first large commission. It opened to international acclaim in 1956, with the press labeling it "the Versailles of Industry." Working in such a beautifully designed environment, where every detail was considered and indeed reinvented for the new modern aesthetic, I developed a curiosity of and an awareness for the design vocabulary of this era, which deepened over the next twenty-five years on the job.

And then there were the cars.

Ultimately, I founded the General Motors Archive & Special Collections (GMDASC), the official repository for the history of design at GM. As my staff began to reach out into the design community to document this history, the most amazing and luscious artifacts that stood out were from the postwar era, infused by hopeful optimism and futuristic fancy. It is the visual and visceral embodiment of a time when everything was being redefined and redesigned.

It's hard not to fall in love with this movement in America, where experimentation and individualism harnessed an ideal or utopic vision of what modern life should be. This vision pervaded every part of our society, from science, art, architecture, literature, religion, and political and social constructs to the activities of daily life. And in this redefinition, beautiful forms emerged that awakened consumers' pent-up desires. Aspiration to this ideal became a marketing tool. People bought in.

It was through my study of the GMTC, and ultimately the publication of my book on its history, *Where Today Meets Tomorrow* (Princeton Architectural Press), that I landed in the mecca for modernism—Palm Springs, California. Presenting at and attending Modernism Week for several years has given me the opportunity to learn and comprehend the larger context of this movement in America. This led me to a surprising discovery: the important role that my home state has played in this story. Michigan designers and architects and the automotive and furniture industries were crucial to the design, development, and manufacturing of midcentury products in America. Institutions such as Cranbrook laid the groundwork by developing a design curriculum supportive of this new aesthetic exploration, and the Detroit Institute of Arts furthered the conversation by sponsoring the groundbreaking 1949 *For Modern Living* exhibition. Midcentury master designers such as Alexander Girard, Minoru Yamasaki, Eero Saarinen, and Charles Eames came together to create a "new concept of beauty" for the modern era, with a focus on design for the home.

In my role as the manager of the GMDASC, I often visited retired or former designers to document their careers and stories, and sometimes to visit with historic-car enthusiasts. I was always amazed at how passionate many of these collectors were, with their detailed mastery of automotive everything. This is how I met Jeff Stork and Tom Dolle. Their enthusiasm and vast knowledge of design and car history are deepened by their gracious engagement and acknowledgment of some of the important designers who lived and worked in this milieu, many of whom ended up in Palm Springs in their retirement. This book certainly serves as a love letter to them.

This book is also a celebration of the often-illusory and romantic attractiveness of the midcentury era and provides the reader with a unique vantage point to jump in and explore. It is beautifully designed and illustrated extensively, with a visual fancy that explains and contextualizes their unique point of view. More than just a *car book*, it is a deeper dive into how the design world became a catalyst for change, and explains how women, fashion, and the advertising world profoundly contributed to the social realignment in American culture.

But it is also just plain fun to look through. The highly stylized photography and illustrations, even the advertising copy itself, paint a rich portrait of desire and aspiration. The effective use of these visual tools was the means to introduce this new way of looking, and drove sales by capitalizing on the fashion and color industries. The importance of the commercial art and design world's influence is often underacknowledged in historical discussions on this subject. However, the important role the advertising industry played is given its due in this book and provides a deeper understanding of the connections between the pop art scene and the commercial-art juggernaut, each co-opting the ideas of branding and style for the other's gain.

And again, there are the cars.

If you're a seasoned midcentury scholar, you will likely learn something new. If you're just delving into this world of glamour and appeal, you will likely be swept away. For everyone in between, this is a wonderful document that celebrates what modernism meant, and continues to mean, in America.

Susan Skarsgard, designer and author,
Where Today Meets Tomorrow: Eero Saarinen and the General Motors Technical Center

INTRODUCTION

Jeff in a 1956 Packard Caribbean with interior detailing by MaryEllen Green

◀ *Postevent photo shoot for Cul de Sac Experience, Palm Springs, 2017, produced by Tom Dolle & Jeff Stork. Photography and models by JEVPIC.*

▶ *Jeff at VIP Night, the 1992 Milwaukee Auto Show*

This book has been more than forty years in the making. I've been accumulating stories for it since childhood.

I was a car crazy kid in Flint, Michigan—home of Buick Motor Division. I listened to the *Buick Factory Whistle Show* on the radio each morning while getting ready for school. They played songs like "Glide Along in Your Buick" and "Quality Makes Our Buicks Great." I still recall the lyrics. They also read the ten- day sales reports three times per month. The whole town felt strongly invested in the success of Buick.

I was the one who knew every car on the road, hounded my father to take me to the new-model announcements, and even strategically chose TV shows to maximize exposure to the new cars. I knew the drill—*Bewitched* for Chevrolets, *Hazel* for Fords, *My Three Sons* and *I Dream of Jeannie* for Pontiacs. I built my first model car (with hundreds to follow) at age four. My mother set up a card table in the living room, and we (okay, mostly she) built a very detailed model of the Chrysler Turbine Car. I was very proud of it. From the look of my bookshelves when I was a teen, one would think I was operating my own tiny automobile factory.

I came by it honestly. My father was a Classic Car collector, and so I grew up as a car club brat. Our adventures included the Auburn Cord Duesenberg reunions in Auburn, Indiana, the CCCA Grand Classics in suburban Detroit, and CCCA Caravans across the Midwest, which were weeklong tours in which everyone drove their 1925–48 automobiles as sole transportation for the journey. I became adept at roadside repairs, like the time I repaired an overheating 1929 Cadillac with a vegetable brush and some electrical tape. Many of Dad's club friends were prominent in the industry—Jack Humbert and David Holls of GM, Jim Quinlan of Ford, even Dick Teague of American Motors.

I was eleven when I first met iconic GM design chief Bill Mitchell, who wheeled into a Grand Classic at Cranbrook School one Saturday morning in his customized "Blue Boy" Eldorado convertible, wearing a leisure suit that matched the electric robin's-egg-blue paint precisely.

Dad had great cars—Packards, Cadillacs, twelve-cylinder Lincoln Continentals, even an Auburn speedster and a Cord 812. It was an idyllic childhood for a gearhead boy north of Detroit. By my teenage years, I found that my tastes ran about fifteen years newer than his—he loved the late thirties and forties; I gravitated toward the fifties with their tri-tone paint finishes and Lurex woven interiors, Cadillac Eldorados, Packard Patricians and Caribbeans, and long, low, lovely Lincolns. I was hooked on the glamour. My first collectible car, at age nineteen, was a one-owner, slightly worn 1956 Continental Mark II—the most expensive American car of its day. I was stylin'. I loved that car.

After college, I ended up in the corporate sales staff of General Motors, where I spent twenty years moving metal

Introduction | 11

to GM dealers and working with them to sell the cars to the public. I have driven a new GM car in just about every place imaginable, including Lambeau Field in Green Bay, on the ice during hockey games while being chased by a Zamboni, and in just about every hotel ballroom there is. I've worked the floor of major auto shows, driven cars in commercials, and stood by them being blown up on film. General Motors brought me to Milwaukee, to Chicago, and ultimately to Los Angeles, where I fell desperately in love with California car culture.

After a couple of decades with the General selling the sizzle, I went into dealership management and spent a decade with upscale products such as Cadillac, Saab, Jaguar, and Land Rover. After the 2009 crash, I changed gears and moved to Palm Springs, the midcentury mecca itself, where I began managing a private collection and writing about automotive history.

Palm Springs is paradise, a glistening city of midcentury jewel boxes nestled up against the mountain. A haven for car collectors and an artists' colony as well, Palm Springs is full of creative people in all phases of their lives. It was here that I realized how intertwined the midcentury design world really was, and that many of the prominent names were involved in projects that reached across the spectrum of commercial applications, including the automotive industry.

Here I befriended retired GM designer Blaine Jenkins and soon realized that we had lived 20 miles apart for many years and never met. I even had pictures of his cars I had taken at shows back in Detroit. We spent many afternoons together discussing General Motors back in the day. He knew how Harley Earl liked his coffee and how Bill Mitchell liked his women. Blaine was at ground zero at one of the most dynamic times in the history of the automobile. He always said he was the luckiest man in the world, and I have to agree.

Cul de Sac A Go-Go, 2019. Photo by Bobby Dezarov.

It was Blaine who put me on the topic of the Damsels of Design, which led me down a two-year rabbit hole that resulted in an article for *Automobile* magazine called "Harley Earl's Designing Women." That article caught the eye of the undefeatable Tom Dolle, and we quickly discovered we were kindred souls who viewed the industry from the viewpoint of the marketer and were mesmerized by the glamour. We stumbled into the Cul de Sac Experience Fall Modernism Week Event pretty much by accident, and it became a big hit. Tom always wanted to do a book, but it hovered somewhere in the future, "when things slow down." Then in the spring of 2020, things slowed down. He was persistent and I was out of excuses. A year later, forty years' worth of stories are down on paper, and I hope you find them as wild and zany and fabulous as we did.

Jeff Stork, author

12 | GLAMOUR ROAD

◀ Tom in his 1964 Ford Country Squire

▶ Announcement for the 2001 show at the Pratt Graduate Communications Design Gallery

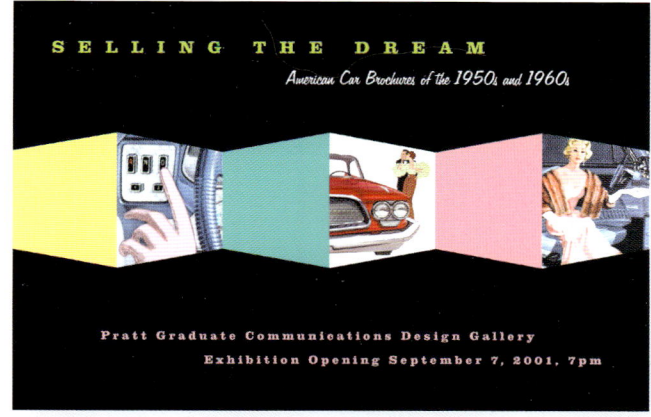

Growing up in suburban Ohio, I (like Jeff) was one of those annoying kids who dragged my parents to every car dealer in September and October to see the new cars. I collected the brochures and studied them for hours, choosing the perfect models, colors, and features for the next family car purchase (they humored me without ever taking my advice). That was the start of a lifelong fascination with marketing, branding, and print media that served me well in my career as a graphic designer.

During my twenty-plus-year stint as a professor at Pratt Institute, I revisited those old brochures, plus others I had collected over the years, and produced a gallery show in 2001 in lower Manhattan, where Pratt had its graduate departments. I painted the walls in pastel colors to display the beautifully illustrated brochures, with blown-up quotes from the breathy prose. To me it wasn't just about the cars—it was the elegant images, the lush formats, the glamorous fashion, the colors and features, all from a time when the entire country became mesmerized by the promise of planned obsolescense. The opening was a big success, but my timing was not—four days later, the Twin Towers fell and the building was closed while the city recovered.

Years later, as my husband and I were planning a move to Palm Springs, I contacted Jeff Stork. He had a blog called the Palm Springs Automobilist, and I sensed he and I were on the same page about cars. He had years of experience and contacts in the Detroit auto world, the automotive press, and the Palm Springs classic car scene. We hit it off and started conceptualizing a book, not sure of where it would take us.

Along the way, our house in Canyon View Estates was chosen for a Modernism Week tour, and I asked Jeff to bring over some cars from the Prescott Collection he manages to use as props. Designed by Palmer & Krisel in the early '60s, Canyon View Estates is the iconic Palm Springs midcentury complex, with white shadow block facades; dramatic umbrella-shaped, double-gabled roofs; walls of glass; clerestory windows; elegant carports—totally intact and surrounded by palm trees and mountain views. Our home is on a cul de sac, so it's like a big stage set.

Once the cars were placed in the neighboring driveways and we looked out the window, a lightbulb went off—the cul de sac was totally transported back to 1964. Jeff said, "I have a terrible idea . . . ," which I've learned usually leads to something big. So the next year we created the "Cul de Sac Experience," a Fall Modernism Week event—we closed off the street, filled the driveways with perfectly curated cars, opened six homes for tours, had a live DJ with period music, and gave out Creamsicles. By the third year, we added go-go platforms with dancers, along with a revolving '66 Charger on a turntable, for "Cul de Sac A-Go-Go." Ticket holders showed up in period clothing, and a unique annual street party was born. Branded to within an inch of its life, it was a groundbreaking success and made us committed to include classic cars as integrated components in larger narratives.

When connected to midcentury modern design and architecture, classic cars become a key visual design element that helps define the period. As we explored how fashion, glamour, and styling had influenced both midcentury car design and marketing, we discovered more information than we ever imagined and, by connecting the dots, quickly had enough to fill a book (or two).

The biggest challenge in designing this book was the sheer volume of imagery—we've included over 500 images from numerous sources, the vast majority from period ads and brochures. We made connections to a treasure trove of private collectors, online resellers, amateur archivists, and professional archives. They are the true heroes of our quickly vanishing print culture, preserving printed history for future generations.

Most of these pieces of ephemera were yellowed with age, stained, or creased and had been mass-printed over fifty years ago at various levels of quality. Do we show them in their current state (as a true archivist might), or do I retouch, descreen, and color-correct to make them look as they may have appeared originally? I chose the latter, and my goal with each retouching was to present the ad or brochure page as if it were new today—crisp, clear, with vivid colors on white stock, often with the text left off to focus on the imagery. I felt it was the only way that a modern audience could truly appreciate the glamour and excitement that these pieces generated in their day. It was a monumental task but worth the effort—we hope you agree.

Tom Dolle, Designer

Introduction | 13

Chapter One

DRIVING TOWARD TOMORROW

POSTWAR AMERICA UNDERGOES A MAJOR SOCIAL REALIGNMENT

The postwar world was dramatically changed. Johnny and Jane came marching home to a world that was very different from the one they left behind. The mobilization of defense production, the likes of which the country had never seen, altered the country and the world in ways both social and economic.

It was wartime mobilization that ended the Depression. Government spending took on a win-at-any-cost philosophy after the attacks on Pearl Harbor, and the federal budget increased tenfold. The economy found itself at full employment, with millions of women entering the worforce. Unemployment, which peaked at over fifteen million workers in 1933, was practically nonexistent in 1945—a meager 1.4%—and consumer savings rates as a percent of income soared to 21% by the war's end, some seven times the rate in the 1920s. Americans were working long hours and saving their money in anticipation of the life they would live when the war ended.

Peacetime arrived, and all of those deferred plans came to the forefront. The soldiers returned home by the millions, and many had wives or sweethearts waiting for them. For those who shopped abroad, the troop ships *Queen Mary* and *Queen Elizabeth* were chartered for transporting European brides home to start a new life in America with their now ex-GI husbands.

And what a life it would be. The economy made a remarkably smooth transition to peacetime production. Four years of wartime rationing had created a huge, pent-up demand for household goods. Production lines that had made airplanes, tanks, and missiles were refitted for automobiles and home appliances. There were waiting lists for automobiles, of course, but also even for toasters—and for new homes for all these newly minted families to live in.

The homes would predominantly be in the suburbs, which was a major shift. In 1940, only 19.5% of Americans lived in the suburbs. By 1950, it jumped to 30.7%, and between 1950 and 1970, 83% of all American population growth occurred in the suburbs. The Servicemen's Readjustment Act of 1944, commonly known as the GI Bill, provided tuition assistance, short-term unemployment benefits, and government-backed mortgage loans. So the path to home ownership was now easy—and millions took advantage of the benefits.

William Levitt of Levitt and Son brought mass-production techniques to residential construction. They created the first Levittown community in the country in 1946 on Long Island, New York. They bought huge

▲ Lakewood, California, was one of the first suburban developments to attract buyers with a street of completely furnished and landscaped model homes, seen here in 1950. (City of Lakewood)

◀ Illustration by Tom Dolle

Driving toward Tomorrow | 15

> Right: *Major Deegan expressway, 1957. Highways changed the American landscape in the 1950s, but it wasn't without controversy.* (Everett Collection Historical / Alamy Stock Photo)
>
> Center right: *The Congress Expressway opens to fanfare in 1960.* (Photo courtesy of Central Electric Railfans' Association Archives)
>
> Far right: *This Seattle protest of 1961 was in response to the destruction of urban neighborhoods by highway construction.* (MOHAI, Seattle Post-Intelligencer Collection 1986.5.4018.1)

tracts of acreage, subdivided them, mass-produced houses—completing as many as thirty per day—and made affordable housing for the mostly GI Bill buyer. All told, they built three Levittown communities consisting of over 17,000 homes. Cities like Levittown on the East Coast and Lakewood in California sprung up, and planned communities spread from coast to coast. Home construction in the suburbs accounted for an astonishing 76% of all residential construction in the 1950s.

Ribbons of Concrete

The suburban explosion created additional demands for both automobiles and highways. Not only was having a car deemed all but essential in the suburbs—the percentage of households owning a car soared from 54% in 1948 to 75% by 1959—but in addition, the multicar household was born. A lack of public transportation created an entirely overlooked market—the married suburban woman as the primary driver of an automobile. This would prove to be an enormous opportunity—and indeed one that the auto companies would not always handle well.

And, of course, a massive population shift toward suburbanization in a very short period of time—less than a decade—and dependence on the automobile as primary transportation would require a complete overhaul of the nation's highway system. When President Dwight D. Eisenhower signed the Federal Aid Highway Act of 1956 on June 29 of that year, it was the single-largest public works project of all time. The act provided for the construction of the Interstate Highway System, a connected roadway of some 41,000 miles that carried an estimated completion time of ten years and an original price tag of $25 billion dollars. Financing would largely fall to the federal government through the creation of the Highway Trust Fund, which included a three-cent-per-gallon gasoline tax. And while that may seem meager, gasoline consumption in the postwar decade soared—from around 22 million gallons in 1945 to some 59 million gallons in 1958. While not sufficient to pay for the new roads, it indeed provided enough political cover to get the bill passed.

The proposed highway routes were published in the 1955 *General Location of National System of Interstate Highways*. Also known as the "Yellow Book," it shared with the motoring public the proposed Interstate Highway System of 1965. It's not incidental that one member of the planning committee was no less than Defense Secretary Charles E. Wilson, "Engine Charlie" himself, who had previously been the president of General Motors. It was Wilson who was quoted as saying that "what's good for General Motors is good for the country" in his confirmation hearings, although he later claimed that he actually said the opposite. Either way, there was certainly plenty in it for both parties, and for

▲ *This 1953 Lincoln ad taps into the excitement of a car-based future.*

16 | GLAMOUR ROAD

◀ Suburban strip malls, such as this one in Monroeville, Pennsylvania, made car ownership a necessity. (Ryan Khatam, flickr.com)

▶ 1952 Nash ad directly targeted women with the need for a second car.

developers as well. It was pretty easy to look at the "Yellow Book" and start shopping for land, because easy freeway access would become a major selling point in the explosion of suburban growth. Once the bill was passed, construction crews wasted no time getting started—in several states, highways were under construction by late summer, and by 1957, the project was in full swing.

It's important to note that the rising tide didn't raise all boats equally—minority communities were often denied access to the bright, shiny, new suburban world, there were protests against the highway system, and there were charges that the routes were laid out with underlying racism as a factor in which neighborhoods the highways would ultimately bisect. Over time, the contentions have pretty much shown themselves to be true, causing urban issues that the planners did not anticipate at the time, including displacement of residents and the acceleration of urban decay.

Strip Malls and Parking Lots

Perhaps no city best exemplifies the dramatic transformation of empty fields to a fully functioning city better than Lakewood, California. In early 1950, the Lakewood Corporation broke ground on 2,350 acres of plowed bean fields near Long Beach. Three years later, Lakewood was a community of 17,500 homes. Lakewood was actually very well planned—twenty-two different styles of houses were offered, along with parks and sixteen neighborhood strip shopping centers, as well as the Lakewood Center, a mammoth shopping mall (California's first) located in the middle of the development on a massive lot at the corner of Lakewood and Del Amo Boulevards. The main building was set back 300 feet from the street and featured parking for 10,000 cars. The anchor was a 345,000-square-foot May Company department store—the largest retail store in the nation. It was an immediate success, with over 200,000 customers swarming in on opening day in early 1952. The store itself was a box in the international style, with four 16-foot-tall yellow neon "M"s as a calling card that was visible for miles. But of course, not every errand necessitates a trip to an enormous shopping mall, and that's where the strip mall came into prominence. The Lakewood development included no fewer than sixteen of them, with important services such as small grocery stores, drugstores, and even hair salons and shoe repair. The strip mall would become a part of the American landscape that would endure long after the mall itself went out of favor.

The history of the strip mall dates back at least as far as the 1920s, when the automobile became a sufficient societal force to begin altering traditional patterns of retailing. It was then when the buildings themselves began to be built set back from the curb, with room for automobile parking in front. Hamady Brothers Supermarkets, based in Flint, Michigan, went so far as to spell out "Automobile Shoppers" in neon tubes on the full-width enameled sign across the storefront.

And while the earliest versions may have served customers who arrived on foot or by streetcar as well as automobile in the earlier urban setting, the postwar versions were primarily designed for those arriving by car. The automobile would be the primary instrument of mobility in the suburbs, and commercial architecture would be designed around the concepts of automobile accessibility and generous free parking.

Waiting Lists for Toasters

The postwar consumer demand was unprecedented. The population had been under consumer rationing for four years, and at war's end, people had plenty of money and lots of household wants. A postwar newsreel advertisement for bond sales included the line "Got your car and toaster ordered," disclosing that indeed there were waiting lists for both. And while the waiting lists for automobiles was as well known as it was notorious, the waiting lists for appliances are less remembered. But in reality, it's not surprising. The entire force of American production capacity was focused on war needs for four years, and even though it adapted back to peacetime with remarkable pace, there was pent-up demand from households old and new. The

Driving toward Tomorrow | 17

▲ This 1953 International Harvester ad showed how you could easily custom-upholster your refrigerator to match your decor.

Top: A 1957 Sheer-Look kitchen from Frigidaire, a division of General Motors

new war brides had sparkling new kitchens to outfit, and the established households had grown weary of mending the frayed toaster cord. And once those production lines were converted, they needed a lot of sales to keep them humming—so even toasters and kitchen appliances had annual model changes and advertising campaigns to keep demand healthy.

Appliances Become Fashion

It's probably no coincidence that some popular appliance brands were owned by automobile manufacturers. Frigidaire was a division of General Motors, Kelvinator was owned by Nash, and even International Harvester made refrigerators and freezers in the postwar decade. So it's certainly no stretch of the imagination to see the same marketing techniques for automobiles being applied to the so-called "white goods" market.

First, we should stop calling them "white goods," because, in the 1950s, they came in rainbow colors. Leafing through the 1956 Hotpoint dealer album, we find the full Hotpoint line offered in Star Shower Colortones of Seafoam Blue, Meadow Green, Sunburst Yellow, Woodland Brown, and, of course, Coral Pink—plus metal finishes of coppertone or stainless steel—and for the truly unstylish, white enamel. Indeed, full kitchen ensembles could be ordered in these fashionable hues, and two-tone portable televisions completed the look.

International Harvester, best known for tractors and farm combines, produced a line of home refrigerators and freezers from 1946 through 1956. Not one of the major players in home appliances, they nonetheless had excellent name recognition in rural markets. IH advertised their refrigerators as being "femineered," meaning that they were somehow designed for women's needs, although there is no evidence that any women were involved in their design process. They further attempted to appeal to women in 1951 by offering ten different color door handles for the white refrigerators, inviting women to "pick a color from the Rainbow." They stepped up their game in 1953 by announcing the "Decorator Refrigerator," whose door could be redecorated by covering with 1.75 yards of any fabric in only seven minutes.

General Motors rocked the appliance industry with the Sheer Look in 1957. GM had been investing in home appliance design in the mid-'50s. Two of the groundbreaking Damsels of Design (see chapter 8) were assigned to Frigidaire to work on a project called the Kitchen of Tomorrow. They created "dream kitchens" for the General

Keep your parfaits perfectly chilled in a Colortone 1956 Hotpoint refrigerator, shown here in Meadow Green.

Television sets became the must-have item in well-off households in 1949, but this Capehart Symphony set was the equivalent to a staggering $8500 in today's dollars.

Motors Motorama traveling exhibitions and worked on designs for production kitchens as well. The Sheer Look was a dream kitchen that made it to market. This look replaced the outmoded rounded-top refrigerator with the perfect rectangle—a look so sharp you could poke your eye out with it, but in reality, it tended to *catch* the eye instead. The Sheer Look offered a futuristic new style that lent itself well to built-in installations, which was a very profitable segment of the home appliance market. The Sheer Look was a hit, launched with ads that showed a glamorous gowned model holding her gloved hands at a perfect 90-degree angle. The look included a full line of appliances, from refrigerators and food freezers to washers and dryers, electric ranges, wall ovens and matching cook tops, dishwashers, and even air conditioners—all with those stylishly severe square corners.

Frigidaire reached its pinnacle in 1960 with the introduction of the fabulous Custom Imperial Flair range. Looking like it just landed from outer space, the Flair featured double, side-by-side, eye-level ovens with upward-sweeping, tempered glass doors. Beneath were slide-out electric burners that nested when not in use, with a storage cabinet conveniently located below. Add dial controls worthy of a Gemini space capsule and those de rigueur square corners, and you have the Flair, possibly the most amazing range ever created. The Flair would achieve immortality in Samantha Stephens's kitchen on the hit 1960s sitcom *Bewitched*. Flairs are highly collectible today.

For marketing these new appliances, manufacturers turned to the newest medium of all, television. A young actress named Betty Furness filled in at the last minute on a live Westinghouse television ad in 1948. Her easy manner proved a perfect fit, and she remained with Westinghouse through 1960, earning over $100,000 per year at her peak. Another actress, this one named Lucille Ball, had pitched Hoover vacuum cleaners during her *My Favorite Husband* radio days but also joined up with Westinghouse during her *I Love Lucy* stint. Bess Myerson, Miss America 1945, was a pitch woman for Frigidaire in the mid-'50s, while dancer Thelma "Tad" Tadlock frolicked to the Kitchen of Tomorrow in the 1956 GM Promotional Film *Design for Dreaming*.

Green Glow in the Living Room

But indeed no appliance matured so quickly as the television itself. The path from its public introduction at the RCA Pavilion of New York World's Fair in 1939 to America's living rooms was swift in the prosperous postwar era. At the end of 1946, about 44,000 American homes had television sets. By the end of 1949, the number had exploded to over 4.2 million, and almost every major city had at least one TV station. By 1956, most cities were linked to television network programming, and by 1959, half of American households had a TV.

In addition to the have and have-not households, beginning in 1954 there was an additional element—households with color TV receivers. So by the mid-'50s, merely having a television wasn't the ultimate in prestige—having a color TV was. And of course, as the product matured, it became larger as picture tubes got bigger; console televisions appeared with large and imposing cabinets, many with radio tuners and phonographs built in. These consoles offered both up-to-the-minute home entertainment and bragging rights throughout the neighborhood.

Space-age styling was taken to the extreme in the Philco Predicta of 1958, which featured a floating picture tube positioned above a box containing the tubes. While it looked like it stepped right out of an outer-space movie, there were reliability issues that haunted it through its short production run. The Predicta was quietly discontinued in 1960, and the Philco company itself was acquired by Ford in 1961.

ARCHITECTURE

DESIGN

As builders from coast to coast scrambled to meet the demand for new homes, cutting-edge architects and designers were redefining how modern homes would look and feel, inside and out. It was John Entenza of *Arts and Architecture Magazine* in Los Angeles who created a competition to design the postwar house in 1945. The magazine was a major force in the emerging West Coast modernism movement, and the Case Study House Program would allow emerging architects to further their reputations with modern home designs. The architecture was of the exposed post-and-beam style, with expansive use of glass and integrated indoor and outdoor spaces. While the contest rules stated that the houses should be reproducible, they were in reality higher-end, one-off residences.

In all, just over two dozen homes were built, all but two in Southern California. The residences were widely published and widely influential. Among the most-notable creations are the Eames House by Charles and Ray Eames, and Entenza's own house by Eames in conjunction with Eero Saarinen. The homes were built next door to one another on a bluff overlooking the ocean in Pacific Palisades. Both were completed in 1949 and are extant today. The Eames house is a time capsule, having survived with its original furnishings still in place.

▲ *The Eames Foundation in Pacific Palisades is the original Case Study house and residence of architects and designers Charles and Ray Eames. (Stephanie Braconnier / Shutterstock.com)*

Modern Living was a watershed moment. Directed by Alexander Girard, *An Exhibition for Modern Living* was presented at the Detroit Institute of Arts from September 11 through November 20, 1949. If it's possible to change the world in sixty days, Girard succeeded. The forward-looking exhibition, whose executive committee included not only Girard but also Eero Saarinen and Minoru Yamasaki, showcased the latest in home furnishings and product design.

In his forward, Girard wrote: "Here is a representative selection of products gathered from all over the world. Each one shows the results of a good understanding of a special individual problem... and each presents a solution that is both direct and honest. They all share a common, unconscious pride in developing new values rather than depending only on the thought and effort of the past."

The exhibition itself was wide ranging. It featured a lengthy gallery tracing the evolution of modern design, and

20 | GLAMOUR ROAD

▶ *The exhibition catalog for An Exhibition for Modern Living included many of the top names in modernist design of 1949. The room settings and products on display would influence design for decades to come.*

For Modern Living *marshaled midcentury masters Alexander Girard, Minoru Yamasaki, Eero Saarinen, and Charles Eames to create a "new concept of beauty" for the modern era—with a focus on design for the home.*

an enormous Steinberg mural telling the story in his own whimsical illustrations. It showcased home-furnishing galleries from all the emerging modern designers of the era, including George Nelson, Charles Eames, Alvar Aalto, Jens Risom, Bruno Mathsson, and Richard Stein. Rooms of upscale, breezy informality by Florence Knoll included works by Pierre Jeanneret, Richard Stein, Franco Albini, Abel Sorensen, Eero Saarinen, Isamu Noguchi, and Hans Bellman; outside her gallery was a patio by Van Keppel–Green. The exhibition concluded with a Hall of Objects that ranged from glassware and flatware to lamps, salt shakers, ceramics, textiles, and even jewelry, which literally represented the works of over a hundred designers.

It was a spectacular and groundbreaking show that set the tone for modern design for the decade to come. And as you will see in chapter 3, it provided the inspiration for what was possibly the most important automotive marketing campaign of the decade.

Driving toward Tomorrow | 21

FURNITURE & HOME GOODS

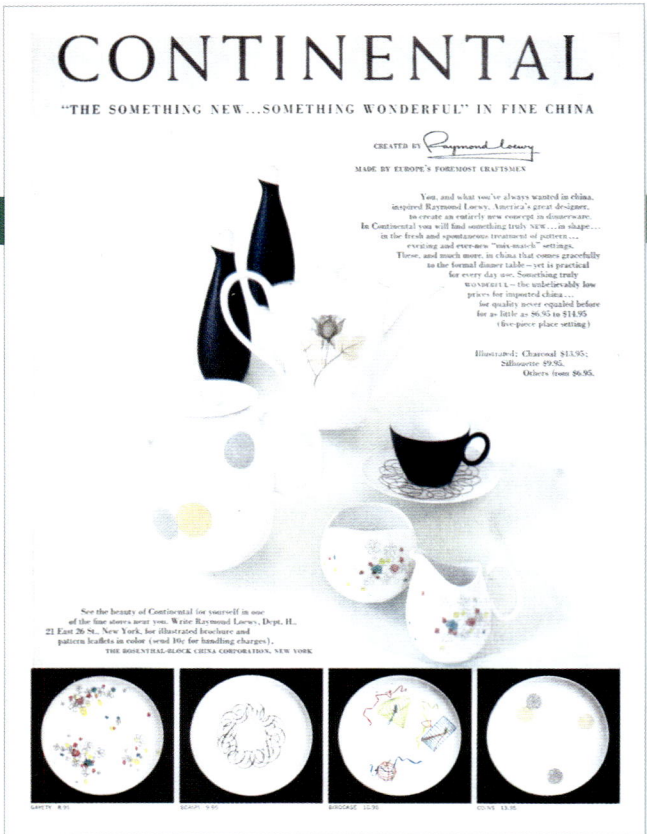

▶ 1953 ad for Continental china designed by Raymond Loewy, who went on to design the Studebaker Avanti in 1962

House and Garden magazine did a special "U. S. Taste" design issue in the summer of 1949. The feature article was called "Only in the USA," which highlighted emerging modern designers and introduced them with the following missive, which brilliantly encapsulates the mood and mission of the postwar American designers:

"Some of the designers on these pages you know. All of them, in a sense, know you, since they work for you. Because each of them has a very personal point of view, we asked them to tell you how they feel about present-day design. Since their work speaks for them, you will find it photographed here. You will see refrigerators, wallpapers, telephones, fabrics, ceramics, shaped by their personalities and their talents. You will also see furniture which fits our present way of living. Some of it is mobile, mounted on wheels and so light that it can be rolled from place to place. Some of it offers engineered storage facilities. Some of it takes up a minimum of space. Some of it capitalized on new methods of fabrication and materials. All of it is calculated to make your life more comfortable and your house more attractive. House and Garden has only one word to add: it could only happen in the U.S.A. Here, in a country which is a vast melange of cultures and viewpoints, where everyone can say his say in words or wood or plastics or whatever he likes best, there is no single party line. Here we have the techniques to improve on life, hourly and daily, and the imagination and spirit to do new things constantly. These designers have one trait in common: they are the unmistakable product of a democracy. They have one object in common: to make American homes the envy of the world."

The article then went on to name the designers and their fields of design, significant in not only displaying the products but in demonstrating a sea change in which the designers themselves became part of the product. When the Herman Miller Company hired George Nelson as creative director in 1945, he began promoting the designer as part of the product pitch. Their groundbreaking 1948 catalog lists George Nelson, Charles Eames, Isamu Noguchi, and Paul Laszlo prominently as furniture designers. When the postwar designers set out to make a name for themselves, they did so quite literally.

◀ The Eames fiberglass shell chair, first sold in 1950

Among those featured in the article were furniture designers T. H. Robsjohn-Gibbings, Florence Knoll, William Pahlmann, Paul McCobb, Jens Risom, Isamu Noguchi, and Edward J. Wormley, and textile designers Dorothy Leibes, Joseph B. Platt, Doris and Leslie Tillett, Virginia Hamill, Marion V. Dorn, Tammis Keefe, and Vera Neumann (who would become a sensation in the '70s for her brightly colored scarves). Henry Dreyfus even made the list with his iconic Dreyfus 500 telephone, and Raymond Loewy and Harold Van Doren were noted for their industrial designs. A separate section called California '49ers highlighted seventeen designers and craftsmen from the Golden State, including interior designer to the stars William Haines, furniture designers VanKeppel-Green, and pottery maker Sascha Brastoff. All and all, it was a *Who's Who* of the up-and-coming designers that would shape the American look in the postwar decades.

22 | GLAMOUR ROAD

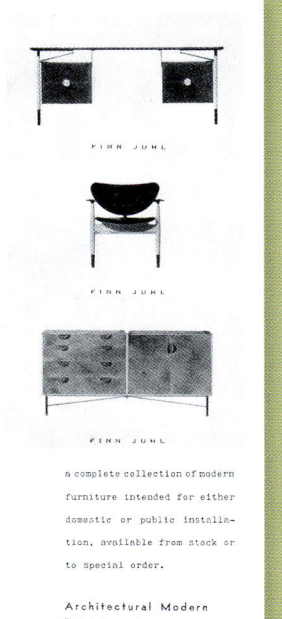
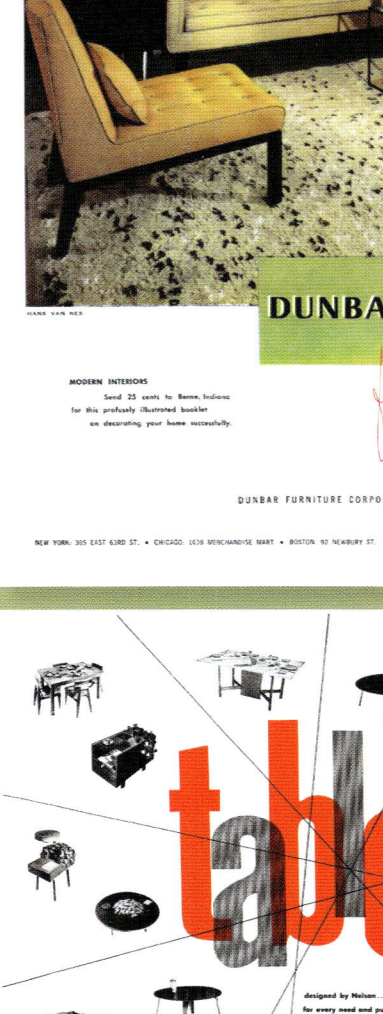

Clockwise from top left: Raymor, 1952; Dunbar for Modern, 1951; T. H. Robsjohn Gibbings for Widdicomb; Paul McCobb for Directional, 1953; Herman Miller, 1951, featuring Nelson, Eames, and Noguchi designs; Knoll, 1949; Baker Furniture featuring Finn Juhl, 1953

◀ One of the biggest changes in fashion was the adoption of casual sportswear, which suited the new modernist ideal of relaxed, informal living. Left, ad for a Claire McCardell gamin suit from 1947. Lower left, ad for Jantzen swimwear in a provocative ad from 1949.

FASHION

For American women, the postwar look was defined by sportswear, and Claire McCardell was a driving force. Her design philosophy was described as an ingenious pairing of function and style. Her works were versatile, easy to wear, and imaginative. It was she who laid the foundation for sportswear by imagining taking a dress and cutting it to pieces. She also chose playful fabrics such as ticking stripes, calico, and denim for day wear.

To quote the *New York Times* in a retrospective show about her: *"From the 1930s through the '50s, McCardell's casual, modern clothes urged women toward greater freedom and flexibility in fashion and promoted an aesthetic that Americans can now claim as their own. Through McCardell, fashion kept abreast of changes like jazz, realism, women's war-time emancipation and an optimistic postwar nationalism."*

Valerie Steele of the Museum of the Fashion Institute of Technology called McCardell "the founder of democratic American fashion." Of course, McCardell was not the only advocate of sportswear—there were others, including Tina Leser, Bonnie Cashin, Elizabeth Hawes, and Tom Brigance. But McCardell is said to be the one who took the carefree and simple look most to heart and inspired thousands of women with a distinctive and informal postwar look.

The New Look

The 1943 Fats Waller song "I'll Be Happy When the Nylons Bloom Again" was a lament to one of the material shortages of particular interest to women in World War II—that of the Dupont wonder fabric used to make hosiery. It was no laughing matter to them—nylons traded at high prices on the black market during the war, and in fact there were "nylon riots" in 1946 when peacetime production did not resume as quickly as promised.

While nylon production did finally resume, it's a metaphor for women's fashion during the war—material shortages, dark maudlin colors, and styling that was clearly military-inspired with boxy lines that were designed to conserve precious fabric. The concept of fashion took a back seat to wartime—indeed, Coco Chanel even closed her fashion house in 1939, and the others operated on a reduced scale.

More than the nylons were blooming in early 1947. It was then that a young Christian Dior introduced a revolution. He called his line Corolle, meaning a ring of flowers—but the editor of *Harper's Bazaar* tagged it "the New Look," and the name stuck. It was indeed new and brought about a fashion revolution. Dior used rounded shoulders, cinched waists, and broad, expansive A-line skirts to emphasize the feminine figure. The clothes were expressive, colorful, and feminine. Dior himself wrote:

"In December 1946, as a result of the war and uniforms, women still looked and dressed like Amazons. But I designed clothes for flower-like women, with rounded shoulders, full feminine busts, and hand-span waists above enormous spreading skirts.

"We were just emerging from a poverty-stricken, parsimonious era, obsessed with ration books and clothes coupons. It was only natural that my creations should take the form of a reaction against this dearth of imagination."

Dior's tight-waisted women-as-fleurs look wasn't for everyone—Coco Chanel for one was particularly nonplussed—but his colorful and feminine clothes struck a chord with women and inspired designers on both sides of the Atlantic.

Branding guru Ross Klein adds an additional note of importance to the New Look—he notes that the New Look in its own way ushered in "fast fashion" and the promise of high fashion without high price tags. Klein notes that "buyers from Alexander's and other US powerhouse

▶ Right: *Julius Garfinckel & Co. ad, 1950, featuring a Christian Dior asymmetrical suit*

Below right: *Studebaker adopts the "new look" headline for its 1948 Champion, one of the first new postwar cars to come to market.*

retailers, along with independent dressmakers, immediately set off 'interpreting' the Dior designs to get them into the closets of regular American women who would never have had such access pre-war."

The parallels of the fashion industry to the American auto industry are what we'll explore in the chapters ahead, and what drove us to write this book in the first place.

Studebaker Wraps Itself in Dior

Given the general consumer climate of waiting lists for toasters and riots over nylons, it will come as no surprise to learn that there was strong consumer demand for automobiles. New-car production had ended in early 1942, and no new automobiles were seen until late 1945. It was beyond a seller's market, with long waiting lists and people hiring brokers to buy them a new car at practically any price. Retired GM designer Blaine Jenkins liked to tell the story of his grandfather, a loyal Buick driver at the time, hiring a broker to get him a new Buick. When he got the call that the car had arrived, he drove over to see it, and waiting there was a new Dodge. He took the car anyway. This almost circus atmosphere would endure until the 1949 model year, when the competitive market resumed.

Studebaker was first to market with an all-new car in 1947, which was a noteworthy feat for a smallish independent. They cribbed on the publicity surrounding Dior with a headline of "Low swung new look!"—and used the tagline "First By Far with a Postwar Car." They clearly borrowed the thunder from Dior, and although of course they lacked the cinched waistline and flowing skirt, they were notable as an automobile clearly aligning itself with a current fashion campaign. Much more would come in the following decade, as the automobile and fashion industries would find themselves on parallel paths.

Driving toward Tomorrow | 25

THE GM MOTORAMA

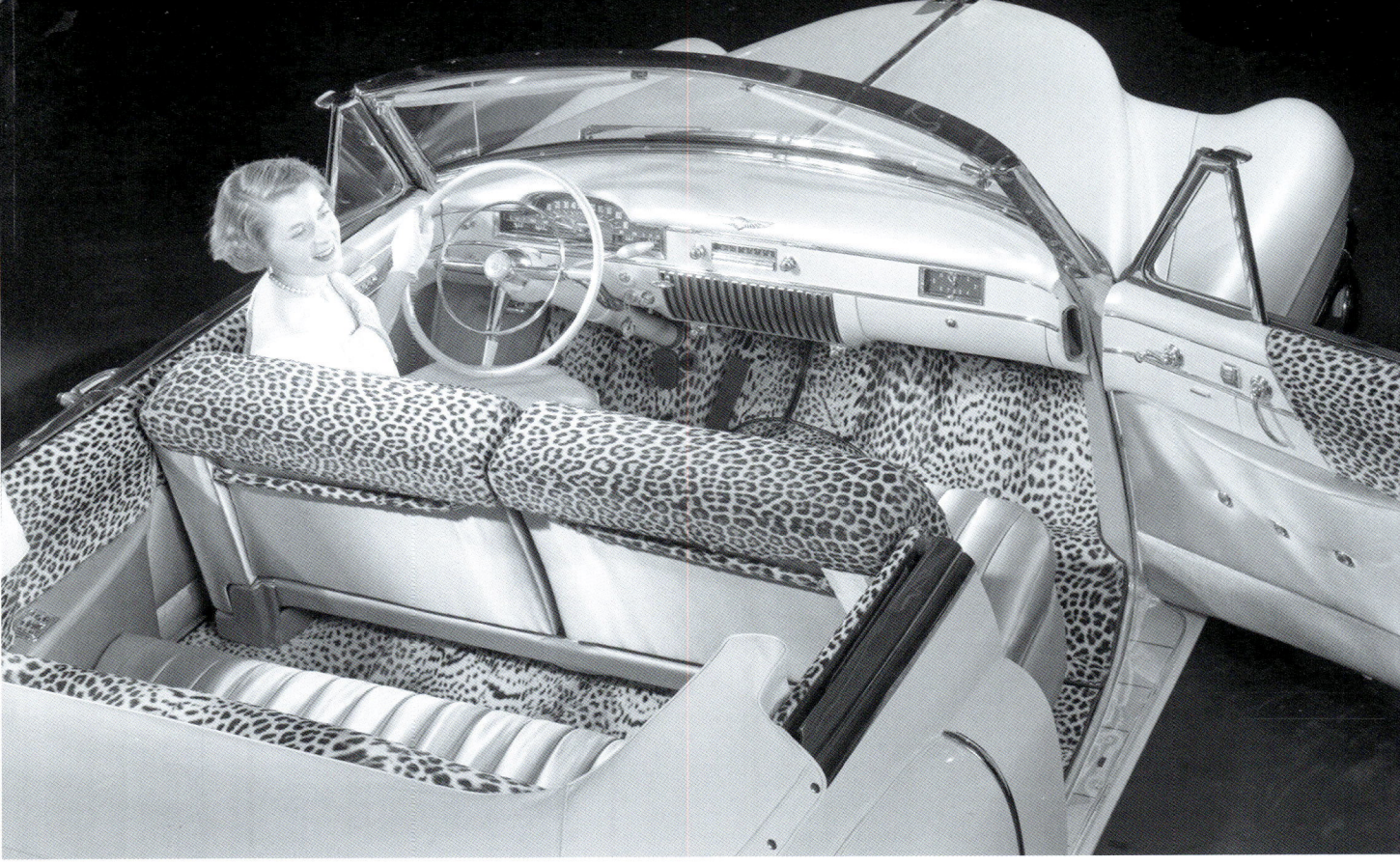

While the auto industry could certainly sell absolutely anything with four wheels at war's end, it was commonly understood that the competitive market would resume by 1949 at the latest, and then it would be up to the automakers to take the reins to aggressively market their cars. A plethora of redesigns appeared by 1949, and the competition was fierce—every automaker was looking for a way to stand out.

Fashion Show with Wheels

General Motors created what amounts to nothing less than a fashion show with wheels. It wasn't a totally new idea for them. Alfred P. Sloan himself began hosting "Industrialist's Luncheons" at the Waldorf dating back to 1931. It was a combination of product exposure to the movers and shakers and inspiring confidence in the potentially nervous investment bankers on Wall Street in the Depression. The display was simple—new GM cars and floral displays. But it wasn't open to the public.

The postwar experience would be greatly enhanced. GM Styling had a Product and Exhibit Studio. They created exhibit designs and sent them to the H. B. Stubbs Company in Warren, Michigan, where display materials were created.

The first show opened in the Grand Ballroom of the Waldorf Astoria in New York in January 1949. The display featured twenty-six new GM cars, along with feature displays and a stage show with a cast of twenty actors who performed six thirty-minute shows daily. The cars were mostly production offerings with the exception of Cadillac, which showed four customized cars out of its six. This led the way for the dream cars of years to follow. The show was a hit, drawing 300,000 attendees in its eight-day run. Everything seemed to work, except for the name. The show was called Transportation Unlimited. Lacking excitement, it was changed the following year to the Mid-Century Motorama.

Motorama. Yes, GM's fabulous assemblage of glitter, girls, gowns, and gladiolas. The Motorama was the automobile show that married the fashion show, with specially created one-off "concept cars" flanked by attractive young female narrators in designer gowns. The newsreels of the shows are fascinating, when the clothes get almost as much mention as the cars.

Planned Obsolescence Creates Demand

It seemed inevitable that automobile marketing and the fashion industry would align. It was GM's Alfred Sloan who introduced the concept of planned obsolescence to the automobile industry to sell products back in the

▲ *The Cadillac Debutante was displayed at the 1950 Motorama. The interior was upholstered in leopard skin, with 24-karat gold fittings. Below: Pretty young women in glamorous gowns surround a Chevrolet Bel Air at the 1953 Motorama.*

26 | GLAMOUR ROAD

The 1954 Motorama at the Waldorf-Astoria featured revolving car displays and elaborate production numbers. (all photos: General Motors Archive)

1920s. His goal was to sell cars to repeat customers more frequently than mere utility would dictate. The natural demand curve for automobiles has a single peak—the demand is highest in the springtime, when the snow disappears. The annual model change adds a second peak in the fall, when the new models make their debut, much like spring and fall fashions. This second peak allows for more even production and sales volumes through the year and—again in a nod to fashion—encourages people to trade perfectly good cars for new ones to have the latest style.

And the Motorama was the perfect place to see the latest fashions in both automobiles and couture. Each year showcased the newest production designs of General Motors, along with experimental concepts to test the waters for the future. Some, such as the original Corvette, drove almost directly from the Waldorf to the Chevy dealer's lot. Others weren't fully realized, by GM anyway.

It's been noted that the highly successful 1958 four-seat Thunderbird could well have been inspired by the concept cars at the 1955 Motorama. And many design concepts appeared on future GM models.

Spin and Grin Girls

But the cars weren't the only stars. The narrators, nicknamed the "spin-and-grin girls," wore the latest in designer gowns and posed alongside the cars on the turntables. They also had roles in the Motorama production numbers, which ran the gamut from song to ballet and interpretative dance. A *Fashion First* fashion show onstage paired the cars and the narrators in their special gowns by top-tier designers, including Christian Dior and Sophie for Saks Fifth Avenue.

The shows, which always originated at the Waldorf-Astoria, traveled across the country, with alternating stops (depending on the year) in Miami, Los Angeles, San Francisco, and Boston. In addition to newsreel films, GM made two full-color films themselves based on the Motoramas, 1956's *Design for Dreaming* and *A Touch of Magic* in 1961. Both feature dancer and choreographer Thelma "Tad" Tadlock—in the former she dances with a masked Marc Breaux, and she appears with actor James Mitchell in the latter. The films were created primarily for markets that the Motorama did not travel to.

There's no way to do justice to a topic as important as the Motorama in this short space—some truly excellent books have been written about these legendary GM shows. Our point is not to describe every detail of the beautiful cars on display, but rather to present the Motorama in the context of what it was—*a fashion show with wheels.*

Driving toward Tomorrow | 27

Chapter Two

KAISER-FRAZER LEADS THE WAY

FASHION AND STYLING HELP A STRUGGLING COMPANY GET NOTICED

▲ 1948 Kaiser-Frazer ad featuring the fashions of Norman Norell

◀ The 1951 Kaiser Golden Dragon in a dramatic two-page ad designed by Paul Rand

Of all the startup attempts to enter the postwar auto industry, Kaiser-Frazer came the closest to actually pulling it off. While others dreamed about air-cooled rear engines, cyclops headlamps, or three-wheeled wonders, Kaiser-Frazer came to market with a conventional four-door sedan, a brand-new, surplus ex-bomber plant, and the financial backing of a well-respected industrialist named Henry J. Kaiser. And while Kaiser could build Hoover Dam, he would have more trouble trying to build cars.

It seems the car was just *too* conventional. It was offered in one body style, a four-door sedan—and with one engine, an anemic six-cylinder most commonly used in farm implements. The styling was clean for the time and inoffensive, with flow-through fenders and a roomy interior, but the overall appearance was dowdy and drab. It was monochromatic in look, with almost no chrome trim except for the bumpers, and a typically uninspiring interior in the industry standard of tan and gray. That would soon change due to one pretty remarkable man—Carleton B. Spencer.

Beyond Basic Black

But first a little overview. Even Henry Ford was forced to backtrack on his "any color as long as it is black" edict by the mid-twenties, when fast-drying automotive paints and changing public tastes created a demand for color. The final two years of Model T production listed seven colors in addition to his iconic black. But inside he held to two choices—taupe and gray. The industry pretty much went along until 1936, when the dramatic Cord 810 appeared. Legendary designer Gordon Buehrig created paired combinations for the car and introduced dramatic dark interiors. A deep-blue broadcloth interior could be had with either Cadet Gray or Geneva Blue exteriors. Similarly, a maroon broadcloth was paired with exteriors of Rich Maroon or Palm Beach Tan. It was dramatic, it was exciting, but, like the Cord itself, it was just a ripple on the waters.

Chrysler made the lightbulb flicker in 1940 with an interior program that added red, blue, and green fabrics to their offerings, and introduced their legendary Highlander Scottish plaid interior in red and blue. A 1941 advertisement foreshadowed Burger King with a

Kaiser-Frazer Leads the Way | 29

Introduced in the spring of 1947, the Kaiser Manhattan launch brochure described a distinctive interior of "custom loomed wool, 'built-in-sheen' worsteds and satin finish broadcloths in exclusive blends matched with fine quality harmonizing carpets. The color symphony of each model is carried out even in such detail as the new steering wheel and chrome-trimmed instrument panel."

headline of "Have It Your Own Way." The Highlander was a success and lasted well into the postwar era, but again they didn't stand the industry on its head. Tiny Kaiser-Frazer would do that themselves.

Carleton Spencer understood color. He had previously worked as a blueprint artist at Fisher Body and then for the Ditzler paint division of PPG, where he developed an interest in color and trim. In 1939 and 1940, he edited a newsletter called *Colors and Contours*, which was a monthly trade publication published by *Ward's Automotive Reports* covering trends in automotive styling and color. He had what was known in the day as "flair." In other words, he was the perfect antidote for the dowdy K-F product line.

Spencer joined Kaiser-Frazer in 1946 and knew what lay in front of him. "From the first, my responsibility was selecting color and material," he said in a 1973 interview. "We didn't have a bunch of different engines—only a flathead six. And we had only one basic body, a four-door sedan. We were working on a future V-8 and other body styles, but among 1947–48 models, this was all we had. The easiest way to add variety was through color and trim."

What Do Women Want?

One of his earliest projects was a survey of color and trim preferences of women. He found their tastes to be remarkably well aligned with a study of home furnishing by *House and Garden* magazine. As a result, he began working with the magazine to develop colors and textiles with both automotive and home applications. For example, what *House and Garden* called Flame and Hot Chocolate became Indian Ceramic and Saddle Bronze at Kaiser-Frazer.

His first automotive contribution at Kaiser-Frazer was the smartly trimmed Frazer Manhattan, introduced in the spring of 1947. As described in the launch brochure, the Manhattan was a decidedly upscale offering and featured a distinctive interior of "custom loomed wool, 'built-in-sheen' worsteds and satin finish broadcloths in exclusive blends matched with fine quality harmonizing carpets." It went on to say, "The color symphony of each model is carried out even in such detail as the new steering wheel and chrome-trimmed instrument panel." The interiors themselves were dramatic two-tones and featured a contrasting color inset on the door panels and headliner.

Like Gordon Buehrig before him, Spencer created paired color combinations for his new flagship, six in total—Teal Blue with a matching interior contrasted in Doeskin Beige, Gunmetal with an interior of Emblem and Wedgwood Blue, Doeskin with Hickory Brown interior, Linden and Turf Green with matching interior, and Doeskin with Burgundy interior contrasted with Doeskin. The Manhattan was an instant hit—12,000 orders flooded in against a projected build of 3,000 cars.

Spencer's creations were also presented in a way that was very fashion friendly. Even before the public debut of the Frazer Manhattan, Henry J. Kaiser somehow managed to have the Fashion Academy of New York present it with a gold medal at a luncheon honoring the Best Dressed Woman of 1947—who happened to be none less than arts patron and Standard Oil heiress Millicent Rogers.

Top Designers Endorse Kaiser

To supplement the effort, an entire ad campaign aimed at women was launched, featuring the top designers of the day praising the styling and smartness of the Kaiser-Frazer line. Lily Dache, Claire McCardell, John Frederics, Tina Leser, Valentina, Omar Kiam, Nettie Rosenstein, Maximilian, and even the auto industry's own per diem princess, Pauline Trigère, all lent their name and likeness to the couture chorus singing the praises of Kaiser-Frazer. Spencer turned down the volume of black and cranked up the pastels.

Special brochures supported seasonal color combinations—such as "Autumn is a Frolic," promoting autumnal tones. But the crown jewel was a 5-inch-square direct-mail piece called "Custom Styling for Fashion Alert Women." It took the form of a pink makeup compact that folded out, and described the many charms of Kaiser-Frazer products to a feminine prospect.

And he was just getting started. Henry Kaiser had always groused about having his name on the lower-priced car, so Spencer came up with the Kaiser Custom, which featured extra chrome trim on the outside and an interior on par with the Manhattan on the inside. And for 1949, knowing that the rest of the industry would have new sheet metal, Spencer shifted into high gear. He either hit his stride or completely lost his mind, depending on whom you ask..

The most unique example of early Kaiser marketing was a 5" square direct-mail piece called "Custom Styling for Fashion Alert Women." It took the form of a pink makeup compact that folded out, and described the many charms of Kaiser-Frazer products to a feminine prospect.

"THE BEAUTY AND DISTINCTION OF CUSTOM CAR STYLING"

Tina Leser

COMMENDS THE NEW STYLING OF KAISER AND FRAZER CARS

FAMED designer of glamorous play clothes for American women, Tina Leser not only knows, but establishes, styles. "In the lines and colors of my beachwear," she says, "I try to capture the spirit of leisure and play in which it is worn. Successful design always reflects purpose. To me, the design, styling and colors of the new KAISER and FRAZER cars appeal as a most successful effort to make distinguished beauty reflect luxurious transportation."

KAISER   FRAZER

THE STYLING of the new KAISER and FRAZER is 100% postwar. Designers, given a free hand—unhampered by tradition or prewar tools—have created a masterpiece of functional beauty. These cars establish a new style trend which other manufacturers are sure to follow. And they are totally new in performance and ride, as well. For their engineering is as ultra-modern as their lines, colors and appointments. In them you truly ride in luxury, framed in beauty.

KAISER-FRAZER CORPORATION • WILLOW RUN, MICHIGAN

Beachwear by Tina Leser

"THE BEAUTY AND DISTINCTION OF CUSTOM CAR STYLING"

Valentina

CALLS THE KAISER AND THE FRAZER "AMERICA'S SMARTEST NEW CARS"

Internationally famous for her creative talents in theatrical and opera costuming, Valentina is recognized as one of the most influential leaders of high fashion in the world. Her taste in line, color and design has been acclaimed by the greatest stars of stage, screen and opera. Madame Valentina has called the KAISER and the FRAZER "America's smartest new cars." She adds: "I hope other designers follow such fine elegance of line and color."

Valentina herself models a formal evening dress of white silk damask, of her design

The new beauty of line and color which distinguishes the KAISER and the FRAZER from all other cars, has set a fashion which manufacturers of cars designed before the war will surely follow. Currently, these 100% postwar models stand out like a beautiful woman in any gathering—attract admiring comment from everyone. You are invited to *drive* one of these cars and learn how easily it handles—how wonderfully it rides. Just call your nearby dealer.

 KAISER-FRAZER CORPORATION
WILLOW RUN, MICHIGAN

An entire ad campaign aimed at women was launched in 1947, featuring top fashion designers of the day praising the styling and smartness of the Kaiser-Frazer line.

32 | GLAMOUR ROAD

"THE BEAUTY AND DISTINCTION OF CUSTOM CAR STYLING"

Omar Kiam

RECOGNIZES "THE FUTURE TREND" IN KAISER AND FRAZER DESIGN

Important and versatile creator of women's fashions, Omar Kiam is now designing for Ben Reig, Inc. in New York, after years in Hollywood. His style judgment is considered infallible by fashion experts the world around.

Asked to comment on the styling of the new KAISER and FRAZER cars, Omar Kiam said: "These automobiles are outstanding in beauty of line. And the good taste of their designers is evidenced also in color, trim, and interior upholstery and appointments. Unquestionably, they establish the future trend in fine cars."

You, too, will instantly admire the new beauty of the KAISER and the FRAZER. But only a *ride* can give you an appreciation of their supreme comfort and remarkable performance.

A checked taffeta dress, with matching coat lined in red wool... a Ben Reig original by Omar Kiam.

KAISER  **FRAZER**

KAISER-FRAZER CORPORATION · WILLOW RUN, MICHIGAN

Nettie Rosenstein

Defines the Style Ingredients of the New Kaiser and Frazer Cars

Born with an instinct for design, Nettie Rosenstein began by making dresses for her dolls as a little girl in Austria — became an international success as a fashion arbiter in New York.

Asked to tell the secret of good style, Nettie Rosenstein said, "Style is more easily recognized than defined. As evidenced in the new KAISER and FRAZER motor cars, I would say it includes beauty of line and fine craftsmanship, as well as pleasing color of body and interior."

A dashing medieval red coat for town wear, by Nettie Rosenstein.

KAISER  **FRAZER**

KAISER-FRAZER CORPORATION · WILLOW RUN, MICHIGAN

Style-conscious women have been among the first to admire and acquire these totally new, 100% postwar cars. They recognize in the KAISER and the FRAZER a design trend — far in advance of the industry — that combines greater beauty with more roominess, more comfort, and a smooth, gliding ride never before known.

P. S. Husbands know that the KAISER and the FRAZER **are as** advanced mechanically as in exterior and interior styling.

"THE BEAUTY AND DISTINCTION OF CUSTOM CAR STYLING"

"THE BEAUTY AND DISTINCTION OF CUSTOM CAR STYLING"

Lilly Dache

Praises the Continental Styling of the KAISER and the FRAZER

Head of the largest high-fashion millinery business in the world, Lilly Dache is internationally acclaimed as the foremost designer of chapeaux for discriminating women. Even in Paris, where she spent her apprenticeship, her hats are copied. Her latest, named in honor of the Frazer Manhattan, is pictured here. "Europe will copy the new, most-modern design of these postwar cars," she says. "Both the KAISER and the FRAZER are truly continental in their suave lines, their supremely good taste and fashionable color ensembles."

The "Manhattan," a green wool beret with plaid wool insertion and long scarf, by Lilly Dache

KAISER FRAZER

The KAISER and the FRAZER definitely "do something" for their feminine owners. No woman could be more envied for the beauty and good taste of her personal transportation. No woman ever commanded a sweeter, smoother, more easy-to-handle motor car. Here stylish lines and fashionable colors reflect the utmost in smartness, safety and luxurious riding qualities.

P. S.—They actually cost very little more than pre-war cars.

KAISER-FRAZER CORPORATION, WILLOW RUN, MICHIGAN

"THE BEAUTY AND DISTINCTION OF CUSTOM CAR STYLING"

Pauline Trigère

APPRAISES THE "BASIC STYLING" OF THE KAISER AND THE FRAZER

Parisian-born Pauline Trigère's early teachers included several of the masters of French couture. Upon reaching New York, she rapidly made her presence known in the realm of high fashion and founded her own establishment in 1942. Since the beginning, Trigère has put emphasis on "Simple and basic design that must always be *right*." This same idea occasioned her comment about the KAISER and the FRAZER, "Such basic styling is right, and will set the pattern for other new cars in the modern trend."

The new "basic" postwar design of the KAISER and the FRAZER begins with *beauty*. It brings an unprecedented combination of *comfort*, *safety* and *handling ease* to motor car transportation!

Summer dinner dress of Chinese natural silk Shantung with fichu décolleté.

KAISER  **FRAZER**

KAISER-FRAZER CORPORATION · WILLOW RUN, MICHIGAN

LADIES' HOME JOURNAL

Claire McCardell
SAYS KAISER AND FRAZER BEAUTY COMBINES STYLE WITH UTILITY

The vast success of Claire McCardell as designer for Townley Frocks, Inc., is the result of her talent for putting youth and glamor and style into the practical work and play clothes of American women. Her fashions are always useful—and enormously popular! So it is not surprising that McCardell sees her own philosophy of design in KAISER and FRAZER cars. Of them, she says, "The beauty of these original designs is based on utility. No wonder women fall in love with them."

The beautiful lines of the KAISER and the FRAZER are the result of postwar engineering that gives you more room, greater safety, and the most restful ride you have ever enjoyed in an automobile!

KAISER-FRAZER CORPORATION
WILLOW RUN, MICHIGAN

KAISER **FRAZER**

Sunburn-brown jersey beachwear designed by Claire McCardell

VICTOR KEPPLER

"THE BEAUTY AND DISTINCTION OF CUSTOM CAR STYLING"

"THE BEAUTY AND DISTINCTION OF CUSTOM CAR STYLING"

JOHN FREDERICS
DISCERNS "TECHNICAL MASTERY" IN THE DESIGN OF THE KAISER AND THE FRAZER

Renowned creator of fashionable millinery, artist John Frederics has long been a noted world authority on design. His fertile imagination has produced many innovations which have led to revolutionary style trends.

Frederics' practiced eye instantly discerned correspondingly important innovations in motor-car design which you will also see when you inspect the KAISER or the FRAZER. He said, "These cars are the magnificent result of fine artistic conception and technical mastery, with the careful emphasis on detail that means continuing enjoyment to owners."

Your own appreciation of beauty and craftsmanship is bound to be pleasingly stimulated when you inspect the KAISER or the FRAZER. And your first ride will be *a ride you never forget!*

Modern carriage hat and accessories, a John Frederics creation in rough straw with black maline veiling.

VICTOR KEPPLER

KAISER **FRAZER**

KAISER-FRAZER CORPORATION · WILLOW RUN, MICHIGAN

Kaiser-Frazer Leads the Way | 35

Kaiser-Frazer offered 17% of the total exterior colors in the industry, and an eye-popping 41.6% of all the interior fabric choices in the entire domestic market—50% more than industry leader General Motors.

◀ *The 1949 Kaiser Color and Trim Guide is an impressive piece. Covered in red leatherette with an artist's easel on the cover, it measures just over 4 inches thick. Inside are paint and fabric samples—thirty-seven solid exterior paint colors and nine two-tone combinations, along with an unprecedented choice of sixty-two fabrics.*

Thirty-Seven Paint Colors and Sixty-Two Fabric Choices

The 1949 Kaiser Color and Trim Guide is an impressive piece. Covered in red leatherette with an artist's palette on the cover, it measures just over 4 inches thick. Inside are paint and fabric samples, thirty-seven solid exterior paint colors, and nine two-tone combinations. For perspective, luxury leader Cadillac was tied for second place at seventeen. But the fabrics look like a whole fashion show unto themselves. The fabric samples represent Corundle Cords, Nocturne Cloth, Beaumont Cloth, and broadcloths in both solids and pinstripes. The range of colors offered is simply an unprecedented rainbow of textiles that include light and dark shades of blue, multiple greens, Dark Hickory Brown, Rich Turquoise, and two shades of Rose—and we haven't even gotten to leather yet. Of particular interest is the Nocturne Cloth, which was the automotive equivalent of deep-cord chenille. Spencer touted the ease of mending when torn as an unusually practical selling point. All in all, they represented sixty-two different fabrics. To add context, Cadillac had twelve interior fabrics in 1949 and Buick had four. Kaiser-Frazer offered 17% of the total exterior colors in the industry, and an eye-popping 41.6% of all the interior fabric choices in the entire domestic market—50% more than industry leader General Motors.

And just when you thought it couldn't get crazier, Spencer decided that the Kaiser Custom owners needed a little added distinction—so he spelled out each of the fourteen available color names on the front fender in chrome script. A new Kaiser could say anything from Onyx to Flax to Clay Pipe Gray on the fender. Even Indian Ceramic and Caribbean Coral were among the offerings. It was no small burden on the production folks, who had to figure out

▶ Details from a 1953 Kaiser Dragon. Note the Bambu vinyl on the roof and the interior, including the dashboard, door panels, seat bolsters, and ceiling. The geometric-patterned cloth was called Laguna. Car courtesy of the Prescott Collection.

how to inventory and install fourteen different emblems (which required holes in fourteen different places) on the front fenders. It shall not surprise you to know that this did not become an ongoing tradition.

Along Came a Dragon

One might think that the totally restyled and quite handsome Kaiser line for 1951 would take the spotlight off the Color and Trim Department, but that was not the case. While the color name scripts did disappear from the fenders, the new car continued to be offered in colorful and numerous combinations—and one very noteworthy model, the Golden Dragon.

Announced in November 1950, the Golden Dragon was a very special limited-production option package on a Kaiser Deluxe. Finished in Arena Yellow with a black-painted top, the Dragon was made possible by a special cold-embossed, simulated alligator vinyl that Spencer named Dragon Vinyl so as not to mislead customers into thinking it was actual alligator hide. It covered every soft surface inside the car—the dash, the package shelf, the door panels, the 2½" pleats, and bolsters of the seats. It made the entire interior into a giant faux alligator handbag and was attention-getting and popular enough that it was ultimately offered in nine different color and trim combinations based on interiors of Black, Burma Brown, Cape Verde Green, Scarlet, Tropical Green, and even Caribbean Coral.

By February 1951, he changed it all again with the Second Series Dragons. The Dragon Vinyl was replaced with another vinyl product called Dinosaur Vinyl, which was now applied to the roof as well as the seats. They had three combinations—the Golden Dragon in Arena Yellow and Black, the Silver Dragon in Mariner Gray and Scarlet, and the Emerald Dragon in monochromatic Cape Verde

This 1952 ad for the Kaiser Manhattan featured graphics by Paul Rand.

Green. A fourth, the Jade Dragon, featuring a once-again-revised, long-grain vinyl called Tropical, was released in Tropical Green with Straw in April.

As if that weren't enough, Spencer created an exhibit for the 1951 Chicago Auto Show called "Worldways in Motoring," featuring cars of the four corners of the globe (subject to interpretation, of course). From the North came the Kaiser "Explorer," finished in deep Academy Blue with a white sealskin padded top and an interior of genuine polar bear hides. A finishing touch was a pith helmet on the front seat. Amazingly, this car is known to have survived. The plains of the Serengeti inspired the "Safari," which was trimmed in a uniquely juxtaposed interior of predator and prey featuring seats of lion and zebra skins. From the American West came the cowboy-modern "Caballero" with an interior of calf and palomino hides, and door-mounted saddlebags with western spur window handles. Three Caballeros were ultimately made, for Roy Rogers, Gene Autry, and a wealthy rancher.

The fourth was the rarest and also the most PETA friendly. The "South Seas" captured the spirit that was sweeping the nation in the wake of the James Michener book *Tales of the South Pacific*. The book was a sensation that would ultimately culminate in a Broadway show, major musical, Polynesian Modern craze, hula hoops, and, indirectly, Hawaiian statehood. The "South Seas" show car featured exotic, tiki-themed, multicolored Hawaiian linen upholstery trimmed in straw-like tropical vinyl; a floor covering of woven straw strips; a fishnet headliner; and a Lucite rear picnic table with a barometer and compass.

Couldn't Compete with the Big Three

It's no secret that the Independents (Kaiser, Hudson, Nash, Studebaker, Packard, and the like) were under considerable financial pressure in the early 1950s. The technological advances that made cars more pleasurable to own, such as powerful high-compression engines, power steering and automatic transmissions, came at a high development cost. Meanwhile, Henry Ford II decided to try and catch Chevrolet in 1953 and did so by building large quantities of unordered cars and shipping them to dealers who hadn't asked for them. He paid huge amounts of cash under the table to Ford dealers to sell them cheap and buy market share. Chevrolet didn't blink an eye, but it caused enormous economic damage to the independents who simply couldn't keep up.

Production fell dramatically for Kaiser in 1953 but Spencer had one more trick up his sleeve. Kaiser-Frazer might be on the way out but they were going in style with the 1953 Kaiser Dragon. He reached out to fashion consultant Marie Nichols who contributed a geometric cloth she called Laguna which he paired with a new long-grain vinyl called Bambu. In true Dragon fashion, this vinyl covered the roof, the dash, the doors, and the package shelf and bolstered the seats. It even lined the glove box. He set it off with a mouton style Calpoint carpeting and added gold plated nameplates, hood and trunk ornaments, and an owner's nameplate on the dash. He created color combinations of Jade Tint Green with Green, Onyx Black with Black, Stardust Ivory with Black, and Maroon Velvet with Maroon, Spencer's own personal favorite. They would be his swan song.

The 1953 editions were the final Dragons. Shortly after, that the lights went out at Kaiser-Frazer and Spencer went into semi-retirement. Their brief era in the automobile business was over, but the Dragon has earned a spot in history and it is not forgotten that one man in a tiny company changed the industry for decades to follow.

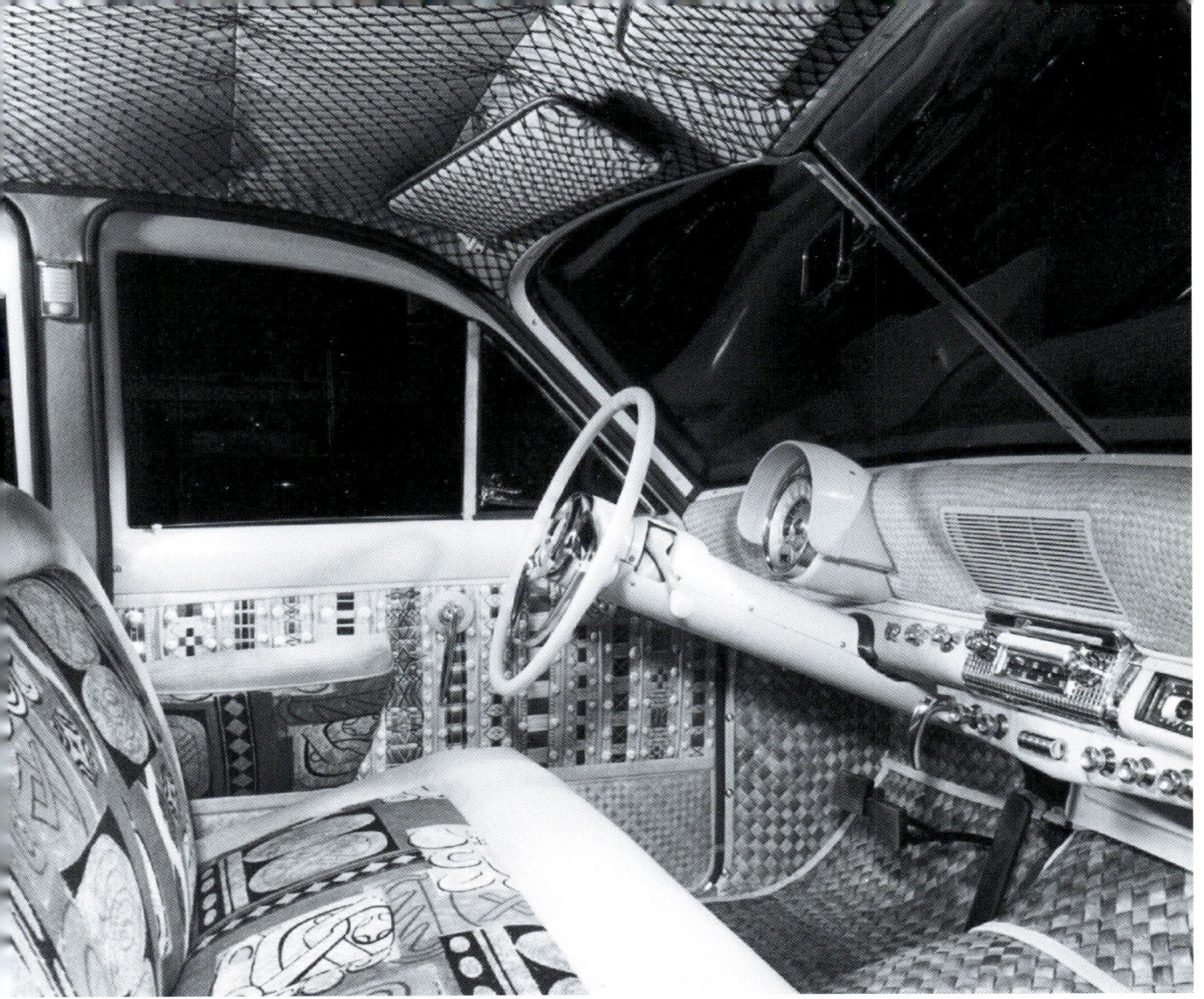

◀ Created for the 1951 Chicago Auto Show by Carleton Spencer, the "South Seas" captured the spirit that was sweeping the nation in the wake of the James Michener book Tales of the South Pacific. The book was a sensation that would ultimately culminate in a Broadway show, major musical, Polynesian Modern craze, hula hoops and, indirectly, Hawaiian statehood.

▶ The "South Seas" show car featured exotic, tiki-themed, multicolored Hawaiian linen upholstery trimmed in straw-like tropical vinyl; a floor covering of woven straw strips; a fishnet headliner; and a Lucite rear picnic table with a barometer and compass.

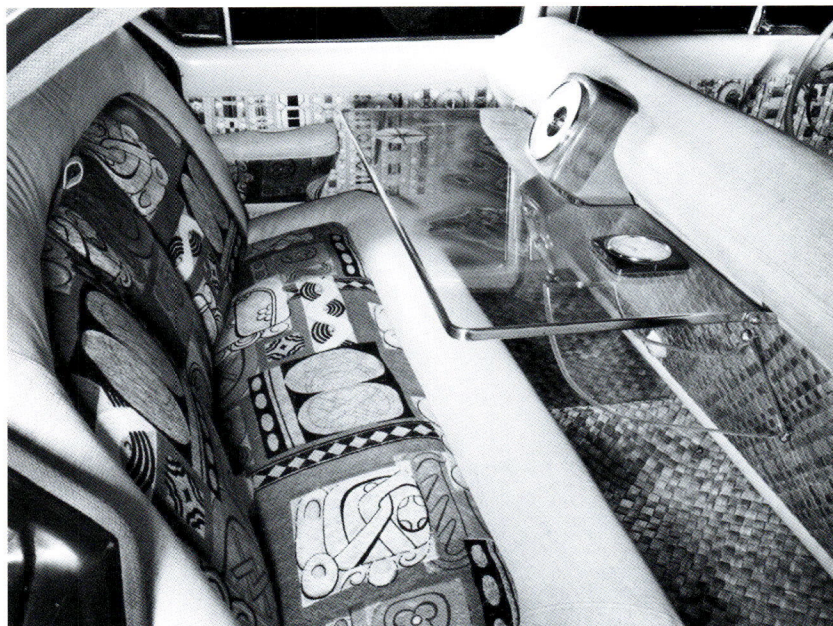

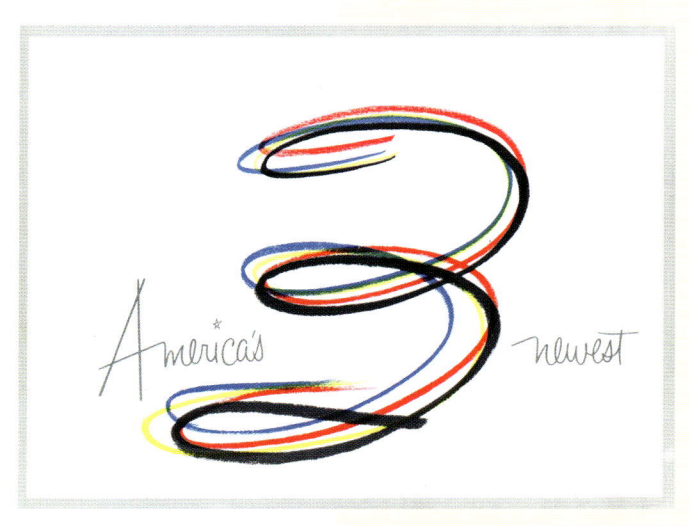

Cover of a 1951 Kaiser-Frazer brochure designed by Paul Rand

Paul Rand refashioned the advertising industry in New York City and introduced the concept of branding and logo recognition.
—SUSAN HENSHAW JONES,
MUSEUM OF THE CITY OF NEW YORK

PAUL RAND ACHIEVES THE IMPOSSIBLE: MAKING KAISER LOOK COOL

There's an unwritten rule in the auto industry that the worse the financial position of the automaker, the better the ad agency has to be. And by the spring of 1949, the pudgy little car from Willow Run needed all the help it could get. It wasn't the fault of the design department or Carleton Spencer, but old Henry J himself had made a couple of critical financial mistakes—mainly overestimating sales volume for 1949—that had left them cash-strapped and stuck with carryover styling in a sea of all-new cars.

It was at some point in 1949 that K-F found top-tier help indeed with the services of the William H. Weintraub agency. Weintraub was a cutting-edge organization full of talented people. They had a creative director named Bill Bernbach—the man Don Draper was modeled after, and the same guy who later would tell you to "Think Small" with the Volkswagen Beetle. Weintraub allowed full artistic freedom to its talented art director, who was none other than the young Paul Rand himself. Rand was well established by then as one of the very finest graphic designers on Madison Avenue, but he had not yet attained the godlike status he would achieve when he opened his own design-consulting firm in 1955 and went on to design the IBM logo.

Rand, who has more than once been called the Picasso of graphic design, changed everything in the advertising business. It was Rand who placed the art director above the copywriter. Automotive advertising, especially before the war, was often rote and uninteresting, with a hard-sell approach and virtually every square inch covered with copy. It had as much allure as an eye chart. Rand, with his concept of "bold simplicity," changed that.

To quote from the 2015 show *Everything Is Design: The Work of Paul Rand*, at the Museum of the City of New York. "Paul Rand refashioned the advertising industry in New York City and introduced the concept of branding and logo recognition," said Susan Henshaw Jones, the Ronay Menschel Director at the City Museum.

Rand treated the Kaiser in a playful way, with bold, colorful graphics and daring fonts. Like many of his works of the era, they were more like a modern art painting that happened to include a Kaiser automobile. His work for Kaiser was prodigious, creating not only advertisements for the cars but also logos, dealer showroom materials, posters, billboards, and even the Kaiser-Frazer annual report.

"Paul Rand once said, 'The problem of the artist is to defamiliarize the ordinary,' and it's a motto he took risks with throughout his career. For example, he would pair images of radically different scale or media, unusual color combinations, and bold typefaces with delicate hand lettering," said Donald Albrecht, the Museum of the City of New York's curator of architecture and design. "The result would be a visually stimulating, memorable, problem-solving approach to a design."[1]

Even the genius of Paul Rand couldn't alter the ultimate destiny of Kaiser-Frazer, but his colorful graphics and attention-grabbing layouts undoubtedly helped in catching the eye of an increasingly distracted public. In the end he couldn't make people buy one, but he certainly made them take notice, and their moment of intersection—albeit on differing trajectories—is one of the fascinating moments in the postwar industry.

Many images in this section are from Danny Lewandowski, curator and archivist at paulrand.design

Kaiser

for 1951

Built to better the best on the road

KAISER

"Hardtop" Dragon

for gracious living
for luxurious driving

Paul Rand

◀ The bold graphics on this 1953 Dragon brochure show an amazingly modern approach to automotive marketing, with no car in sight.

◀ Modernist artist Henri Matisse was creating his famous cutouts just before Rand designed these 1950 posters, and the influence is clear. The typography has a constructivist look and is radically different from the hand scripts that were popular for advertising then.

Kaiser-Frazer Leads the Way | 43

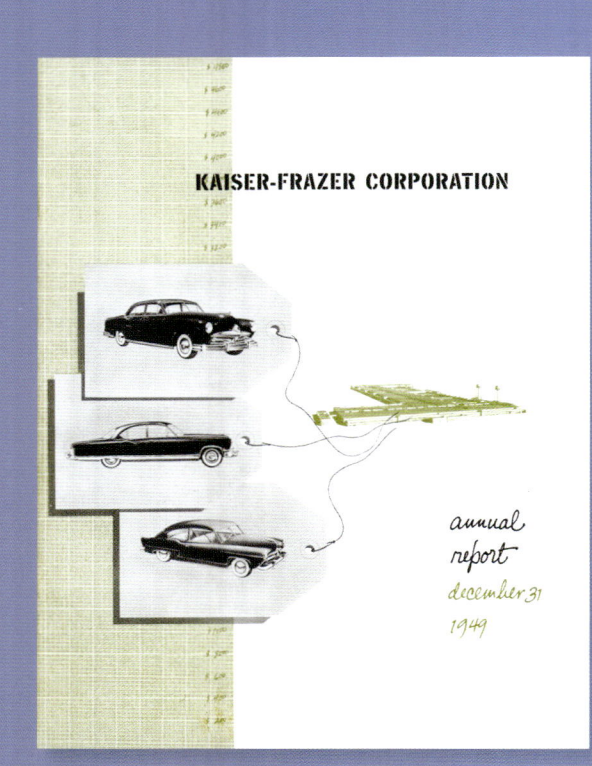

▶ Rand's strong graphic approach was applied to advertisements, posters, and even annual reports.

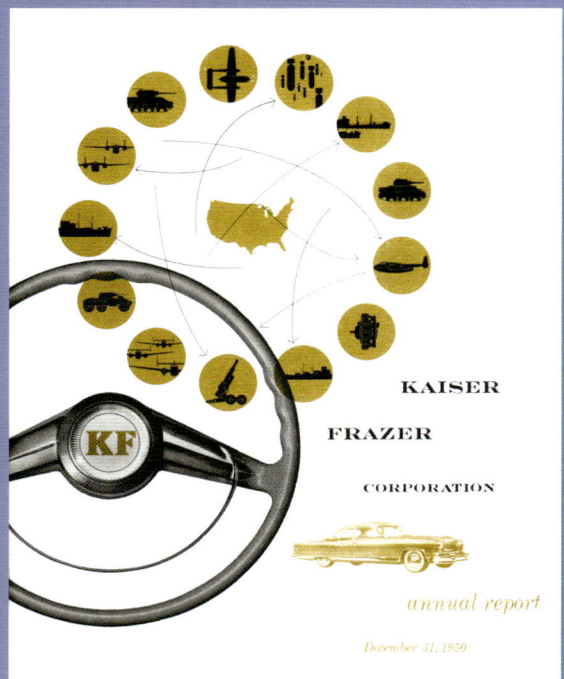

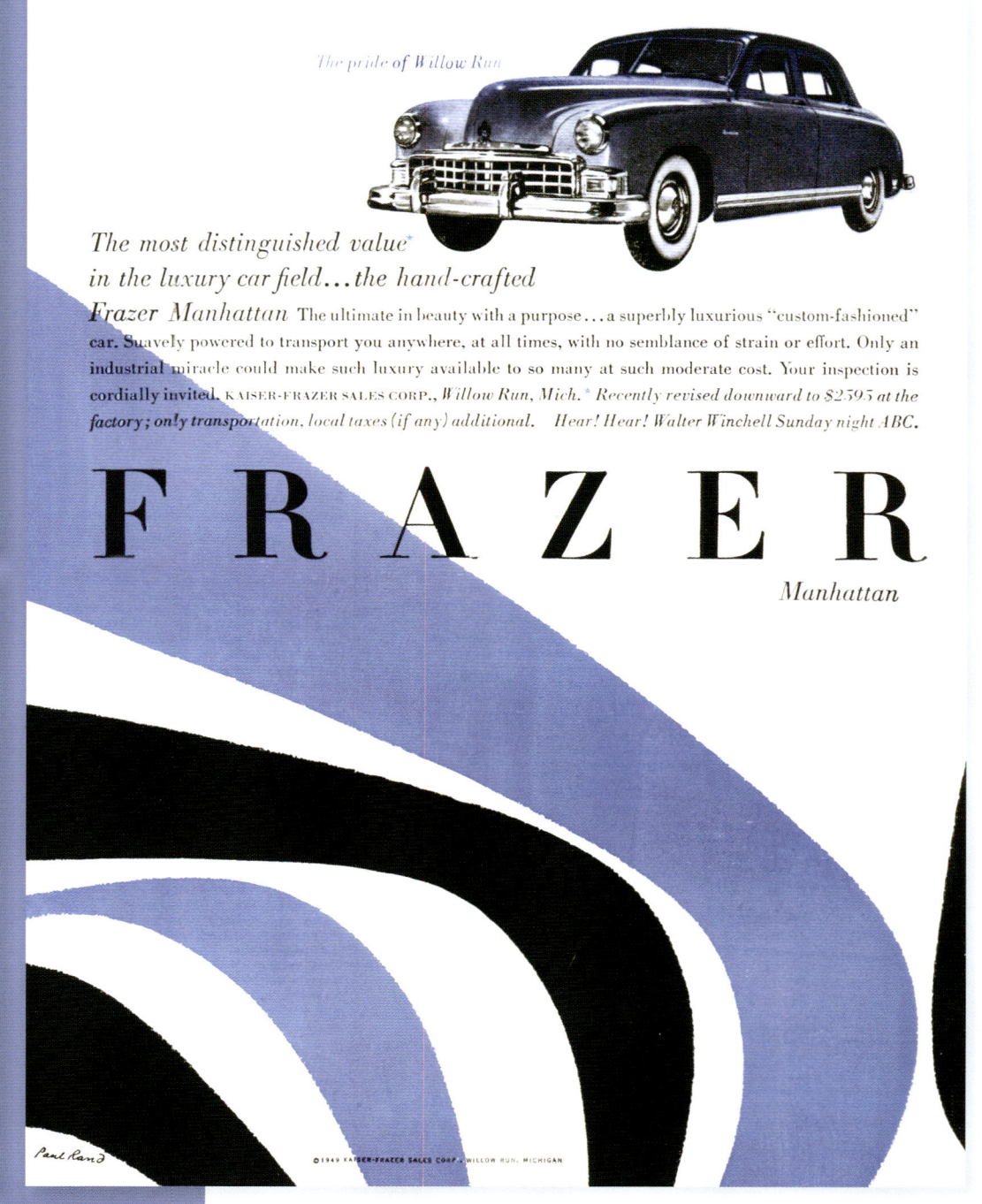

The pride of Willow Run

The most distinguished value
in the luxury car field...the hand-crafted
Frazer Manhattan The ultimate in beauty with a purpose...a superbly luxurious "custom-fashioned" car. Suavely powered to transport you anywhere, at all times, with no semblance of strain or effort. Only an industrial miracle could make such luxury available to so many at such moderate cost. Your inspection is cordially invited. KAISER-FRAZER SALES CORP., *Willow Run, Mich.* * *Recently revised downward to $2395 at the factory; only transportation, local taxes (if any) additional.* Hear! Hear! Walter Winchell Sunday night ABC.

FRAZER
Manhattan

44 | GLAMOUR ROAD

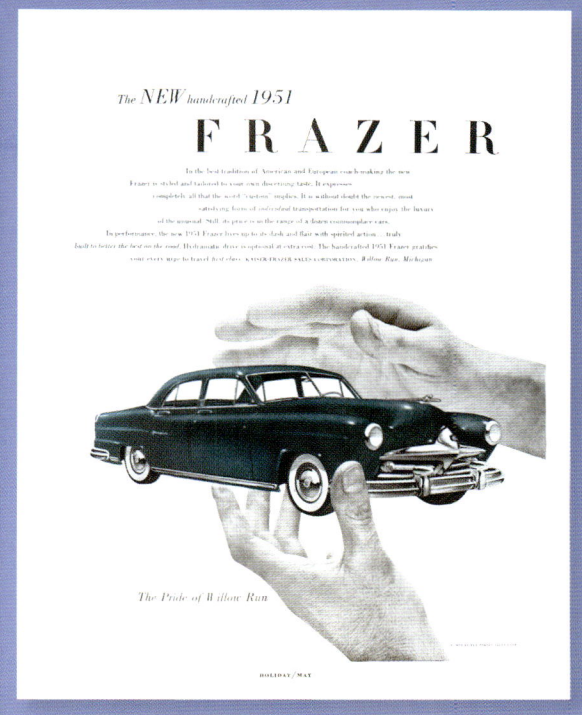

▶ These ads show an influence of surrealist Man Ray. Surrealism was becoming a strong art movement in the US in the late 1940s and was often applied in cinema.

Kaiser-Frazer Leads the Way | 45

46 | GLAMOUR ROAD

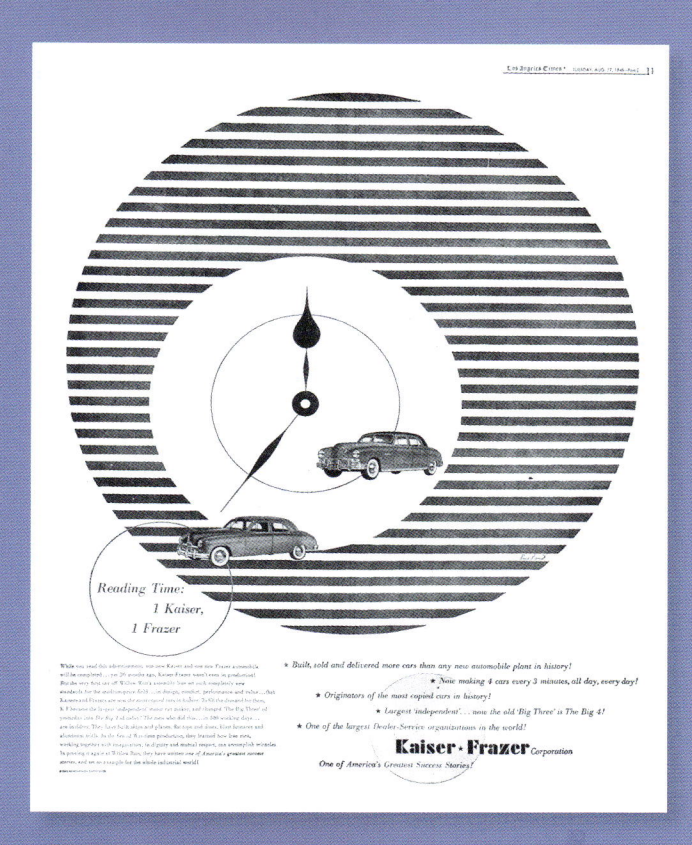

Black-and-white newspaper ads are one of the most difficult formats to design—you have black ink, the reproduction is coarse, and most advertisers want to jam the page with information since the ads are expensive. And in Rand's case, he was given a rather pudgy-looking car to promote. His solution? Clever use of large graphic gestures, smart concepts, elegant but playful typography—and a very small image of the product being advertised—make these ads bold and exciting. Imagine opening a newspaper in 1949, with pages jam-packed with text and ads, and then coming across these fun, energetic pages!

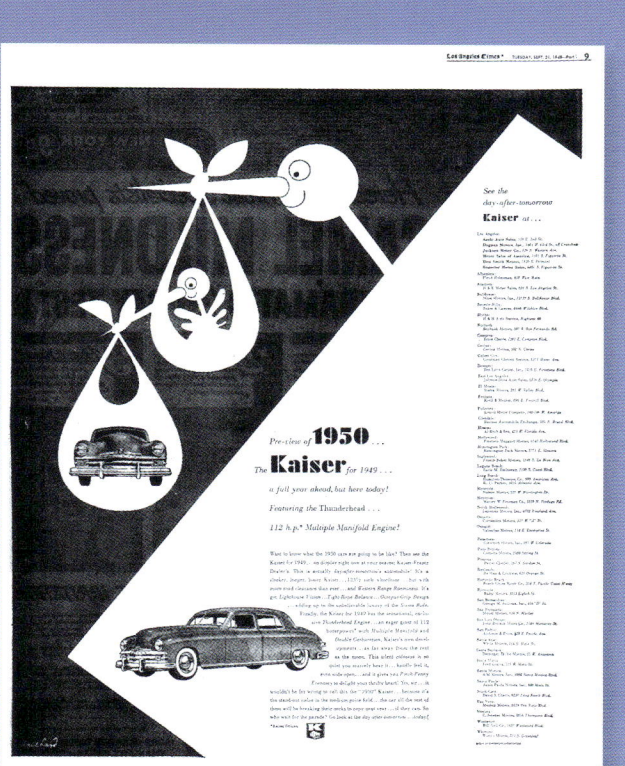

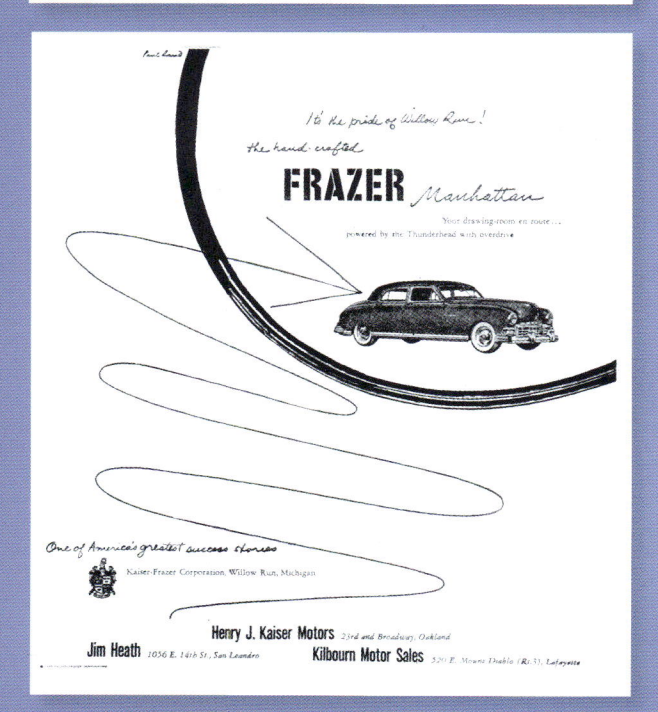

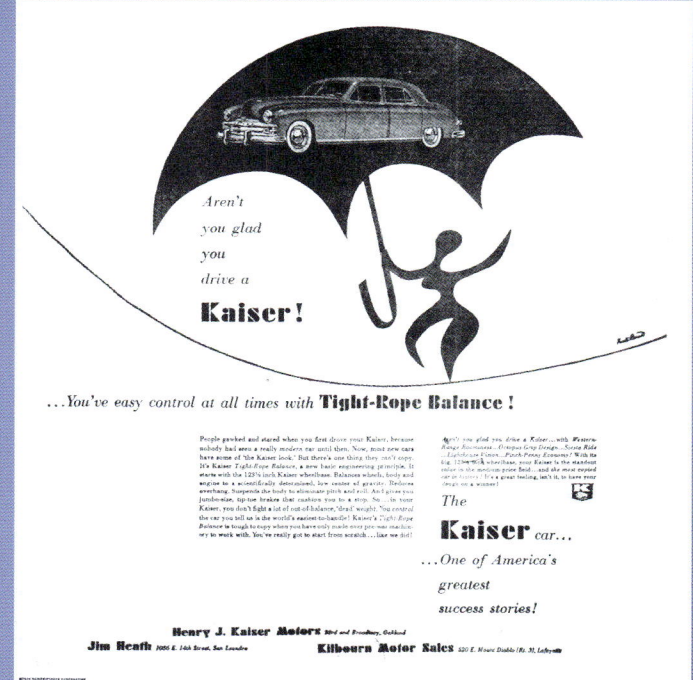

Kaiser-Frazer Leads the Way | 47

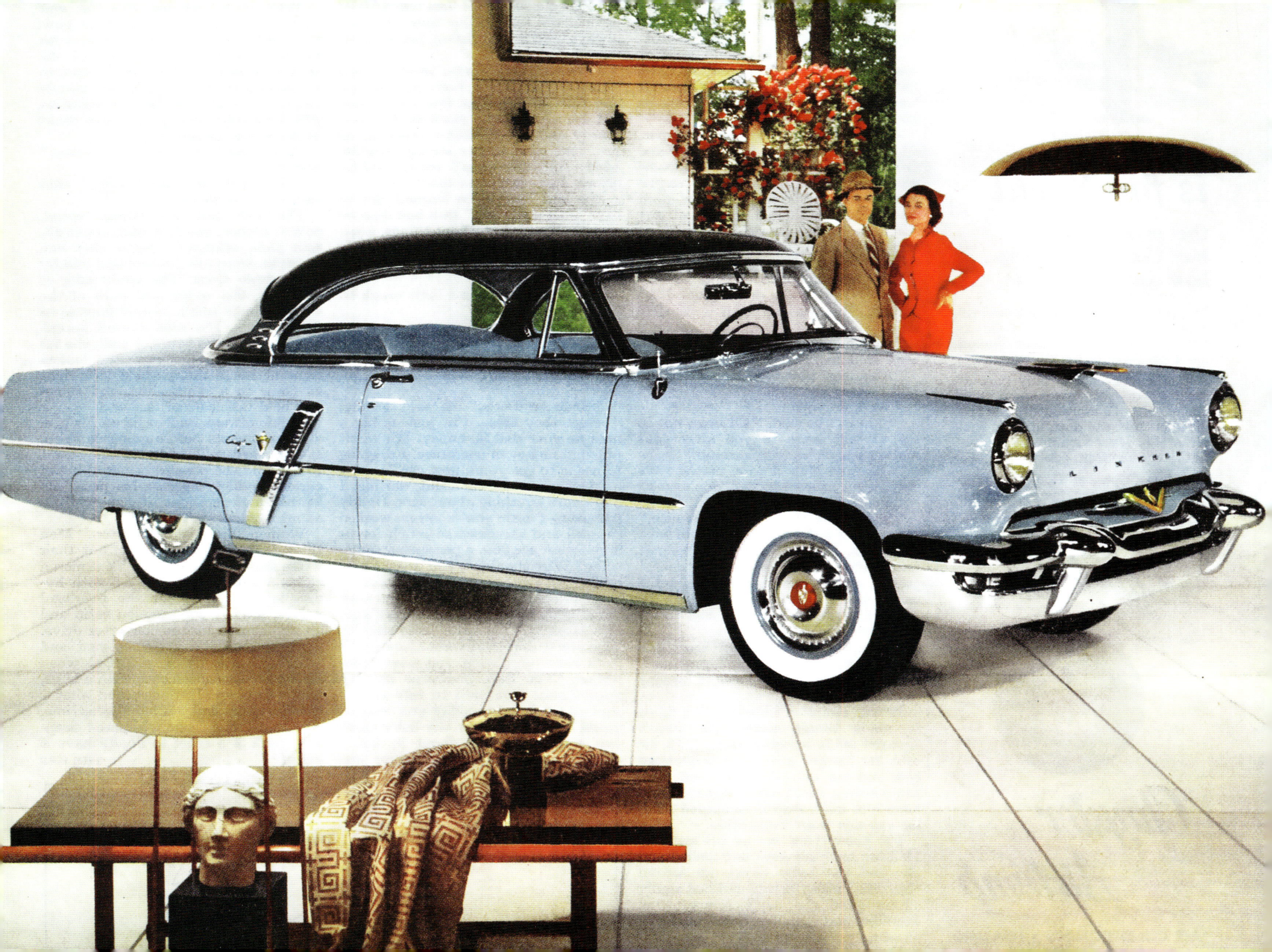

MODERN LIVING

LINCOLN IS INSPIRED BY A PIVOTAL 1949 DESIGN SHOW IN DETROIT

▲ *Spread from the 1952 Lincoln brochure*

◀ *Starting in 1952, Lincoln took a revolutionary approach to marketing by presenting their luxury cars as part of the new casual, elegant, modern lifestyle. Here, a 1953 Lincoln Capri is shown with iconic elements of midcentury decor.*

Billy Wilder's iconic 1950 film *Sunset Boulevard* told the tale of a glamorous silent-movie star who peaked in the Roaring Twenties but was thoroughly out of date by 1950. In truth, he could have made the film about Lincoln. Under the protective tutelage of Edsel Ford, the car was both beautiful and exclusive in the twenties—offering a catalog full of custom body styles—and could even be custom-ordered to suit. Lincoln was a favorite of the movie star set in the twenties and early thirties, but the Depression shook it to its core. Never a volume offering, Lincoln survived the Depression by the introduction of a midpriced production car, the Zephyr, which offered handsome styling and a popular price. While the mechanical underpinnings were unimpressive, with transverse, solid axles (a.k.a. "buggy springs") that were more at home beneath a Model T than a luxury offering, and a flathead V-12 engine derived from a Ford V-8, the Zephyr bought time.

It was a Zephyr that Edsel had customized into a cabriolet for his own use in 1939. His instruction that the look was to be "strictly Continental" gave the car a name—the Lincoln Continental—and all his society friends wanted to buy one. The production version that quickly followed, with its long hood and rear-mounted spare tire, is remembered as one of the loveliest cars of its era. In tribute to its enduring beauty, it remained in production through 1948, having outlived its inspirer—Edsel Ford himself died in 1943.

The restyled Lincoln lineup for 1949 had a more modern chassis, up-to-date suspension, and a flathead V-8 engine that developed a respectable 152 horsepower, but the timeless Continental was no more. In its place were the streamlined Cosmopolitan and the medium-priced, Mercury-based base Lincoln. They were attractive-enough cars, despite their oddly recessed headlamps and frowning grilles, but they did not captivate the motoring public. The advertising was likewise unremarkable, showing the car but giving it no real positioning. Headlines clamored, "Lincoln has a new idea," but no one seems to recall what it was. Like many faded movie stars, Lincoln needed a makeover.

And in 1952, it got one.

Modern Living | 49

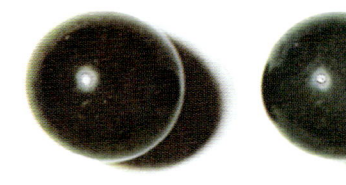

CHOICE

Lincoln for 1952 provides a wide range of exterior color selections, including a host of two-tone color combinations to help you make your new Cosmopolitan or Capri exactly the car of your personal choice.

Inside, too, you may choose from an extensive range of interior selections that harmonize with the exterior hues you like best.

And this year, an even greater array of fine leathers and choice fabric combinations also serve to make Lincoln ownership still more distinctive, more highly personal than ever before.

Lincoln Gets a Makeover

It was more like a reinvention of the brand than just an all-new car. The Ford family had taken a personal interest in the Lincoln nameplate and installed Benson Ford as vice president of the Lincoln-Mercury Division back in 1948. He arrived too late to make any changes in the 1949–51 models, but there was plenty of time to plan the new '52s. The goal was to get Lincoln out of the medium- priced market and close the perceived gap between it and Cadillac.

The whole Ford Motor Company product line was restyled for 1952. The Ford, the Mercury, and the Lincoln received not only new body styling for 1952, but an all-new chassis underneath as well. The base Lincoln was dropped, leaving them to compete only in the luxury car class. The new Lincoln Cosmopolitan was both shorter and lighter than before—6 inches shorter and 500 pounds lighter than a comparable '51, and thoroughly modern throughout. It featured a brand-new, 160-horsepower, high-compression V-8 engine and standard automatic transmission. The engine had more torque and less weight than the previous year, and the suspension was all new and state of the art, which gave the car superior handling and roadholding abilities. In one year, it had gone from dowdy to lithe and athletic.

The styling was low and clean, with squared-off fenders and hood line, and sparing but effective use of brightwork, including a distinctive chrome slash across the rear fender. The hardtop coupe, Lincoln's first, was especially attractive. The look was further enhanced with handsome interiors, an aircraft-inspired instrument panel, and a rainbow of colors—no fewer than fourteen exterior color choices, twenty-seven two-tones, and even five convertible top colors.

50 | GLAMOUR ROAD

COLORS

...and CHOICEST

of interior trims

◄ *The large-format 1952 Lincoln sales brochure is elegant and modern, with none of the trappings of traditional luxury excess. The clean graphic design combines paint colors as floating spheres, fabric choices as photographic swatches, and illustrated renderings to show colors on the coupe. The typography is spare and reserved.*

Harry Walton remarked in *Popular Science* that "hardly anything but the name remains of Ford Motor Company's upper-bracket automobiles."[1] The car was universally praised, both for its appearance and for its performance—especially its handling—so much so that Lincoln would become prominent in the Mexican road races of the early 1950s.

Designed for Modern Living

It was a very special car, and they needed an ad campaign that was just as fresh and modern as the car itself. Lincoln-Mercury's advertising agency, Kenyon and Eckhardt, was handed a very tall order, and this time they knocked it out of the park. The theme was Modern Living, and it was a fully integrated campaign—the print advertising, dealer brochures, direct-mail pieces, and dealer support materials were all designed around the Modern Living theme. Many buys were placed in women's periodicals. Creative director Bill Johnson was a big believer in photography and began utilizing it in the campaign. The campaign showed the modern lifestyle—with up-to-the-minute midcentury architecture, furniture, and fashion. It was breezy, uncluttered, and in very upscale yet informal good taste. Cars were even placed in mockups of modern living rooms. The ads stressed that the cars were "luxurious yet functional," with "ample room," but not "oversized, heavy and hard to park," and the Lincoln "completely matches the characteristics of modern living." The illustrations showed women behind the wheel as well as men. It was a groundbreaking campaign and won advertising awards each year. Direct-mail pieces included themes of "Modern Women" and "Modern Home," which were targeted at women buyers.

No small part of the magic came from the art director, Chauncey Korton. He didn't have an agency background;

Modern Living | 51

he had been an interior decorator, graphic designer, and illustrator before, but he demonstrated an understanding of modern architecture and furnishings that matched the need precisely. Korton held the key to the look that was the Modern Living campaign.

We have not located a torn ticket stub that proves unequivocally that Korton attended Alexander Girard's groundbreaking *For Modern Living* exhibition at the Detroit Institute of Arts in 1949, but given the circles in which he moved, it is all but impossible that he did not attend. All of the arrows line up. The exhibition would have reached throughout the design community in the Detroit area and

▶ *The first ads from 1952 utilized illustration exclusively, highlighting how elements of the new modern lifestyle were represented in the new Lincolns—"Beautiful, functional, like today's new homes," "New glass-wall visibility," "Easygoing comfort of outdoor living."*

all of lower Michigan and across the region for that matter, and while we can't lift the fingerprints, the influence is undeniable. Furthermore, it's impossible that Lincoln-Mercury would have simply borrowed the name of Girard's breakthrough exhibition from under his nose. It would have required his consent if not indeed his active participation.

A Groundbreaking Exhibition

As we noted in chapter 1, Alexander Girard's *An Exhibition for Modern Living* was presented at the Detroit Institute of Arts in the late fall of 1949. It was forward looking and wide ranging in its scope, presenting a wealth of household products ranging from sofas to salt shakers, all reinterpreted through a postwar eye. And it's likely that most of the automobile designers of the day saw it. In addition to Girard, the executive committee included Eero Saarinen—who would go on to design the GM Tech Center as well as the Gateway Arch in St. Louis (notably, Alexander Girard was also on that team) and the space-age TWA Flight Center at JFK Airport in New York—as well as Minoru Yamasaki of World Trade Center fame. It was an exhibition of rising talents.

To reprise Girard's forward, he wrote: "Here is a representative selection of products gathered from all over the world. Each one shows the results of a good understanding of a special individual problem…and each presents a solution that is both direct and honest. They all share a common, unconscious pride in developing new values rather than depending only on the thought and effort of the past."

The exhibition itself showcased home-furnishing galleries from many young and rising modern designers of the era—George Nelson, Charles Eames, Alvar Aalto, Jens

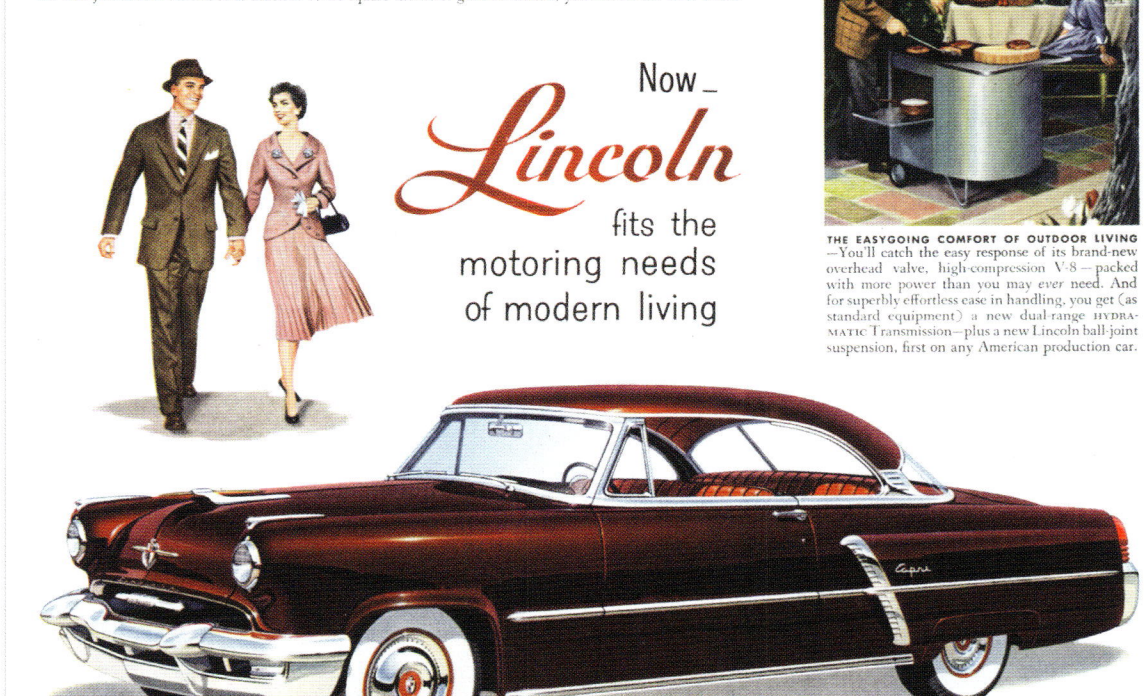

Modern Living | 53

THE EASYGOING COMFORT OF OUTDOOR LIVING —You'll catch the easy response of its brand-new overhead valve, high-compression V-8 — packed with more power than you may *ever* need. And for superbly effortless ease in handling, you get (as standard equipment) a new dual-range HYDRA-MATIC Transmission—plus a new Lincoln ball-joint suspension, first on any American production car.

BRINGS THE OUTDOORS INDOORS—Moving walls of glass give new dimensions to the homes of today. Lincoln mirrors this trend with 3,721 square inches of cool sea-tint* visibility — vision that includes both front fenders. Think of what that means when parking, or when you need to see close up.

NOW—a fine car that meets every test of modern living

Lincoln for 1952

IN TWO INCOMPARABLE SERIES —
THE *Cosmopolitan* — THE *Capri*

NEW GLASS-WALL VISIBILITY—There's a new way of life in America—reflected in today's glass walled rooms for modern living. Lincoln, too, surrounds you with glass—3,271 square inches. With chair high seats and down-sweep hood, even the daintiest woman driver can see the right front fender—see the road in front and way ahead. Every line has a reason.

NEW FLIGHT-LIKE POWER—There's ready-to-fly excitement in Lincoln's completely new overhead valve, high compression, V-8 engine—premium product of the company that has built more V-8's than all other makers combined. With HYDRA-MATIC Transmission (as standard equipment), and new ball-joint front suspension (first on a standard U.S. car), steering and handling are astonishingly effortless.

NEW VERSATILE SMARTNESS—This is beauty with purpose. Right for trip or town, a business car, a family car—with more leg room, more head room, almost 30 cu. ft. in the luggage compartment. Yet Lincoln is smartly sized to thread through traffic, park easily, fit your garage. The one fine car deliberately designed for modern living.

LINCOLN DIVISION—FORD MOTOR COMPANY

These 1952 ads included literal illustrations of modern-living concepts and linked them directly to Lincoln features. Lincoln equated luxury with a relaxed ease, highlighting power features, visibility, and handling that made driving more appealing, especially for women.

54 | GLAMOUR ROAD

TODAY'S PUSH-BUTTON MAGIC—like television—makes life easier, more comfortable. In Lincoln, controls open windows electrically,* provide quick heat and ventilation, automatically adjust car's speed to driving needs (dual range HYDRA-MATIC Transmission as standard equipment). And never before such easy handling, with an exclusive new ball-joint front suspension system, first on a U.S. production car.

THE OUTDOOR FEELING—INDOORS... that is the charm of today's beach club... and of the new Lincoln. Lincoln's 3,271 square inches of glass (sea tint glass available) let you drive with a feeling of sky and space. Low pressure tires, giant springs and shock absorbers, smooth the going... let you enjoy the open road in solid comfort.

LINCOLN
puts life in modern living

A NEW APPROACH to driver relaxation and ease of handling. In Lincoln, ball joint front-wheel suspension, first on any American production car, takes the effort out of steering. Brand-new overhead valve, high-compression V-8 engine (with dual range HYDRA-MATIC Transmission — standard equipment) whisks you silently up the steepest grade.

The beauty of the outdoors... the feeling of *life* around us—that is the spirit of modern living. You see it in the livable luxury of today's home. In the informal magnificence of today's club. And now you see it, too, in a fine car... in the distinctive new Lincoln.

Lincoln's every detail has a purpose: to add to the relaxation of people on the go ...who think nothing of driving miles away for dinner at the club.

Take its powered-for-action beauty. It gives you the handling ease of a sports car... with the stability of the big car that it is.

Take everything about this Lincoln—from its down-sweep hood... to its strikingly decorated interiors... to its nearly 30 cubic foot luggage compartment—and you have a car as comfortable and as modern as your living.

Visit your dealer's showroom and see the new Lincoln Cosmopolitan and Capri. Above all, let him give you a demonstration drive in *the one fine car deliberately designed for modern living.*

LINCOLN DIVISION   FORD MOTOR COMPANY

Modern Living | 55

▶ At some point after the 1952 ads began, Lincoln switched to a dramatically upgraded campaign using the same modern-living theme but substituting photography for illustration. Note the illustrated ad on the right, and on the opposite page, the identical car shown in a radically different photographic setting.

Risom, Bruno Mathsson, Richard Stein, and Florence Knoll. There were works by Pierre Jeanneret, Richard Stein, Franco Albini, Abel Sorensen, Eero Saarinen, Isamu Noguchi, and Hans Bellman, and even a patio by Van Keppel–Green. The Hall of Objects highlighted over a hundred designers. It was dazzling and memorable, and it set the tone for modern design for the decade to come. The exhibition included almost everything but a car—Lincoln would take care of that themselves.

More Power and More Photography

It is fascinating to watch the campaign evolve. In 1952, the print ads were primarily single pages with airbrushed illustrations, the backgrounds depicting post-and-beam modern homes and brand-new skyscrapers. The brochure uses background photography, but again the principal images are illustrations. Bill Johnson began to exert his influence more in 1953, and we find lavish double-truck ads featuring spectacular color photography, and the brochure is again a mixture but the places are inverted, with the photography being primary and the illustrations in a supportive role. The Lincoln engine was made more powerful for 1953 by no less than 45 additional horsepower, and the tagline reflected the change. It was now "The One Fine Car Designed for Modern Living—Completely Powered for Modern Driving." And completely powered it was, so much so that the division sponsored a four-car entry into the Mexican Road Race and the Lincolns finished 1-2-3-4 in their class. The race-prepared Lincolns appeared alongside the stock ones in some advertisements.

Power became the theme of its own 1953 direct-mail brochure called Lincoln Power, which specifically calls attention to the 205-horsepower engine, power steering, power brakes, and Lincoln's groundbreaking new 4-way power seat.

NEWEST ADVANCE IN MODERN LIVING

The exquisitely simple shapes below, silhouetted summaries of today's design, symbolize your life at mid-century.

For you do not dwell in marble halls or drafty mansion. Your home has walls of glass. Your kitchen is an engineering miracle. Your clothes and your furniture are beautifully functional. You work easily; play hard. And now—now a fine car keeps in step with your living. There has never been a motorcar like this before.

It has a rare beauty that is eminently at home with mid-century living. Beauty of line and form, not of ornamentation, nor of pompous size. It is functional beauty that works for a living; the loveliness of great stretches of gleaming glass that let you see—of clean lines that aid your driving. It is the beauty, too, of effortless handling, of magnificently easy power.

And so—there has never been a reception like this for a fine car. In city after city, department stores have grouped new Lincolns with outstanding examples of modern living. The new Cosmopolitans and Capris are gracing the driveways of country clubs from Greenwich to Beverly Hills. And dealers report amazing acceptance, especially after trial rides.

LINCOLN DIVISION—FORD MOTOR COMPANY

---

1. Cocktail and dinner gowns by Philip Hulitar, with lovely simplicity that distinguishes the new Lincoln. 2. Smart lounge chair by Robsjohn-Gibbings, cleverly constructed for superb comfort and luxury, as are Lincoln seats. 3. Glass walls for new rambling home, with views that inspire the design of Lincoln windows. 4. The tree lamp—functional yet attractive use of light—as carried out especially in distinctive Lincoln taillights. 5. The new-day barbecue, sturdy, with no excess weight—a beautifully useful tool for modern living—à la Lincoln. 6. The new-day kitchen with push-button convenience and helpful placement of appliances—suggesting the new Lincoln dashboard. 7. Storage wall, handsome use of enormous space—like the 30-cubic-foot luggage compartment beneath Lincoln's long rear deck. 8. Capri Special Custom Sports Coupé, by Lincoln, in Pebble Tan with Raven Black Top. Here the feeling of modern living is captured in swift lines, bold masses, with disciplined restraint. Here, too, design is more than eye-appealing; it is surprisingly functional. The sweep-down hood, for example, permits even small drivers to see the road directly ahead, as well as the right front fender.

The light, almost airy, quality of the upper structure comes from lavish use of glass (as much as 3,721 square inches). Inside, Lincoln is equally in step with modern living, with unsuspected roominess, and rich upholstery and fittings that characterize the finest homes.

Finally, there is surpassing power and response. A completely new Lincoln V-8 engineered into the compact space beneath the hood—an overhead valve, high-compression power plant, premium product of the world's largest builders of V-8 engines. Together with shift-free HYDRA-MATIC Transmission—plus the new ball-joint suspension, first on any American production car—you get astonishingly easy response, unlike that of other cars. Your Lincoln dealer will let you have a Lincoln for a week end—<u>a week end of modern living on wheels.</u>

THE ONE FINE CAR DELIBERATELY DESIGNED FOR MODERN LIVING

LINCOLN

IN TWO INCOMPARABLE SERIES—THE COSMOPOLITAN—THE CAPRI

Modern Living | 57

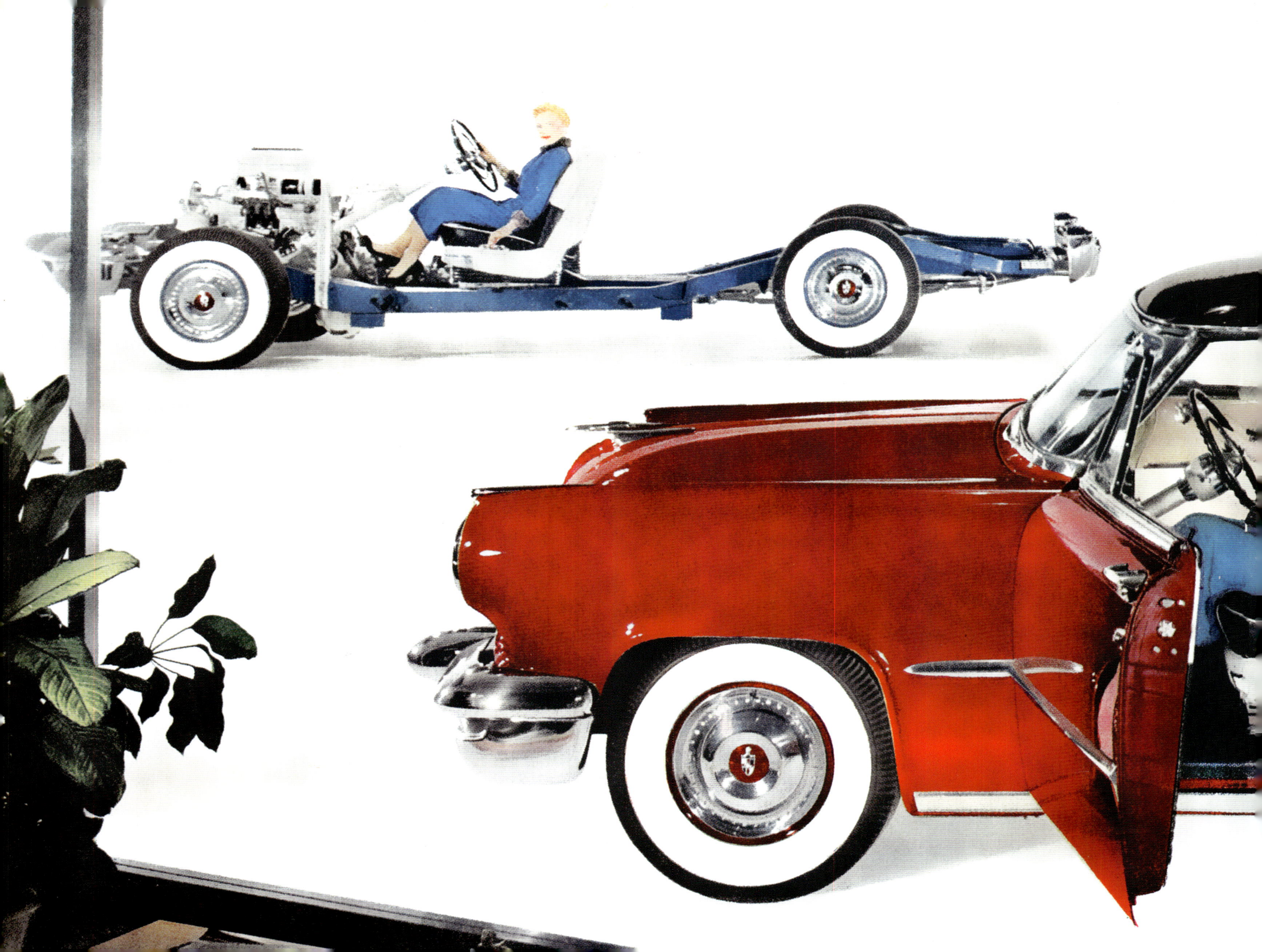

This 1953 Lincoln ad was honored in the Art Directors Club of New York 32nd Annual of Advertising and Editorial Art, 1953. The headline reads, "Powered to Leave the Past Far Behind."

NEW TREND IN MODERN LIVING

OF COURSE YOUR AUTOMOBILE CAN BE AS MODERN AS YOU

Power steering, 4-way power seat, power brakes, sea-tint glass, white side-wall tires optional at extra cost.

1. The great Lincoln taillight, designed for duty as well as distinction. **2.** The Lincoln Capri dinner gown—created by Charles James. **3.** The Lincoln Capri Special Custom Coupe, in Crown Blue and Kingsbury Grey, with the open flair of a sports car crowned by solid steel. **4.** The glass-walled home whose functional elegance inspired Lincoln's advanced design for modern living.

You're living a magnificently casual life in mid-century America. Your clothes reflect it; your home is gracious and glass-walled. You expect push-button convenience and clean-lined beauty in your living—and in your driving. And so this magnificent new Lincoln is the one fine car designed for you.

Its clean lines tell you much of this at a glance. The hood is low so that you see over it—the glass is deep and wide for utmost visibility. There are no pompous bulges—only dramatic, sweeping lines which have been capturing the eyes of connoisseurs. There are new colors and fabrics—rich nylons, sparkling friezes, a rainbow of soft leathers, all the excitement of a modern living room. But Lincoln doesn't rest its case on design alone.

You can have push-button convenience everywhere. Touch a button and the 4-way power seat moves backward or forward; touch another and it moves *up or down*! Touch the wheel and it turns with amazing ease. Lincoln's new power steering, coupled with exclusive ball joint suspension, means exquisite maneuverability. Touch the brake pedal and this sumptuous car stops as you wish, with Lincoln's power brakes doing the work. Then touch the gas pedal—and see how you go.

For beneath that smart low hood is Lincoln's incomparable new 205 horsepower V-8 engine, premium product of the world's largest builders of V-8's. It provides a wonderfully safe reservoir of power. It is the same engine which helped Lincoln capture the first four places among stock cars in the Mexican Pan-American Road Race. What's more—Lincoln also won first place in its class in the Mobilgas Economy Run.

Remember—an early visit to your dealer insures earlier delivery of your Lincoln Cosmopolitan or Capri in the model and colors you wish.

LINCOLN DIVISION—FORD MOTOR COMPANY

LINCOLN

THE ONE FINE CAR DESIGNED FOR MODERN LIVING—COMPLETELY POWERED FOR MODERN DRIVING

Crowning Achievement of Ford Motor Company's 50th Anniversary "50 Years Forward on the American Road"

60 | GLAMOUR ROAD

A TOUCH HERE... A TOUCH THERE... AND

MODERN LIVING COMES TO LIFE

1. NEW 205 HORSEPOWER V-8 ENGINE, WITH HYDRA-MATIC TRANSMISSION. 2. NEW POWER BRAKES. 3. NEW POWER STEERING. 4. WORLD'S FIRST 4-WAY POWER ELEVATOR SEAT.

◀ Lincoln used the Modern Living campaign to define a new type of American luxury. Yes, you could wear a Lincoln Capri gown by Charles James, but you could also buy a Lincoln to make driving more fun, more relaxing than ever before (above). Both ads from 1953.

Along Comes Julia

Another major change for 1953 was the introduction of Julia Meade as the Lincoln pitch woman on Ed Sullivan's *Toast of the Town* TV program. The ads featured Julia on driving adventures in her new Lincoln—demonstrating the power, the handling, the ease of driving, and the smartness of the Lincoln automobile. She called the car "Modern Living on Wheels" and helped establish the trend of a product having a single pitch person. But more than that, the ads showed a modern woman breezing through her day in the new Lincoln—in traffic, even on busy freeways—and praising the performance and specifically the handling of the Lincoln. The commercials were long by modern standards—up to four minutes in length as Julia and her new Lincoln created a travelogue of America. They visited a different city each week and showcased the performance of the new Lincoln. Ed would bring her onstage and ask, "Where are you taking us tonight, Dear Julia?," and the tape would roll. Her adventures were wide ranging, from the Hollywood Freeway to Washington, DC, where she previewed the route of the second Eisenhower inauguration, top smartly down on the frozen January day.

Meade, who was described by Gerald Nachman as "part auto dealer, part chic sexpot," made commercials that ran up to five minutes in length. She told a *LIFE* magazine interviewer in 1960 that while she would prefer to be known as a full-time actress, "I tackle commercials as though I were playing the queen in 'Hamlet.'" *TV Guide* would later describe her as Ed Sullivan's "favorite salesgirl," and she remained on his show pitching a variety of products (even after her Lincoln affiliation ended) for nearly a decade.

Modern Living | 61

NEW INSIGHT into mobile interiors

...colors to go with modern living

▲ The 1953 Lincoln sales brochure is a triumph of modern graphic design, with an elegance and sophistication in layout, typography, and photography rarely seen in automotive marketing of the time. Above, photographs of stylish interiors are combined with line drawings of the exteriors, and paint colors are shown as floating spheres atop large Lincoln typography..

▶ The cover of the 1953 brochure features two stylish models without the trappings of the traditional luxury lifestyle—no furs, no gowns, just simple elegance. They look ready for a driving adventure.

62 | GLAMOUR ROAD

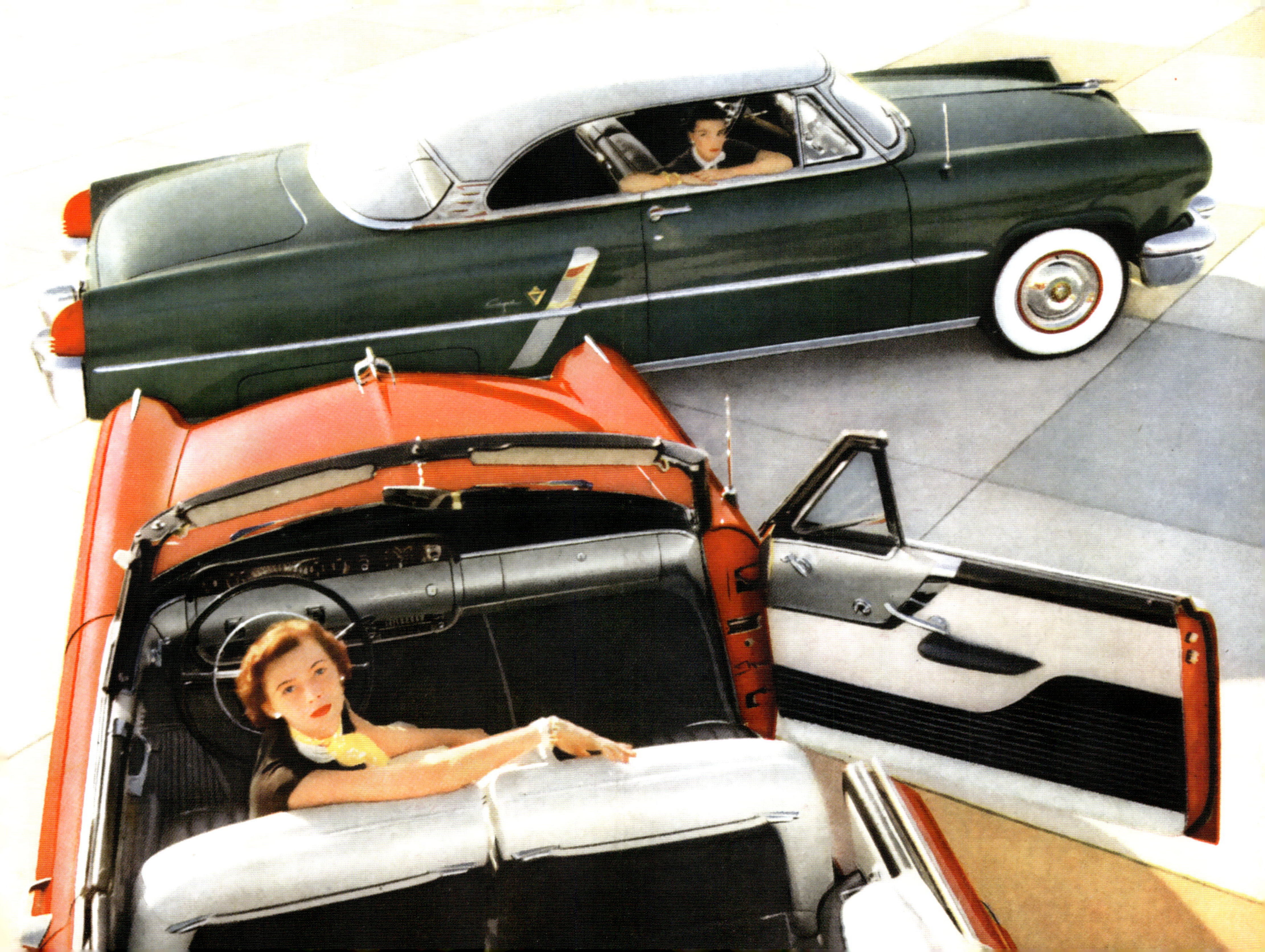

This Lincoln Capri Special Custom Coupe is smartly two-toned. The top is *Regent Black* and the body is *Colony Tan*. The interior upholstery, continuing this color theme, is of *Beige Whipcord* and *Calf Leather*. Interior painted metals are finished in *Embassy Brown Metallic* and *Silver Slurry*.

The wide sweep of open viewing area in this Lincoln is further emphasized by the Lincoln silhouette. Styling details also contribute to this new longer, lower look. Lines of bright metal, sweep of the protective stone shield, new rear-quarter molding—all are elegantly conceived in the spirit of modern living design.

Lincoln performance is traditionally outstanding, and in 1954, more than ever before, Lincoln offers newer, finer performance. Power to take you and keep you out front, power to carry you easily up steep grades, power to call on at every driving range —the true mark of Lincoln superiority.

This interior, designed for the Cosmopolitan series, is color-matched to the *Palace Green Metallic* exterior paint. The dash is *Silver Slurry*. The upholstery is a combination of *Green Frieze* (a beautiful green cloth with flecks of silver thread woven into it) with *Light Green Gabardine* bolster.

The 1954 Lincoln brochure was groundbreaking since it relied almost exclusively on location photography. Also notable is the image of women drivers in a mass-market luxury car brochure—it would be years before Cadillac showed women as anything other than glamorously clad passengers. The fact that the entire setting is on a beach—as opposed to the typical luxury venue of an opera house or elegant soirée—shows how committed Lincoln was to its Modern Living campaign.

A Very Special Brochure

The campaign stepped it up yet again in 1954. This time it was a revolutionary product brochure, which featured a single photography session as its main theme. In the summer of 1953, the agency took five handmade preproduction 1954 Lincoln automobiles—minus drivelines for weight—and photographed them in situ on the fine sands of the Sleeping Bear Sand Dunes in Leelanau County, on the west coast of lower Michigan. Cranes positioned the cars in a circle and the photos were taken. It was noted that the models helped rake the footprints out of the blowing sand. The result was a groundbreaking brochure where one shoot was the theme of the entire piece. It was nothing less than a major advance for automotive photography and remains a dazzling idea to this day. The tagline was simplified to "Designed for Modern Living—Powered for Modern Driving."

Modern Living | 65

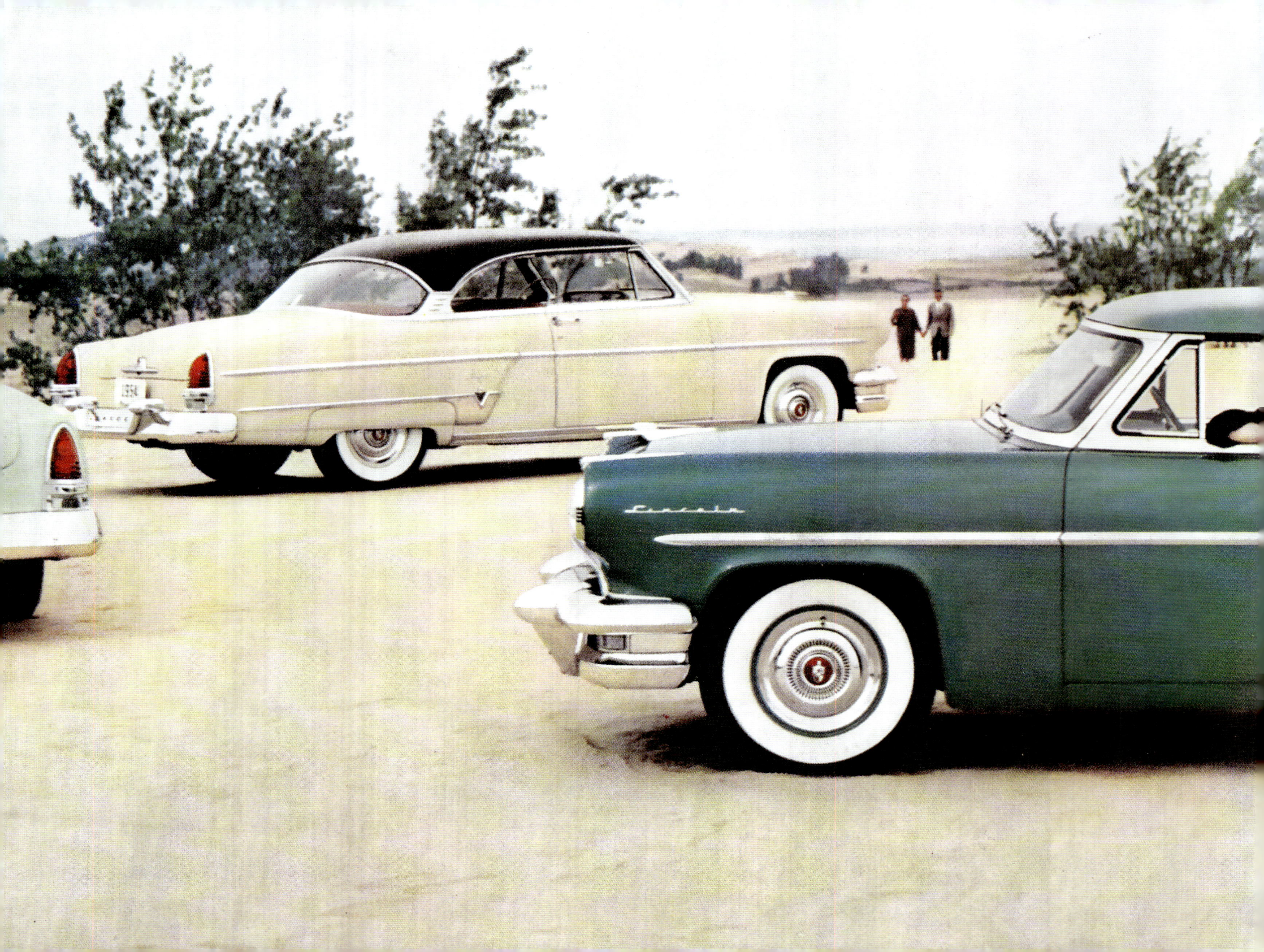
1954

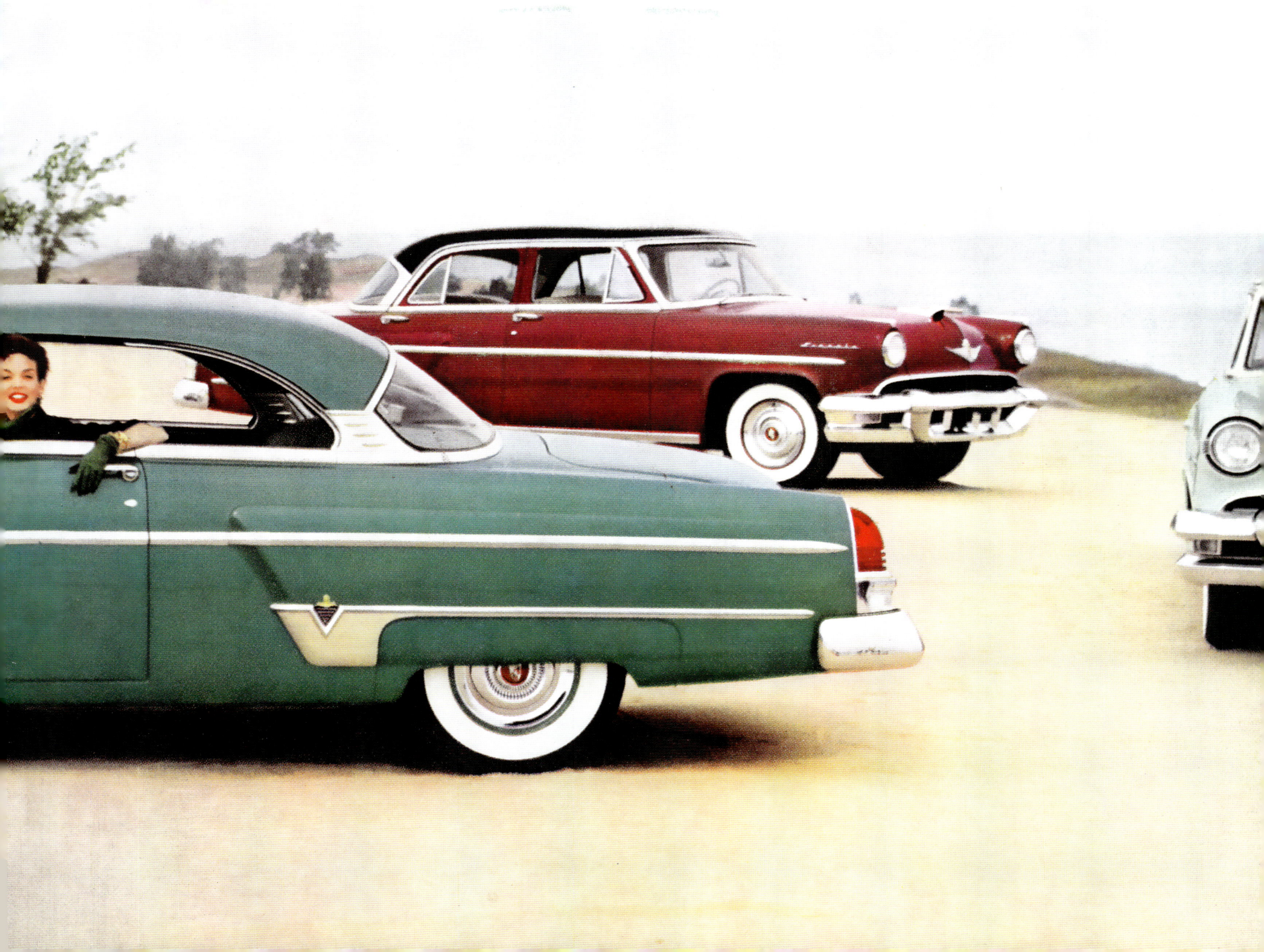

◀ Previous, pages from 1954 Lincoln brochure

1954 Lincoln ad featuring Juila Meade (blue dress)

68 | GLAMOUR ROAD

1954 Lincoln ad featuring a stylized midcentury modern setting

1955 Lincoln ad, featuring Lincoln pitchwoman Julia Meade with Ed Sullivan

Modern Living | 69

Sadly, by 1956, the Modern Living campaign was abandoned for a more conventional luxury campaign featuring columned mansions and furs.

Modern Living Bids Adieu

The Modern Living campaign itself was in its twilight in 1955. The campaign had been very good indeed for Lincoln and had helped restore much prestige to the dog-eared brand, but changes were afoot. Lincoln had been spun off into a separate division in early 1955 and had a new general manager, Ben Mills. They were planning a move even farther uptown with a restyled and even-grander model for 1956—a truly magnificent, longer, lower, lovelier Lincoln.

As a glimpse into what was coming, they introduced the Futura concept car at the Detroit Auto Show in January 1955. Almost 19 feet in length, the pearlescent blue-white beauty featured a power Plexiglas canopy, double-bubble windshield, and a speedometer mounted in the center of the steering wheel. Clearly the future of Lincoln was large.

No more road racing, no more sporty image—instead they were pursuing an image of full-on luxury. Rather than chasing Cadillac, they decided to position themselves as an equal using the tagline of "Unmistakably... the finest in the fine car field." Modern Living gave away to fur coats and manor homes, and midcentury living rooms were swapped out for horse barns while headlines proclaimed "Never before a Lincoln so long... and so longed for!"

As almost a way of closing the door, the 1956 Lincoln brochure itself was composed entirely of airbrushed illustrations with backgrounds of fox hunts and manor homes—and not a photograph to be found. There was a beautifully photographed direct-mail piece introducing the 1956 model at an unnamed Palm Springs resort getaway, and the 1957 brochure was a mixture of approximately 50/50 renderings and photography. It could be that the 1956 piece had to be renderings because the new car wasn't ready in time to photograph. Or perhaps the new general manager was trying to impart his own preferences. Whatever the reason, it remains a disappointment to see what was such a beautiful car in such an uninspiring brochure.

Of course, all campaigns run their course, and four years is a pretty good lifespan for a single campaign, especially in the auto industry, which relies on annual product changes. Despite its disappointing conclusion, Modern Living was easily the most significant and successful automotive marketing campaign of the 1950s. It was truly groundbreaking in both concept and technique, and it became the textbook example of not only a truly integrated campaign but a lifestyle campaign as well. Furthermore, it elevated the art of commercial photography in a printed brochure. It was an award-winning campaign that put Lincoln back in the customer's mindset and drew them nearer to parity with Cadillac—all in all, a well-executed and strategic campaign that is worth remembering.

This page and opposite, *details from 1956 Lincoln ads*

70 | GLAMOUR ROAD

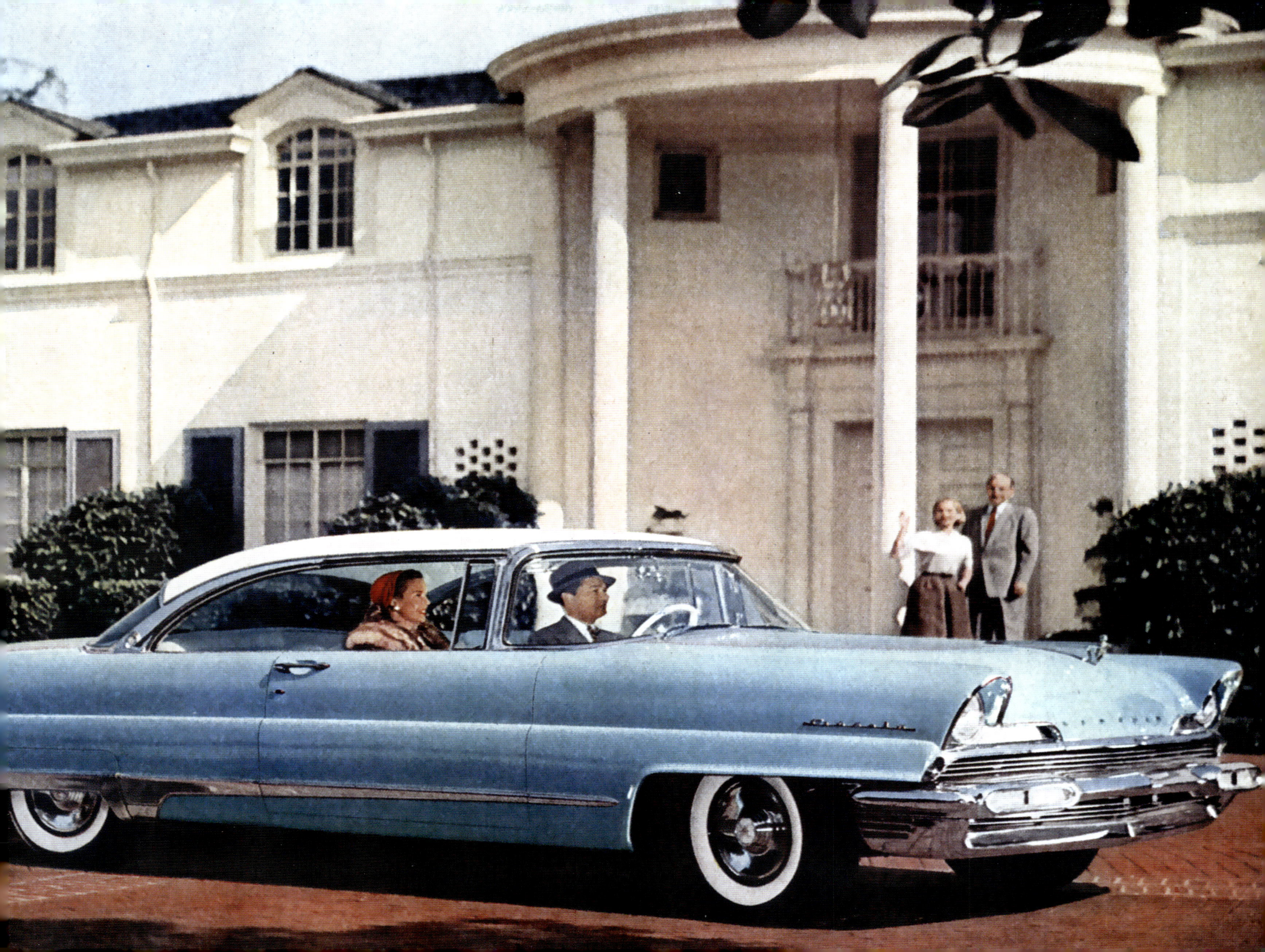

Cadillac

Chapter Four

DIAMONDS ARE A GIRL'S BEST FRIEND

CADILLAC DOUBLES DOWN ON TRADITIONAL AMERICAN LUXURY

Cadillac, the self-described *Standard of the World,* was perfectly poised for postwar prosperity. It came through the thirties as the unchallenged leader of the luxury car field and introduced a smaller but highly luxurious model called the Sixty Special in 1938, which gave the chauffeur a pink slip. It was fitted with an automatic transmission in 1941 that they then war-tested in tens of thousands of Cadillac tanks during World War II, all while becoming a war hero in the process. Cadillac came to the postwar party ready to rumble, with coffers full of cash and a chromium-plated winner's smile.

The postwar advertising portrayed the Cadillac as an undeniable symbol of success. While advertising as recently as 1941 had touted a low base price of only $1,345 and a headline of "Now Nothing Stands in Your Way," by 1946 those egalitarian themes had vanished. The postwar ads had a consistent, if unimaginative, look, with a giant Cadillac crest and the Cadillac name in script, below which was a watercolor rendering of the car and a tagline such as *Standard of the World*. Text, if indeed there was any, talked about the car as a reward for success and took a very soft-sell approach. The lifestyle took precedence over product attributes; those would be saved for the product brochure itself.

The importance of Cadillac to GM in the immediate postwar era can't be overstated. The climate in 1946–48 was one of unprecedented demand, and the buyers were willing to pay. Steel was in short supply, and Cadillac provided the company with the greatest dollar return per pound of precious steel. One need only glance at postwar Cadillac production figures to recognize their impact on GM's bottom line—in model year 1946, Cadillac produced 29,194 cars. In 1947, they made 69,926. By 1949, they hit 92,554, soared over 100,000 units per year in 1950, and broke the 150,000-unit barrier in 1956. It's no surprise that Broadway producer Max Gordon called his 1953 hit play *The Solid Gold Cadillac*, or that Dwight D. Eisenhower rode to his inauguration in a brand-new limited production 1953 Cadillac Eldorado convertible (with a stratospheric price tag of $7,750)—clearly no other make would do. The postwar economy was booming, and Cadillac was riding the crest of the wave.

▲ Above: *In a 1941 ad, Cadillac promoted its low price. (Alden Jewell collection)*

◀ Left: *by 1949, Cadillac unapologetically proclaimed its position as "Standard of the World" in an ad showcasing a diamond-and-emerald necklace by Harry Winston. The Spencerian lettering was drawn by Jerry Campbell.*

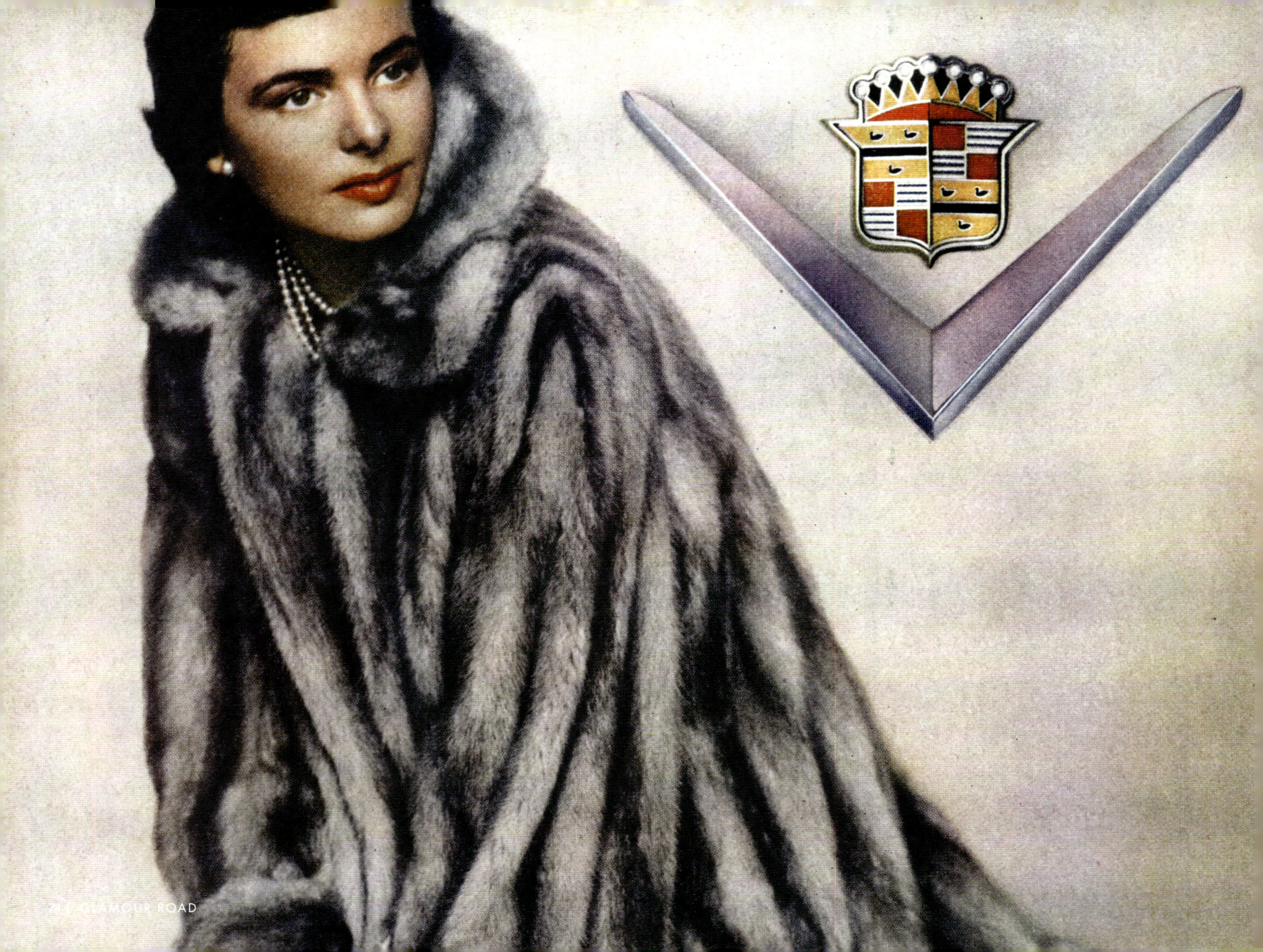

Diamonds and Furs

The unmistakable introduction of fashion elements began to appear in 1949, when the V surrounding the Cadillac crest was replaced by fine jewelry, almost always including but by no means limited to diamonds. The actual pieces depicted were always color-coordinated to the car featured, with emeralds for a green Fleetwood and sapphires for a blue one. And the jewels always came from a top-tier jeweler, one that Cadillac customers would recognize, such as Cartier, Harry Winston, or Van Cleef and Arpels. The jeweler was credited in the ad. Captions were added to the layout in 1950 in the form of enticements such as "What Are You Waiting For" and "No Finer List of Names on Earth," describing Cadillac owners. In an alternate series, furs made their appearance. Glamorous fur-draped models wearing creations by the Ritter Bros., Robert of Detroit, and others became the centerpiece of the ad, with the airbrushed illustration of the car itself. Again the furrier was credited, and while the copy might make reference to women driving Cadillacs, they were not shown behind the wheel in these ads. The women are props in the ads, and while they might drive the car, the pitch is to men to buy it for them.

While it may be difficult to imagine in our current PETA-conscious climate, fur was once considered an important accessory of the luxury lifestyle. This meant not only that Cadillac showed mink-clad models in the ads, but they also tested their upholstery fabrics to make sure that the mink would not become caught, discolored, or unduly worn by the fabric—and they are said to have

◀ *Left, and this page: The Cadillac ad campaign of 1950–51 focused on fine furs to make the connection to upper-class luxury.*

◀ Left, top: *1955 ads with gowns created for Cadillac by Givenchy and Balmain*

Left, below: *1956 ads featuring photos taken at private fashion showings arranged by Cadillac at Balmain and Dior in their Paris salons, and detail (opposite) of private fashion showing in the Paris salon of Jacques Fath. The fashion photographer was Arik Nepo, who worked for French Vogue.*

taken it so seriously that mink-clad models were taken for 50-mile test drives to ensure that the seat upholstery and the expensive mink coats would play nice with each other.

Watch the Birdie

Photography began to appear in Cadillac advertising in earnest in 1954. Glamorous full-color photos show successful couples in high-tone surroundings—impeccably dressed men with coiffed, bejeweled, and fur-wrapped women, inferring no doubt as to what automobile brought them there. We also saw the introduction of what we have nicknamed the Gown Wars—full-color photography with beautiful women in custom creations commissioned by Cadillac, with credit to both gown and jewels, and an illustration of a Cadillac in a complementary color. This series continued through the mid-'50s. It cannot be argued that Cadillac didn't know how to sell lifestyle positioning—they did a masterful job.

The series continued in 1955, with power couples in large lifestyle photos with illustrations of the cars below. Exclusive locales were the focus of 1956, with the cars appearing in places such as Romanoff's restaurant, the Palm Springs Racquet Club, the San Francisco Symphony, and the Boston Museum of Fine Arts. Designers creating custom gowns for this series included Hubert de Givenchy, Pierre Balmain, and James Galanos. The renderings were replaced with photography in 1957, but the theme was consistent. One knew instantly it was a Cadillac ad. Along the way, some interesting variations appeared—a dramatic monochromatic series appeared in 1958 with beautifully gowned models, the cars and the background all in a single yet vivid color statement. Again the ad copy referred to the women in the third person—Cadillac was speaking still *about* them instead of *to* them.

76 | GLAMOUR ROAD

Diamonds Are a Girl's Best Friend | 77

This page and opposite: *1958 Cadillac ads strike a monochromatic mood.*

78 | GLAMOUR ROAD

Diamonds Are a Girl's Best Friend | 79

◀ *Detail from a 1960 Cadillac ad featuring matching mother-daughter leopard coats and hats—"Furs by Robert, Detroit, created expressly for Cadillac"*

Mother and Daughter Dress-Up

The Gown Wars reached an interesting pinnacle in the massively finned years of 1959 and 1960, in which part of the goal was possibly to distract from the outrageous styling of the car itself. A series of ads showed women and young girls in matching dresses, custom-created for Cadillac by various designers such as Jane Derby, Ceil Chapman, and even Scaasi—who again were credited in the ads. The copy of these ads was particularly tone deaf, to the point where we need to visit it:

"One of the special delights which ladies find in Cadillac ownership is the pleasure of being a passenger. First of all there is the sheer physical luxury of riding in a new Cadillac. The car is wonderfully spacious and comfortable—and perfectly proportioned for complete freedom of movement. Then there is its enchanting interior beauty ... the marvelous convenience of its appointments ... its great smoothness of ride ... and its marvelous quietness of operation.

We invite you to visit your dealer soon—with the man of the house—and spend an hour in the passenger seat of a 1959 Cadillac. We know you will agree that it is the world's nicest place to sit."

In the traditional Cadillac ads, the jewelled crest made a return in 1960 (in a V-shaped contrasting canopy of success), and except for the use of photography, the ads looked as they had in 1952. Cadillac went to the opera in 1961—the backgrounds changed to a series of textiles, and locations included opera houses in Vienna and San Francisco, and even La Scala in Milan. They followed in 1962 with more airbrushed illustration—the only photography was the glamorous figures (albeit retouched into soft focus) and the jeweled crest (credited, of course).

Gowns for mother and daughter
created for Cadillac by Jane Derby

One of the special delights which ladies find in Cadillac ownership is the pleasure of being a passenger. First of all, there is the sheer physical luxury of riding in a new Cadillac. The car is wondrously spacious and comfortable—and perfectly proportioned for complete freedom of movement. Then there is its enchanting interior beauty . . . the marvelous convenience of its appointments . . . its great smoothness of ride . . . and its marvelous quietness of operation. We invite you to visit your dealer soon—with the man of the house—and spend an hour in the passenger seat of a 1959 Cadillac. We know you will agree that it is the world's nicest place to sit.

Cadillac

EVERY WINDOW OF EVERY CADILLAC IS SAFETY PLATE GLASS · CADILLAC MOTOR CAR DIVISION · GENERAL MOTORS CORPORATION

1959 Cadillac ads

Gowns for mother and daughter
created for Cadillac by Ceil Chapman

How many ways does a Cadillac delight a lady? Let us count them. There is its great beauty, for instance, to please her eye . . . its wondrous luxury and spaciousness to enhance her comfort . . . its incredible quiet to bring her rest . . . its extraordinary handling ease to assure her relaxation . . . its renowned safety to add to her peace of mind . . . its great fame to inspire her pride . . . and its marvelous economy to satisfy her practical judgment. Have you yet to discover the magic of Cadillac for yourself? Then you should visit your Cadillac dealer soon and spend an hour or so in the driver's seat. It's motordom's most convincing sixty minutes!

Cadillac

EVERY WINDOW OF EVERY CADILLAC IS SAFETY PLATE GLASS · CADILLAC MOTOR CAR DIVISION · GENERAL MOTORS CORPORATION

Diamonds Are a Girl's Best Friend | 81

Mother, daughter ensemble
designed expressly for Cadillac
by Ines da Roma

The great Cadillac car has long been held in deep affection by the American woman. And yet, we believe that she will regard Cadillac with still greater favor during the coming year. For the "car of cars" now offers so much more to inspire and delight her. There's greater beauty and majesty of styling . . . new elegance and convenience of appointments . . . improved Fleetwood comfort and luxury . . . far finer performance and handling ease . . . and an even wider choice of models. So if you've lost your heart to Cadillac, this would be a wonderful year to find yourself at the wheel. Your dealer will be happy to acquaint you with all the new Cadillac virtues at any time.

Cadillac

EVERY WINDOW OF EVERY CADILLAC IS SAFETY PLATE GLASS   CADILLAC MOTOR CAR DIVISION • GENERAL MOTORS CORPORATION

Gowns for mother and daughter
by Alessandra De Paolis
of Ines Da Roma

Whenever a lady rides in a new Cadillac car, she finds the undeniable evidence of quality on every hand—in the faultless tailoring of its fabrics and leathers . . . in the careful crafting of its appointments . . . in the flawless beauty of its finish . . . and in the car's awe-inspiring quietness of operation. A journey in a 1960 Cadillac is the only practical way to appreciate the car's deep, abiding goodness. Why not visit your dealer? The car and the keys are yours for the asking.

Cadillac

CADILLAC MOTOR CAR DIVISION • GENERAL MOTORS CORPORATION

1959 Cadillac ad

1960 Cadillac ad

82 | GLAMOUR ROAD

1960 Cadillac ad

1960 Cadillac ad

Diamonds Are a Girl's Best Friend | 83

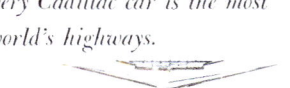

1961 Cadillac ad featuring a matador's cape from the Brooklyn Museum, and jewels created by Harry Winston

1961 Cadillac ad featuring French embroidery from the Boston Museum of Fine Arts, and jewels created by Black, Starr and Gorham

84 | GLAMOUR ROAD

1962 Cadillac ad featuring jewels by Harry Winston, Inc.

Diamonds Are a Girl's Best Friend | 85

LADIES TWIST CADILLACS AROUND THEIR LITTLE FINGERS

That's how easy this great new motor car is to handle. Just the lightest touch of toe and hand, and it goes through its paces as if by magic. With improved Cadillac power steering, all it takes to park it is a nickel and a space. And its brilliant new engine and transmission move it through city traffic like nothing else on wheels. It offers greater beauty—more luxurious interiors—and introduces several significant new extra-cost options, such as the exclusive Comfort Control that enables you to pre-set the car to your desired temperature winter and summer. The Cadillac car for 1964 is more than a hundred ways new. Go see for yourself. *It's more tempting than ever—and just wait till you drive it!*

Cadillac Motor Car Division • General Motors Corporation

CADILLAC LADIES SAY IT BETTER THAN WE CAN!

Besides, you'd think we were boasting. So here are some quotes from Cadillac ladies. "We've had Cadillacs for ten years, but this one is by far the easiest to drive." (A new engine, advanced transmissions, and a true-center drive line do the work.) "If clouds had power steering, they'd handle like this." (She's referring to our improved power steering and advanced suspension system.) "That Comfort Control* is incredible. Dial your temperature and forget it." (And only Cadillac has it.) Your dealer has a lot of other quotes—for Cadillac ladies are wonderfully vocal this year. Visit him soon and hear all the exciting new facts for yourself.

1964 Cadillac ads featuring women behind the wheel

86 | GLAMOUR ROAD

Cadillac Ladies Love to Play Chauffeur

The dam finally broke in 1963 as Cadillac was undergoing a transformation. Even the Cadillac wreath had been redesigned, and Cadillac had taken the opportunity to update its image. Swept away were the airbrushed illustrations and jewels; in their place, a campaign based on vivid, grand-scale color photography, and for the first time in the postwar era, well-dressed women in modern clothes actually behind the wheel of a Cadillac. Under the headline "Cadillac Ladies Love to Play Chauffeur," a blonde in a white dress is seen behind the wheel of a white 1963 convertible, picking up a handsome gentleman caller, luggage and briefcase in hand—in the hills above San Francisco, *as one does*. In the product brochures, these women would be seen in and around the cars and not just posed in front of an opera house.

But while the new campaign was modern and dramatic, transforming women from coiffed props into actual drivers, the copy was still written for men, referring to the mechanical advances as "man talk" and inviting him to visit his Cadillac dealer soon. "And don't forget to bring your loveliest chauffeur with you." Another 1964 ad showed two ladies in a red De Ville convertible under the headline "Cadillac Ladies say it better than we can"; another ad showed a blue Coupe de Ville under the headline "Ladies Twist Cadillacs Around Their Little Fingers," stressing how easily they can control the car. The line had been crossed—women would now be shown not as gowned mannequins but as drivers of Cadillacs. While the copy might still be speaking to the men, Cadillac had acknowledged the modern woman.

▶ *1963 Cadillac ad*

CADILLAC LADIES LOVE TO PLAY CHAUFFEUR. *Unusual? Not at all. For this one is really fun to drive . . . feather-light and sure to handle . . . smooth and effortless on the move . . . quick and nimble in the clutches. The reasons are mostly man-talk: a high performance engine, a true center drive line, a triple braking system, graduated power steering. But the result is eloquent enough for any lady to understand: the finest, sweetest performance in any automobile today. Visit your dealer soon and see for yourself. And don't forget to bring your loveliest chauffeur with you.*

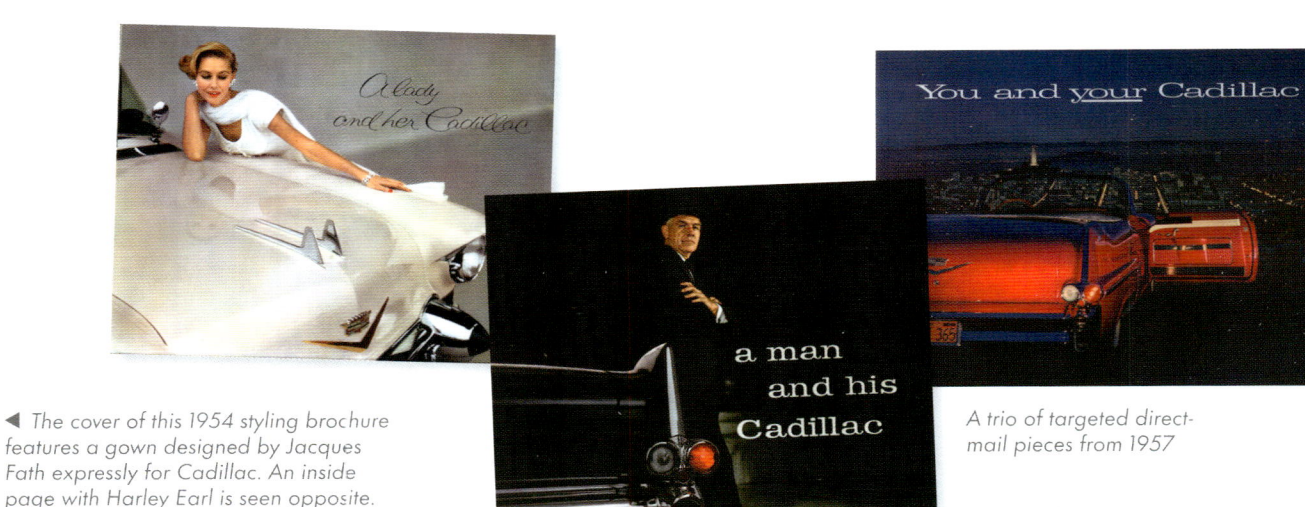

◀ The cover of this 1954 styling brochure features a gown designed by Jacques Fath expressly for Cadillac. An inside page with Harley Earl is seen opposite.

A trio of targeted direct-mail pieces from 1957

A DOUBLE LIFE

Like so many men in the 1950s, Cadillac had a double life. While their public advertising campaign was based on jewels and airbrushed illustrations, they dabbled on the side by utilizing brilliant color photography to create stunning direct-mail pieces as early as the 1954 model year.

It's really a question of why they chose a dual path—unlike Lincoln, which was investing heavily into the new medium of color photography, Cadillac seemed to keep it on the down-low. There were two very different creative teams at Cadillac's longtime agency MacManus—one for advertising, and one for dealer support materials and direct mail. They produced some stunning pieces, and indeed quite a number of them, and while there were too many to offer in detail, here and on the following pages are a few highlights.

Harley Earl Takes You on a Tour

The first piece from 1954 was called "Styled to be copied for years to come." This sixteen-page, large-format brochure (executed in full-color photography throughout—there are no illustrations) is a guided tour of the new Cadillac by none other than legendary GM design chief Harley Earl, whose photo appears in six of the seven dual-page spreads. It's an extraordinary piece that takes the prospect into a deep immersion of Cadillac design philosophy at the hands of Earl himself.

"The requirements of automotive styling are almost as numerous as they are demanding. While artistic beauty is perhaps the primary consideration, it must be beauty which is evolutionary and which grows out of a natural process of design. While design must be reflective and graceful, it must also be keyed to mechanical requirements and to the practical necessities of production. And while styling must be functional and imaginative, it must also be shaped to the tastes of the motoring public. Truly successful automotive styling, then, must be pleasing to the creator ... gratifying to the engineer ... and inspiring to the motorist—a rare and magic meeting of beauty, practicality and popularity. Never, to my knowledge, have these qualities been combined with greater majesty than in the 1954 Cadillac."

Until the 1955 model came along at least. The copy might have been a bit thick, but all in all it's a visually striking piece.

A (Pronoun) and Their Cadillac

The year 1957 was a recession year, and Cadillac created three very notable direct-mail pieces. A full sixty years before people began sharing their pronouns, Cadillac created "A Lady and Her Cadillac," "A Man and His Cadillac," and, for those whose identities were less clear, "You and Your Cadillac." "A Lady and Her Cadillac" showed a blonde woman in a white dress and white scarf leaning against the hood of a white Cadillac. Inside they showed a woman seated behind the wheel of a new Cadillac (remember, that scene won't appear in a print ad until 1963). In a twist reminiscent of western movies, "A Man and His Cadillac" showed a man dressed in black with a black Cadillac. Whether they were paying homage to Johnny Cash or trying to make a statement about the Cadillacs of Good and Evil is not certain. "You and Your Cadillac" is careful not to show anyone behind the wheel—the cover photo of a red convertible has the top down and the door open, but no occupants at all, and indeed the cars inside are all unoccupied.

88 | GLAMOUR ROAD

This brochure is much more than a simple exposition of Cadillac's new styling. It is a "guided tour" of the car, so to speak, by one of the world's most renowned automotive stylists—Mr. Harley Earl, Vice-President of General Motors in charge of Styling. We know that you will find his comments both interesting and educational. And we know, too, that they will give you a greater appreciation of the philosophy behind the car's creation . . . as well as a better understanding of Cadillac's many unique styling characteristics.

(Cover oil by Jacques Lath, designed expressly for the 1954 Cadillac.)

Suzy Parker at the Motorama

And speaking of 1955, the follow-up mailer for 1955 was every bit as dazzling. Again in fourteen pages of full-color photography, it was called "A Trip to the Motorama" and followed supermodel Suzy Parker in a red ensemble by Folcol (with furs by Maximilian, hats by John Frederics) through the Cadillac display at the GM Motorama of 1955. Several special Cadillac Motorama show cars were pictured, including the tone-on-tone red Coupe de Ville "Celebrity" with a red leatherette padded roof, the Eldorado "St. Moritz" convertible in pearlescent white with an interior of English leather trimmed in white ermine and white mouton carpeting, and the 1955 Fleetwood "Westchester" show car finished in Korina Gold with a black-leather-covered top, a built-in telephone and tape recording deck, and a 14" television built into the back of the front seat. All in all, it was a magnificent piece that included photos of the display itself, including the cantilevered arm that majestically swept the cars over a specially constructed reflecting pond—all in the ballroom of the Waldorf-Astoria hotel in New York City. Miss Parker even got to shake hands with Cadillac divisional manager Don Ahrens, sales manager James Roche, and GM president Harlow Curtice, in full color on page 3.

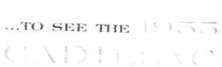

▲ Above left: *The Coupe de Ville Celebrity show car.* Above right: *Suzy Parker tries out the power steering exhibit.*

◀ Far left: *Suzy Parker shakes hands with GM brass.* Left: *A 2-ton Cadillac is cantilevered over a reflecting pond while the orchestra hovers above in suspended pods.*

▶ Right: *The Eldorado St. Moritz show car with seats trimmed in white ermine*

90 | GLAMOUR ROAD

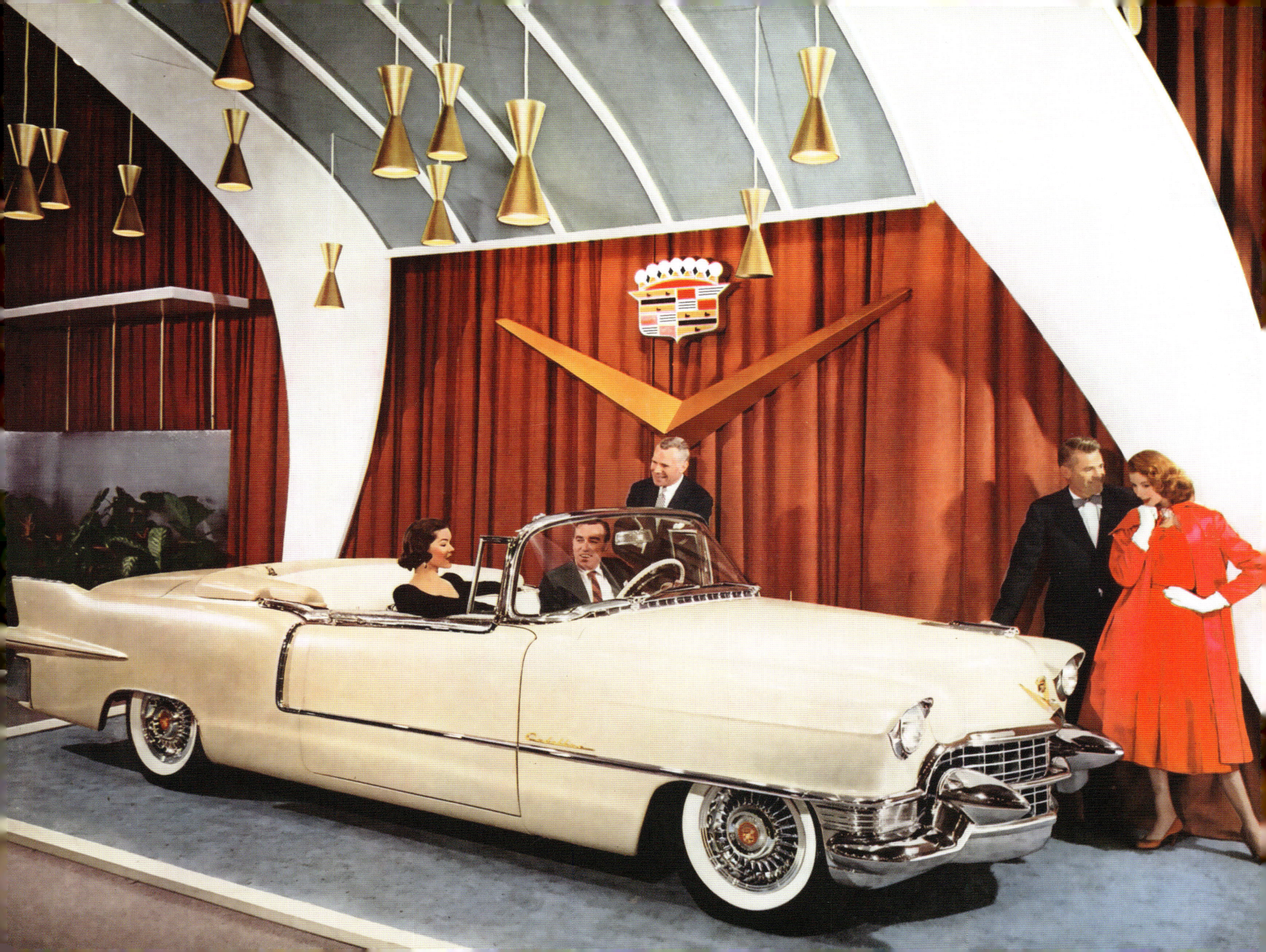

▼ A two-tone Tahoe Blue Sedan de Ville is parked next to the Styling Building.

Bottom: An Alpine White Fleetwood 60 Special parked under the cantilevered entrance to the Service Section Building

▲ A Mandan Red Coupe de Ville graces the base of the floating staircase in the Styling Administration Building lobby.

▶ All of the 1956 Cadillac models beneath the Styling Dome

92 | GLAMOUR ROAD

◀ *A Mountain Laurel Series 62 convertible photographed against the colored glazed brick walls of the Technical Center*

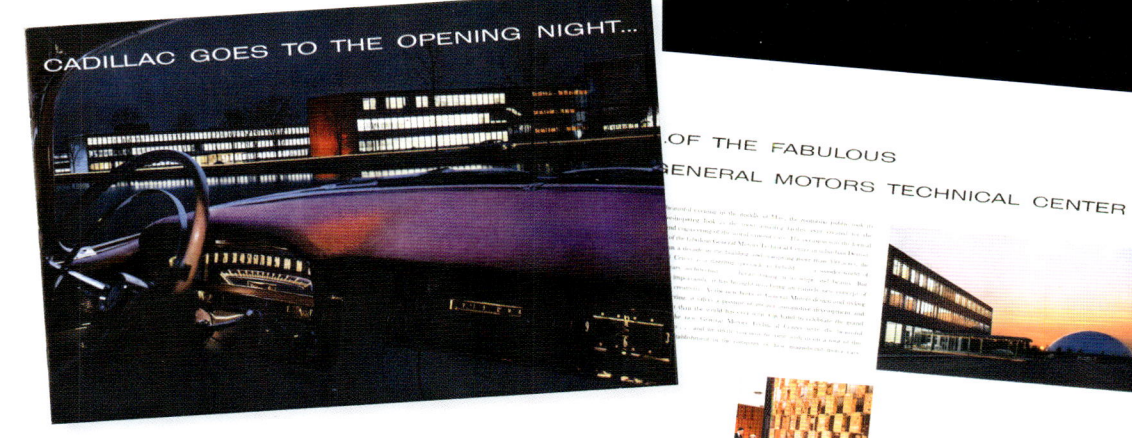

The booklet features romantic photographs of the Eero Saarinen–designed General Motors Technical Center.

Cadillac Goes to the Opening Night

The year 1956 marked the opening of the landmark General Motors Technical Center. Dubbed the Versailles of Industry at the time, the brand-new state-of-the-art campus by architect Eero Saarinen was a technical marvel and an aesthetic triumph, signifiying postwar prosperity and optimism. It was one of the most significant building projects of the decade and was a monument to modern design. A special mail piece toured the campus, showing the new 1956 Cadillac models in key locations. The highlight is on the last spread, where the entire ten-car Cadillac lineup is on display under the styling dome—a place that few mortals have ever been. This was a very elaborate and expensive production utilizing both daytime and nighttime settings. One photograph in particular, of a red Coupe de Ville alongside the floating staircase in the styling center lobby, has become iconic. A breathtaking piece that is highly collectible today, it truly makes one wonder why their advertising campaigns weren't as memorable.

A Goddess Gold Coupe de Ville under the spiral staircase in the Research Administration Building lobby

These are but a handful of many special Cadillac brochures. In 1959, they discovered "Motordom" and created "Motordom's finest hours" and "The wisest investment in Motordom." Whatever "Motordom" was, Cadillac appeared to be the very pinnacle of it. A 1960 piece shows grand homes and asks, "What car lives here?" Finally, for 1963 the advertising took on the full-color photography and modern upscale look of the direct-mail pieces. Both would of course continue, but with a continuous look and feel—Cadillac no longer felt compelled to live a double life.

Diamonds Are a Girl's Best Friend | 93

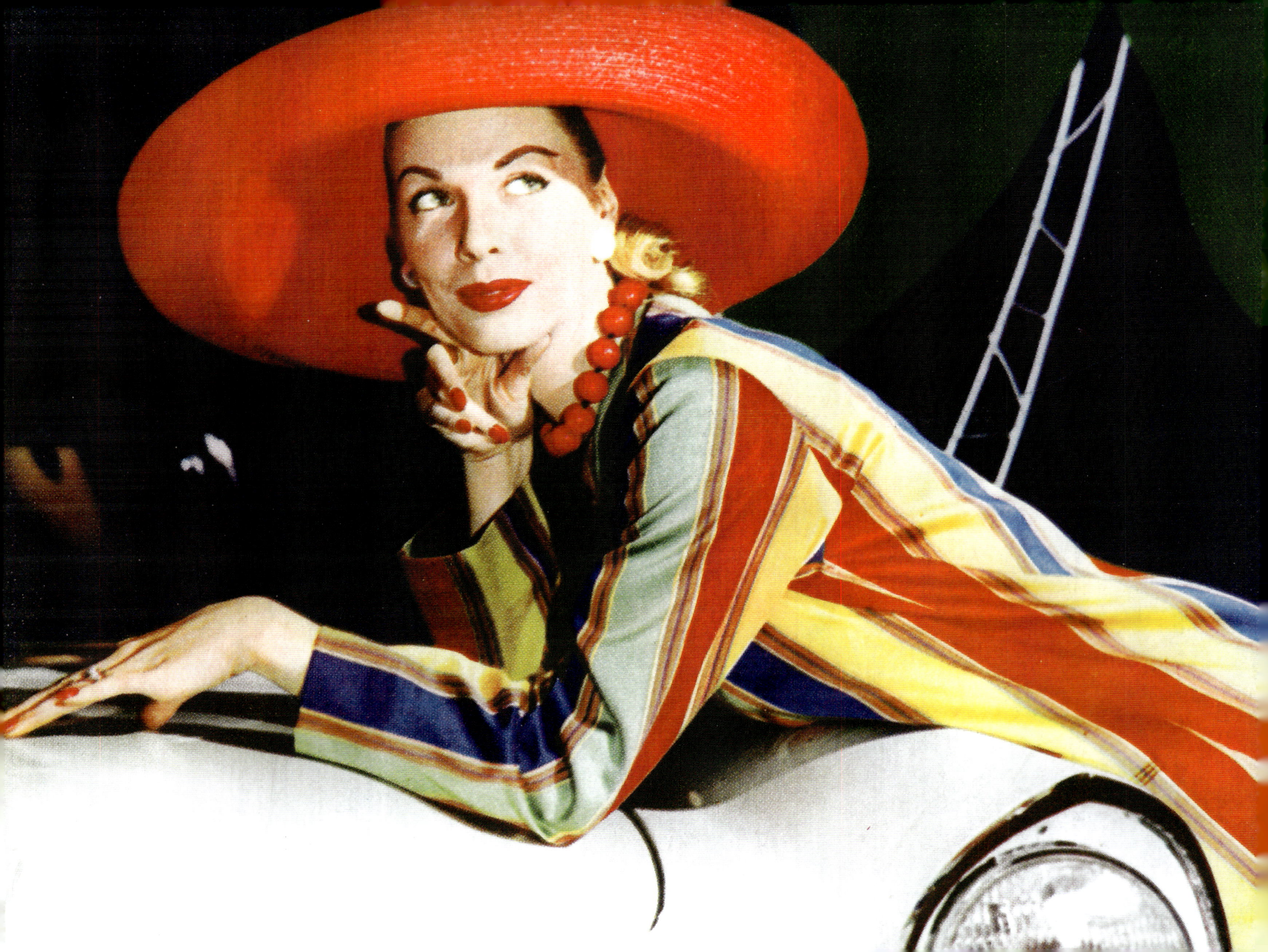

Chapter Five

THE IMPERIAL COLLECTION

FASHION BRAND COMARKETING CONNECTS TO THE FEMALE MARKET

Of the Big Three's luxury car offerings, Chrysler's Imperial needed the most thorough makeover if it was going to succeed in the postwar era. Introduced in the late 1920s as the largest and most powerful of the Chrysler line, the Imperial had been a top-tier prestige offering in the years between the wars. Back then, Imperial came in a full range of models, from large sedans and limousines to dashing roadsters and racy dual-cowl phaetons with custom bodies from coachbuilders such as Le Baron, which they later purchased. They offered a handmade Imperial Airflow Limousine in 1934. But by the late 1930s, the nameplate was pared down to adorn the most-luxurious Chrysler sedans in two sizes—large sedan and even-larger limousine.

While women were indeed pictured in Imperial advertising in the early postwar ads, they were shown seated in the back seat of a Crown Imperial limousine while the chauffeur whisked them smartly away to the opera. It was an elegant depiction, but one aimed at an ever-shrinking target. Things were about to change dramatically, and what had been a limousine would emerge as a high-fashion automobile. But first a few things had to happen.

By 1951, the revamped Imperial lineup still retained the large sedan and the limousine, but now they were supplanted by a sporty coupe called the Newport, with hardtop styling and a luxurious interior featuring seats trimmed in horizontally pleated leather and contrasting cloth. Chrysler's first high-compression hemi engine was newly installed under the long hood, and the styling was modern dignified, and respectable, even if not exactly chic.

A Pink-Gloved Hand

Chrysler Corporation was the first to market with hydraulically assisted power steering in early 1951 under the trade name Hydraguide. It first appeared in the Imperial brochure for 1952, which depicted a steering wheel being guided by the single finger of a gloved hand. It is not random that the glove was pink.

The importance of Hydraguide cannot be overstated. Before the crash of 1929, wealthy families had chauffeurs. But the economic realities of the '30s changed all that, and by the time the postwar era arrived, most wealthy people were driving their own cars. It was of paramount impor-

▲ *Chrysler was the first to offer hydraulically assisted power steering in early 1951 under the trade name Hydraguide. This illustration is from the 1952 brochure.*

◄ *Top fashion model Dorothy Griffith models a brilliantly striped rainsuit of water-repellent cotton by Claire McCardell as part of the 1956 Imperial Fashion Show in Chrysler Events.*

Imperial

BY CHRYSLER

Dr. Walter E. Lammerts introduced a fragrant crimson-red, hybrid tea rose in 1952. The fragrant flower, which was named an All-America Rose in 1953, was called the Chrysler Imperial rose. The famous flower began to appear in Imperial advertising and promotions.

96 | GLAMOUR ROAD

tance to make them easier to manage for drivers of both sexes. Chrysler had a very marketable advantage. From the 1952 brochure:

"With only one finger on the spoke of the steering wheel, you can turn the large 8.20-15 Super Cushion Tires on the Imperial their full travel from side to side, which illustrates the effortless steering made possible by Chrysler's new Hydraguide Power Steering system, available as extra equipment on the Imperial. This remarkable convenience and safety feature requires only one-fifth the effort that is needed to steer and park a car equipped with the ordinary manual steering mechanism. In other words, Hydraguide does four-fifths of the work for you."

Say It With Flowers

The other significant development of 1952 was less mechanical in nature. Dr. Walter E. Lammerts of Descanso Gardens in La Cañada Flintridge, California, introduced a fragrant, crimson-red, hybrid tea rose in 1952. The fragrant flower, which was named an All-America Rose in 1953, was called the Chrysler Imperial rose. The famous flower began to appear in Imperial advertising and promotions. The City of Detroit and Chrysler Corporation sponsored a float named "Life of an American Workman" in the 1954 Tournament of Roses Parade that was covered in 25,000 Chrysler Imperial Roses, each in their own small glass tube of water to keep them fresh. Here is the entry description from the Rose Parade brochure:

"Central figure of this year's entry was a heroic figure of an American workman striding out of the pages of the book and striking an anvil with a heavy hammer. Out of the anvil flow floral 'sparks' and at the end of each of these was some product of Detroit's great workshop—an automobile, a truck, a plane, a tank, a boat."

1954 Imperial ad awash in red to highlight the Chrysler Imperial Rose

The Imperial Collection | 97

1954 Imperial ads show glamorous female passengers.

98 | GLAMOUR ROAD

Ad for the 1953 Coronation Imperial

Like the car itself, the depiction of women in Imperial advertising would undergo a dramatic change. Unlike Lincoln's modern, informal lifestyle, Imperial played to high society. For 1953, Imperial advertising showed a prominent hand, gloved in pearl gray, holding Imperial's distinctive hood ornament. A gold Imperial crown emblem dangled from a gold bracelet at the wrist. The newly introduced Chrysler Imperial rose was prominently included in every layout. A much-smaller-than-customary rendering of the car was added to the lower half of the ad, almost as an afterthought.

Fit for a Queen

A rather playful promotion appeared at midyear. Elizabeth II ascended to the throne of England in June 1953, and Chrysler marked the occasion with the creation of the Coronation Imperial, a one-off special Imperial sedan in royal purple with a white top and genuine wire wheels. Inside was a custom interior of white broadcloth with royal-purple inserts featuring gold embroidered crowns and gold-plated interior hardware. For the special announcement advertisement, the gloved hand wore a royal-purple glove (but the Chrysler Imperial rose remained crimson red). It was, of course, not an official commission, and the young monarch had no connection to Chrysler corporation or the purple car itself. More than likely, she never learned of its existence, and its final disposition is unknown.

Of possibly more lasting significance in late 1953 was the announcement of Power Flite, Chrysler's first fully automatic transmission, which became available on Imperial only very late in the 1953 model year. It would roll out across the Chrysler lineup in 1954. Now with both power steering and a fully automatic transmission, Imperial created a colorful campaign in 1954 showing elegantly dressed women both in the back seat of the luxurious Imperials—and also firmly behind the wheel.

Interior illustration from a 1956 Imperial brochure

The Imperial Collection | 99

THE MAN WHO DRIVES THE IMPERIAL

He has the imagination to be different

Some men have a knack of doing the unexpected. They have the imagination, the daring spirit, and the courage to differ from the crowd. That's one reason they're so successful in everything they attempt.

To these men Imperial comes as a new breath of life in the fine car field, a refreshing new experience.

Nothing about Imperial is commonplace. Among fine cars, it commands immediate attention and respect. Its sleek, flowing lines, the graceful curve of its rear fenders with their distinctive gun-sight tail lights, and the richness of its appointments win universal approbation.

And when you see the Imperial on the highway, winging up a steep grade or gliding serenely past on an open stretch of road, you sense the tremendous reservoir of silent V-8 power.

Here is a car that truly reflects the man it serves... poised, assured, dynamic. Here is "the New Look of Leadership."

Such a car strongly appeals to men of position in their community. They are the natural leaders... the ones who invariably anticipate the trend where others follow. And they have taken Imperial to their hearts.

If Imperial is your car, you will sense it instantly. See it soon at your Chrysler-Imperial dealer's.

IMPERIAL FOR 1956

THE WOMAN WHO DRIVES THE IMPERIAL

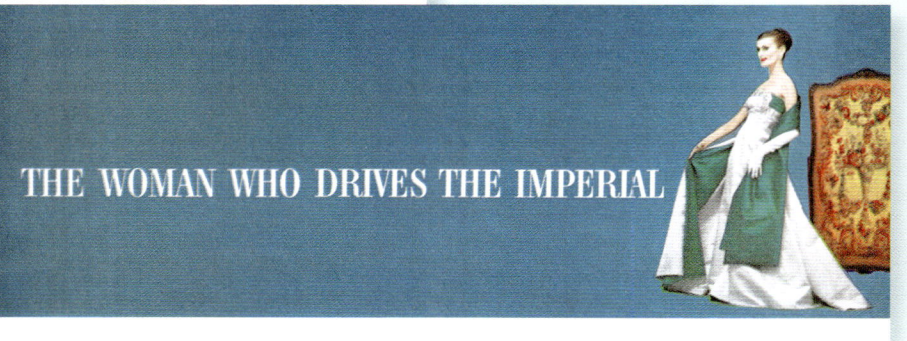

Elegance is her way of life

With some women, elegance is a way of life. Everything about them is elegant — their manner, their possessions, their homes. Nothing about them is commonplace.

Thus it is that more and more such women are today being seen in the Imperial for 1956. For no other motorcar on the American road so completely fits into their way of life.

There is nothing ordinary about the Imperial. It is made in limited quantities for those who can both afford and appreciate the finest. Imperial owners do not have to pay the invariable consequences of mass production.

In appearance, the Imperial is elegance itself, from its dramatic exterior sweep to the richness of its interior appointments.

And the Imperial is elegant in function. The mistress of this magnificent motorcar has at her command the most advanced power features in American motordom. A pushbutton automatic gear shift that is literally under finger-tip control. Power steering that renders assistance every single moment. And power brakes that require but the gentlest touch of the daintiest slipper.

If it can be said of any motorcar, it can be said of this one — in function, in appearance, in true distinction, the Imperial for 1956 is, indeed, elegance on wheels.

Your Chrysler-Imperial dealer invites you to see and drive the new Imperial. We urge you to accept his invitation and then ask yourself if *you* wouldn't rather be seen in an Imperial in 1956.

IMPERIAL FOR 1956
finest expression of The Forward Look

Battle of the Sexes

Chrysler straddled the fence with an interesting series of ad layouts. By substituting the model and changing the tone of the copy, Chrysler had somewhat tailored an otherwise identical ad for each of the sexes.

Although it wasn't unusual for automotive advertising to include different ads to reach specific audiences, this series for the 1956 Imperial took it one step further. Women were usually assumed to be luxury car passengers, not drivers. Here, Chrysler made a case for why a man *or* a women would want to drive an Imperial—notwithstanding the stereotypes that men "have the imagination, the daring spirit, and the courage to differ from the crowd," while women "sense instinctively when it's time for a fashion to change" and need brakes "that require but the gentlest touch of the daintiest slipper."

THE MAN WHO DRIVES THE IMPERIAL

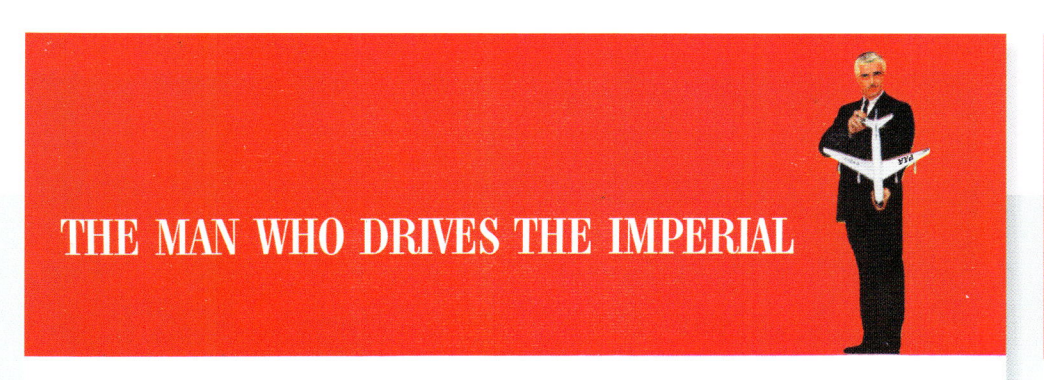

He sees the future taking shape

Some men have the vision to look beyond immediate boundaries, and to foresee new developments. And so, what others will do tomorrow, these leaders are doing today.

This year, in the field of fine motor cars, it is men like these who are setting the trend to Imperial. For, in every sense, the Imperial for 1956 has about it "the new look of leadership."

More and more you will notice the regal crown, emblem of the Imperial, in parts of town where fine cars naturally congregate. More and more you will catch a glimpse of Imperial's distinguished gun-sight tail lights out on the open highway.

The 1956 Imperial will be produced in limited numbers. It is for the man who steadfastly refuses to accept the commonplace. For Imperial's look of fine breeding, its rich and tastefully chosen appointments, its superb engineering and elegant lines truly reflect the owner it serves.

The preference for the Imperial is not taking place overnight. Many men are not fully aware of it. But the trend is here. That is why we suggest that today, you look twice in the fine car field. The Imperial for 1956 is awaiting your inspection now at your Chrysler and Imperial dealer's.

IMPERIAL FOR 1956
finest expression of The Forward Look

THE WOMAN WHO DRIVES THE IMPERIAL

She's seen fashions change before...

Some women sense instinctively when it's time for a fashion to change.

It is these discriminating women who are being seen more and more in the new Imperial. For the magnificent Imperial for 1956 satisfies the discriminating on every count.

It is made in limited quantities for those who can afford and appreciate the finest. Flair and high drama distinguish its exterior lines. And within its spirited beauty, you'll discover a mastery of the road equalled in no other car:

It starts at a fingertip's touch . . . and a completely new power brake system brings it to a graceful stop with the gentlest touch of the toe.

Its automatic pushbutton transmission makes changing gears as easy as tuning a radio. And a unique power-steering system makes it possible to park with a few simple turns of the wheel.

Your Chrysler and Imperial dealer invites you to see and drive this most gracious of automobiles. We urge you to accept the invitation . . . and then to ask yourself:

Don't you belong in the Imperial in 1956?

IMPERIAL FOR 1956
finest expression of The Forward Look

The Imperial Collection | 101

CHRYSLER

Events

FEB.–MARCH 1956

For the 1956 Imperial Fashion Show presentation, Vogue editors have selected smart new costume bathing suits, sheath daytime dresses, organza and printed chiffon short evening dresses with matching stoles and evening coats to be modeled before the socially prominent guests.

FEB.–MARCH 1956 CHRYSLER EVENTS

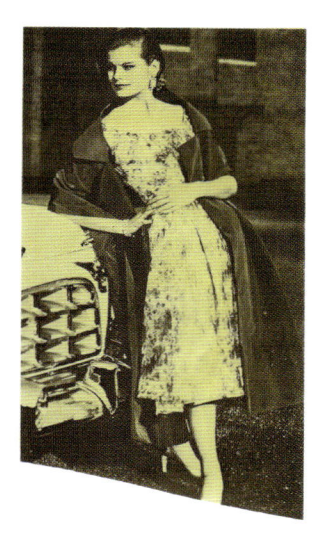

Pages from the 1956 Chrysler Events magazine featuring the Imperial Fashion Show

The High-Fashion Road

Imperial took serious aim at women buyers in 1955 with an Imperial Fashion Show. They teamed up with *Vogue* magazine to create a traveling show that visited seventeen cities in the summer of 1955. Pleased with the reception, they not only repeated the effort for 1956 but stepped up big time on their way to becoming the High Style Car. The 1956 show featured the work of five design houses—Claire McCardell, Brigance of Sportsmaker, Adele Simpson, Luis Estevez for Grenelle, and Ben Reig—and traveled to thirty cities across the US, where they were seen by audiences of up to 2,000 guests at a time. The show had a theme of Nautical-Tropical Vacation travel and showed a total of forty-three ensembles, including "bathing suits, sheath daytime dresses, organza and chiffon printed short evening dresses with matching stoles and evening coats." The fashions themselves were selected by *Vogue* editors and modeled by five of the top fashion models of the day. Backdrops included brand-new 1956 Imperials as well as a three-dimensional ocean liner model.

Vogue editor in chief Jessica Daves wrote the following account in *Chrysler Style* magazine:

"The 1956 Imperial Fashion Show gives women the opportunity to see how they hope to look this winter at southern resorts and next spring and summer at vacation spots from coast to coast. We think it interesting that the makers of a fine American automobile realize the importance of emphasizing the appeal of their cars to smart women by presenting these cars in direct connection with the clothes these smart women will wear."

The Imperial Collection | 103

The New Look of Beauty

The *Vogue* alliance continued through the decade. Notable in the January 1959 issue was a four-page advertising spread called "The New Look of Beauty/The New Touch of Luxury," starring the cosmetics of Elizabeth Arden; the clothes of Ben Zuckerman; the original supermodel herself, Suzy Parker; and two brand-new Imperial LeBaron four-door hardtops, one in Persian Pink and one in Ivory White.

Miss Parker was shown in the shades of the season by Ben Zuckerman—an emerald-green, woolen-tweed, high-waisted greatcoat; a driving suit of deep-violet woolen boucle; and a silk dress of pink, gray, and white covered by a sheer woolen tweed coat "in the freshest pink going" that precisely matched the Persian Pink paint of the Imperial.

The text described the Imperial of 1959 as having

"…calculated simplicity, warmed by accents as arresting as a beauty spot. Length without bulk, size without mass, elegance without opulence, dignity without coldness. Eminently acceptable, totally assured. In finishes so lustrous you look deep down into then… in colors thoughtfully bred to the shades you'll be wearing through the fashion year."

"Calculated simplicity, warmed by accents as arresting as a beauty spot. Length without bulk, size without mass, elegance without opulence, dignity without coldness. Eminently acceptable, totally assured."

▶ Pages from Imperial's Vogue advertising. Supermodel Suzy Parker strikes an elegant pose in Ben Zuckerman's pink wool tweed coat over a watercolor print silk dress.

IMPERIAL OF 1959

. . . calculated simplicity, warmed by accents as arresting as a beauty spot. Length without bulk, size without mass, elegance without opulence, dignity without coldness. Eminently acceptable, totally assured. In finishes so lustrous you look deep down into them . . . in colors thoughtfully bred to the shades you'll be wearing through the fashion year.

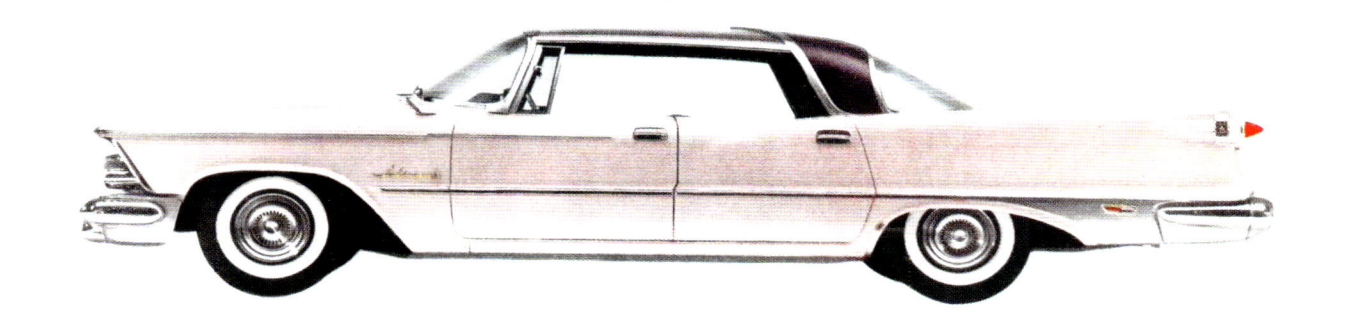

The new look of BEAUTY

ELIZABETH ARDEN

revises your complexion in texture and tone with a treasury of gentling, soothing emollients and a fresh spectrum of eye and skin tints to make the most of your 1959 look of beauty.

Miss Arden, inspired by the elegance of our new Imperial, fits them all neatly into a new Imperial Travel Case . . . the year's most beguiling travel accessory. Slip it into the glove compartment of your Imperial against the inevitable times when ravages demand repair. And for overnight tripping it's next best to an appointment at the Elizabeth Arden Salon.

BEN ZUCKERMAN

master of understatement, gives you the new look of beauty with the calculated simplicity of sheer woollens, spring-splashed silks and high gear color plans.

Right: New Imperial Travel Case designed by Elizabeth Arden contains Velva Moisture Film, Skin Lotion, Veiled Radiance Foundation, Creme Extraordinaire, Cleansing Cream, Eye Shadow, Mascara, Eyebrow Pencil, Cream Rouge, Lipstick, Memoire Cheri Perfume and Invisible Veil Compact. *Left:* Ben Zuckerman's new-season silk dress, drawn close above the waist, printed all over like a water-color wash. The silk-lined coat: sheer woollen tweed, in the freshest pink going.

The Imperial Collection | 105

The copy made note of how male engineers could have devised "so many womanly graces for this gentle vehicle," and went on to extoll the "most obedient power steering in the world," the cushioning effect of torsion-bar suspension, and power brakes "the daintiest foot can operate." It further noted the particular appeal of swivel front seats and Auto-Pilot speed control for the female motorist.

And as a final enticement, Miss Elizabeth Arden announced a new Imperial Travel Case, "this year's most beguiling travel accessory. Slip it into the glove compartment of your Imperial against the inevitable times when ravages demand repair." The white leatherette case contained Velva Moisture Film, skin lotion, Veiled Radiance Foundation, cleansing cream, eye shadow, cream rouge, lipstick, Memoire Cheri Perfume, an Invisible Veil Compact, and something called Creme Extraordinaire. It was practically a beauty salon in a box, and, at times, no doubt, just as essential as an auto club card.

The piece concluded by noting that fashions and the Imperial Travel Case were available at Saks Fifth Avenue, Jules Garfinckel, the Dayton Company, Harzfeld's, Sakowitz, Vandever's, Neusteter's, and Goldwaters, and that "The car, of course, is waiting at your Imperial dealer's."

And if you think they'd gone over the top, you would be distinctly and extravagantly mistaken, because 1960 would bring the grandest Imperial fashion statement yet.

"Each front seat turns gently doorward so you enter or leave gracefully. . . . hat undisturbed, seams straight, hemline decorously in place."

▶ Pages from Imperial's Vogue special advertising section. Suzy Parker shows how easy it is to look glamorous in an Imperial, especially wearing Ben Zuckerman's two-piece driving suit in "deep violet sheer woolen boucle."

The new touch of LUXURY

It may be a source of some little wonderment that male engineers could have devised so many womanly graces for this gentle vehicle. Yet you'll note them gratefully, and enjoy them every mile you drive. The most obedient power steering in the world, to make you a dexterous parker.

A lovely cushioning effect from torsion bar suspension, which makes it unnecessary for you to skirt rough spots in the road. Muscular power brakes the daintiest foot can operate.

IMPERIAL OF 1959 is powerful but well-tamed. It helps you drive . . . does what you ask, instantly, serenely. You can almost feel the tensions melt away.

A touch of your fingertip moves you forward . . . and rearward . . . selects the climate you particularly like to drive in, summer or winter. (Heater and air-conditioner are, of course, optional). The Imperial instrument panel is a delight of clarity . . . controls well in reach and self-explanatory. Yet with all this practicality, a blessing to the eye.

Your foot needn't be welded to the accelerator. Imperial's Auto-Pilot serves faithfully as your speeding conscience, saving you from the ultimate legal embarrassment, and may be set to keep you at a steady pace mile on mile, while your right foot rests. A sensibly luxurious option.

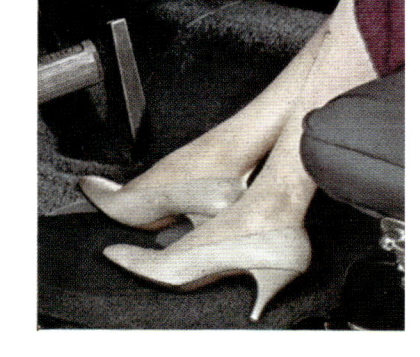

Imperial's specially installed swivel seats hand you in and out in the manner of a well-trained footman. Each front seat turns gently doorward so you enter or leave gracefully . . . hat undisturbed, seams straight, hemline decorously in place.

Left: Ben Zuckerman's greatcoat in tissue-weight woollen tweed, tied easily in front, and so green it fairly grows. *Above:* The slender ease of Ben Zuckerman's two-piece walking (and driving) suit in deep violet sheer woollen bouclé.

Fashions and cosmetics on these pages are available at: Saks Fifth Avenue (*all stores*), Julius Garfinckel, The Dayton Company, Harzfeld's, Sakowitz, Vandever's, Neusteter's, Goldwaters. The car, of course, is waiting at your Imperial dealer's.

Imperial's tonneau invites you to sit gracefully. Puts armrests beneath each elbow. Is prodigal of space for legs and feet. You sit head-high, imperially straight . . . as becomes a woman whose car is so much hers that even the interior fabrics are an obedient and tasteful foil for her ensemble. Glove-soft leathers, textured tweeds, custom-woven broadcloths in the shades you'll see again and again in the 1959 collections of every great couturier, here and abroad.

The Imperial Collection

The Imperial Collection

We'd like to have been in the meeting when this idea was proposed. It's true that Imperial was given its own production facility for 1960, because that year the rest of the Chrysler line went to unibody construction, but the low-volume Imperial did not. As a result, it had the Jefferson Avenue plant with nothing else on the assembly line. And indeed, it could make for an interesting photo opportunity. I'm sure it occurred to very few to actually close the plant and pose supermodels on the assembly line itself. But that's exactly what they did.

Naturally, the magazine was again *Vogue*. The designer was Jules-Francois Grahay of Nina Ricci of Paris. The cosmetics of course were by Elizabeth Arden. The photographer was John Rawlings, with over 200 *Vogue* and *Glamour* covers to his credit. And the photo background was Imperial's exclusive Jefferson Avenue Assembly plant. They did it on a Sunday, when the plant was closed. Models in Nina Ricci fashions were placed at the body drop, standing atop Imperial's reinforced perimeter frame. They posed and twirled at final inspection, to the amusement of inspectors who came in for some easy overtime pay. They were placed outside the paint booth and in the body bank, where newly painted cars awaited their interiors. In one particularly well-composed photo, a model in a silk chiffon dress of Imperial Red posed with a white LeBaron hardtop and a white Crown convertible with red leather that precisely matched the dress. Two matching red sedans could be seen on the assembly line. At six spectacular pages, it was eye catching and dramatic and presented Imperial as the high-fashion car.

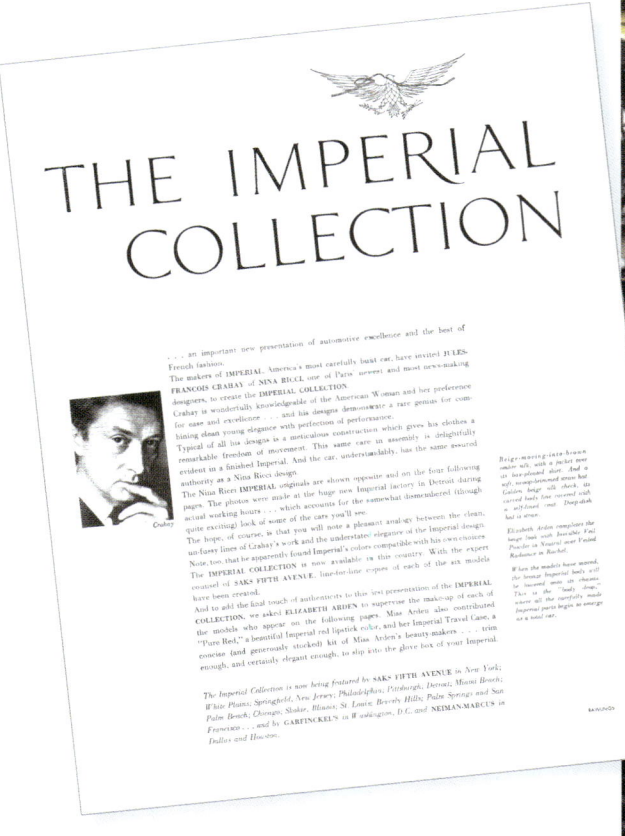

The clothes, dresses, and woolen suit dresses in wool flannel and navy, dramatic black and white for evening, and, of course, that Imperial red chiffon dress, were called the Imperial Collection and were sold at Saks Fifth Avenue, as well as Neiman-Marcus and Garfinckel's. The Elizabeth Arden travel case was back, this year sheathed in Imperial Red. And it featured a new lipstick called "Pure Red."

There is no record of additional Imperial fashion shows or clothing lines after that, but by now it was the 1960s and the industry was about to take off in exciting new directions. It would be a decade that would begin with a space rocket and end on another planet, and along the way a youthquake would occur and society would undergo substantial change.

THE IMPERIAL COLLECTION
See it at all Saks Fifth Avenue stores, at Neiman-Marcus and Garfinckel's.

Glossy black with white interior: Luxe peau de soie costume that gives you almost as many changes as there are Imperial interiors. For your Imperial you can choose from half a dozen leathers (including white), soft broadcloths, handsome ribbed or textured fabrics . . . and your own combinations of them, in tones studiously keyed to what you'll be wearing. In fact, your Imperial dealer has a great handsome book which has samples of the actual materials you can select. And Imperial interiors are, of course, tailored with the careful precision of a Ricci original.

Pages from Imperial's Vogue advertorial shot in the Jefferson Avenue Assembly plant by John Rawlings

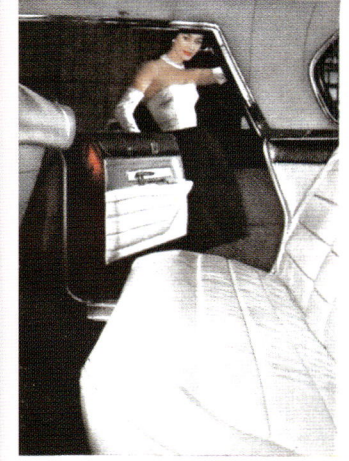

Above: The posh dot-embroidered sash gives way to a trim, shaped patent belt for black-with-pearls affairs and reflecting the color on her lips, the new bejeweled Rolling Mirror Lipstick by Elizabeth Arden. *Below:* Belt and jacket come off to reveal the strapless bodice for evening. The car is a regal red Imperial Crown lined with white leather.

Above: Free-wheeling wool flannel, flashing by in a spin of pleats, is a match for the gray broadcloth Imperial uses. Silk sash, lining and piping are red and white polka dots. The red car body has just come from the drying ovens after a series of sprayings and coatings that give Imperial the richest luster any car ever had. *Below:* Sleek-bodied navy wool, blown back to a gentle blouson with a strip of half-dollar-size white pearl buttons from neck to hem. Matching scarf over bare shoulders. That's Elizabeth Arden's Imperial Travel Case she's looking into. And the bumper-to-bumper Imperials are waiting for interiors to match their colors.

The Imperial Collection | 109

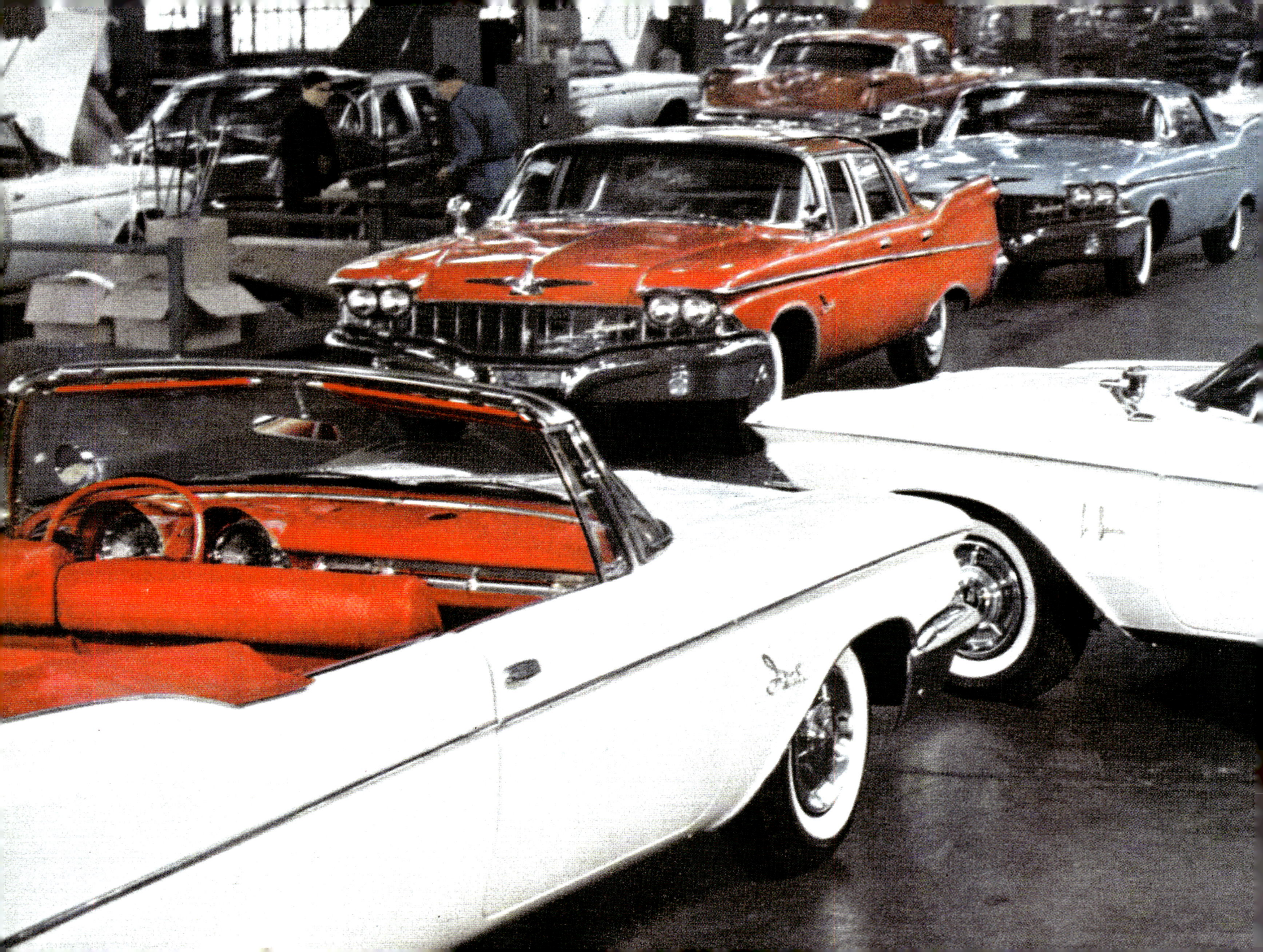

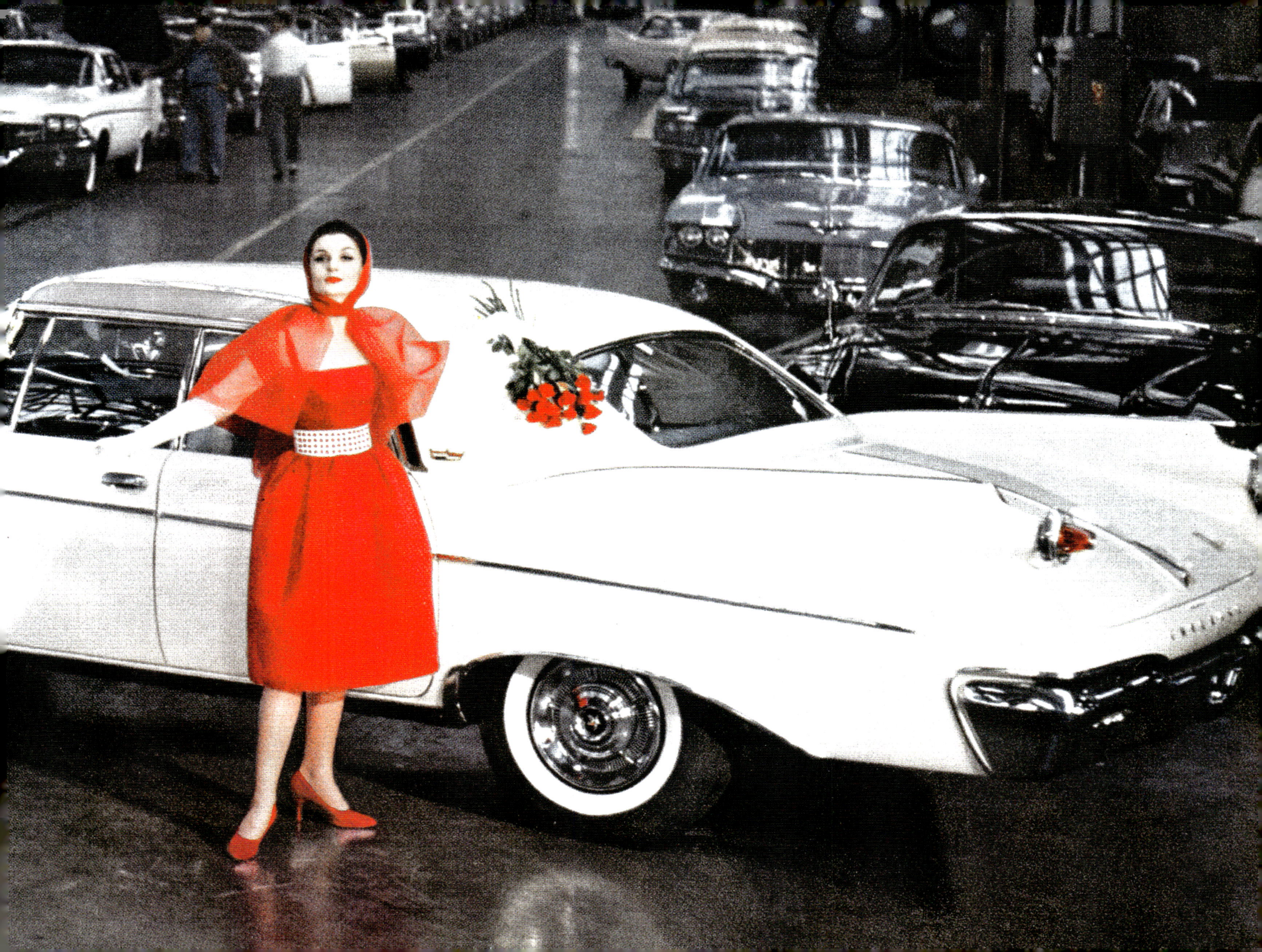

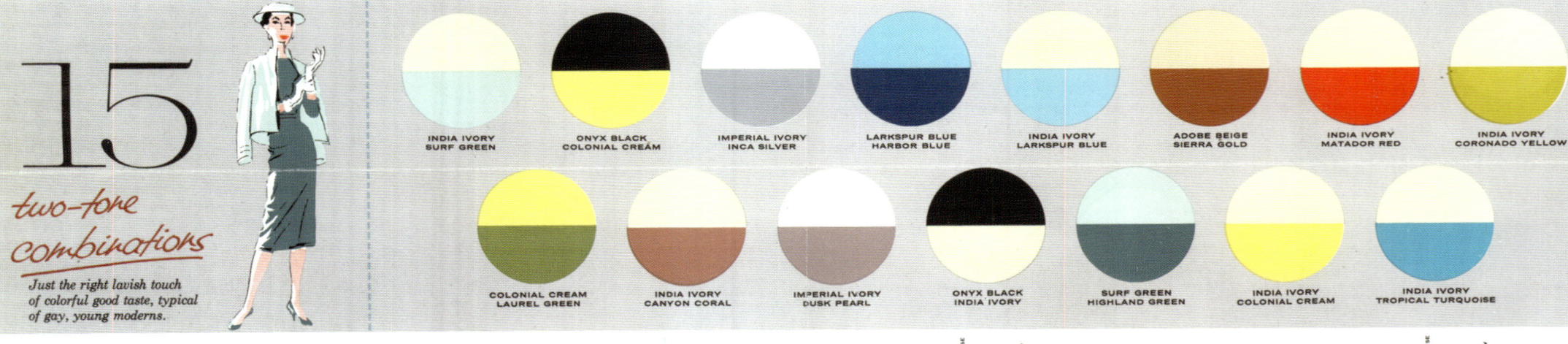

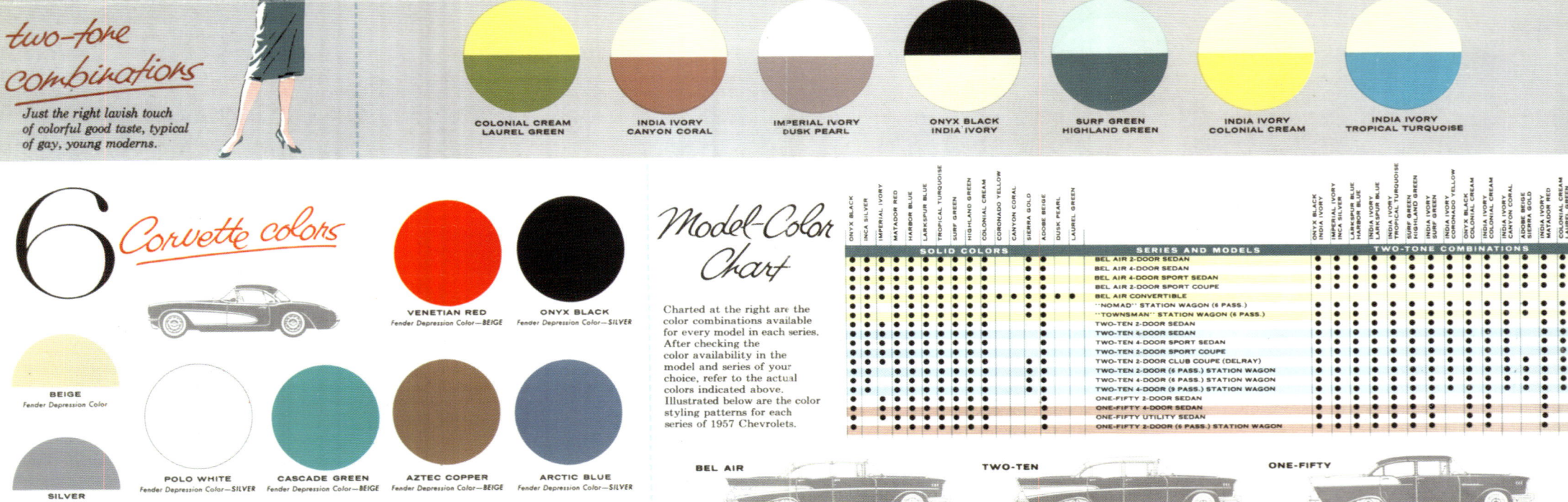

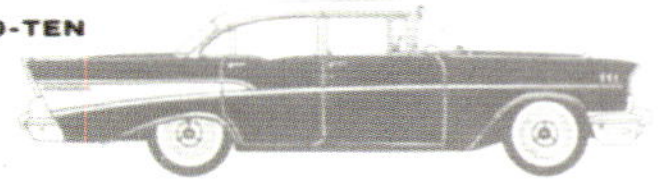

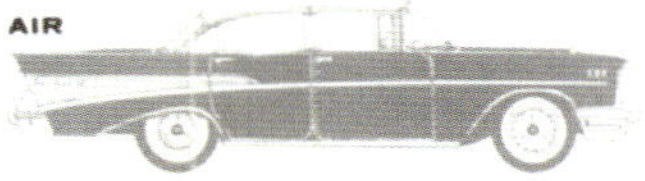

16 solid colors
Exclusive richness in a wide variety of pleasing, complimentary shades.

- CORONADO YELLOW
- LARKSPUR BLUE
- SURF GREEN
- ADOBE BEIGE
- SIERRA GOLD
- MATADOR RED
- ONYX BLACK
- TROPICAL TURQUOISE
- HIGHLAND GREEN
- DUSK PEARL
- COLONIAL CREAM
- CANYON CORAL
- LAUREL GREEN
- HARBOR BLUE
- IMPERIAL IVORY
- INCA SILVER

15 two-tone combinations
Just the right lavish touch of colorful good taste, typical of gay, young moderns.

- INDIA IVORY / SURF GREEN
- ONYX BLACK / COLONIAL CREAM
- IMPERIAL IVORY / INCA SILVER
- LARKSPUR BLUE / HARBOR BLUE
- INDIA IVORY / LARKSPUR BLUE
- ADOBE BEIGE / SIERRA GOLD
- INDIA IVORY / MATADOR RED
- INDIA IVORY / CORONADO YELLOW
- COLONIAL CREAM / LAUREL GREEN
- INDIA IVORY / CANYON CORAL
- IMPERIAL IVORY / DUSK PEARL
- ONYX BLACK / INDIA IVORY
- SURF GREEN / HIGHLAND GREEN
- INDIA IVORY / COLONIAL CREAM
- INDIA IVORY / TROPICAL TURQUOISE

6 Corvette colors

- VENETIAN RED — Fender Depression Color—BEIGE
- ONYX BLACK — Fender Depression Color—SILVER
- POLO WHITE — Fender Depression Color—SILVER
- CASCADE GREEN — Fender Depression Color—BEIGE
- AZTEC COPPER — Fender Depression Color—BEIGE
- ARCTIC BLUE — Fender Depression Color—SILVER
- BEIGE — Fender Depression Color
- SILVER — Fender Depression Color

Model-Color Chart

Charted at the right are the color combinations available for every model in each series. After checking the color availability in the model and series of your choice, refer to the actual colors indicated above. Illustrated below are the color styling patterns for each series of 1957 Chevrolets.

BEL AIR   TWO-TEN   ONE-FIFTY

Chapter Six

READY TO WEAR

POPULAR-PRICED CARS USE COLOR AND FASHION TO BOOST SALES

The postwar market bore great promise. Peacetime had arrived at last, and all economic indicators pointed to blue skies and an almost unprecedented automobile market. There was pent-up replacement demand for the nation's aging automotive fleet, as well as the promise of a huge new market opportunity. But with that great hope came a challenge. Rosie had laid down her rivet gun and reached for the car keys—and automakers had to learn how to sell to women.

Ah, yes, the fairer sex. The one that made up almost 0 percent of the management of the automobile companies but would soon be a substantial part of the market. In the prewar decades, they were rarely depicted as drivers in automobile ads, let alone as purchasers. The marketing plans now had to include pitches to women, and this would be accomplished with wildly varying degrees of success.

As was shown in earlier chapters, luxury brands took an approach of selling lifestyle. Lincoln's Modern Living campaign placed women behind the wheel in the most modern and upscale settings. Imperial presented itself as a carriage fit for royalty, complete with a special car built for the coronation of Queen Elizabeth II, and produced fashion shows and cobranded promotions with upscale women's retailers. And, of course, Cadillac wrapped women in designer gowns and jewels and placed them in front of opera houses (subtlety was never Cadillac's forté).

For every woman who drove her new Cadillac to the opera house in a Scaasi gown or wore smart separates by Sophie for Saks Fifth Avenue, thousands more drove to the brand-new shopping center for sportswear at Woolworth's or S. S. Kresge. But just because those women were on a tighter budget didn't mean they were one iota less fashion conscious than their more upscale sisters, so the lower-priced manufacturers had to make their products just as appealing to style-conscious women of the prosperous postwar economy as the luxury brands did.

They used a variety of methods, from celebrity spokespeople—both Dinah Shore (Chevrolet) and a youthful Betty White (Plymouth) appeared on television programs sponsored by their respective automakers—to specially targeted advertising and even copromotion with moderately priced women's attire. And there could be books written solely on the subject of the fascinating color palette of the fifties, complete with its two-tone and even tritone color combos, which were the secret weapon in the strategy of attracting a lady's eye.

◀ *1957 Chevrolet Color Ideas Brochure, "15 Two-tone combinations—Just the right lavish touch of colorful good taste, typical of gay, young moderns"*

▲ *1962 Buick color- and fabric-styling presentation featuring tartan cloth (General Motors Archive)*

The '58 cars in new Du Pont LUCITE* Lacquer

You'll thrill to color so deep you can "see into" it—and this finish keeps its showroom brilliance three times longer!

When the '58 cars are unveiled, you'll see many styled in startlingly beautiful colors. Easier to care for than any previously known finish, new Du Pont "Lucite" Acrylic Lacquer achieves dramatic new hues with metallic powders and pigments that sparkle in a diamond-clear "Lucite" base. The color effects are so rich and exciting you'll have to see them to appreciate what happens. It's like looking into a pool of liquid color and seeing the subtle changes from pastels to deeper values. And whether in the new metallics, or in traditional colors, Du Pont "Lucite" Lacquer is so *durable* it stays bright and beautiful three times longer than the best conventional finishes. Water rolls off . . . dirt slides off the jewel-smooth surface. So it is easier to clean and stays clean longer. You'll want this remarkable new finish on your new car. Look for the many makes and models that will be available in Du Pont "Lucite."

Wonderful World of Color

It's no coincidence that the colors of fashion are reflected in the colors of automobiles—both tend to reflect the prevailing national mood. So it's no surprise that both reflected the colors of wartime by the time victory was declared. Fashion colors tended to be dark and drab, and the fashions themselves reflected the lines of military uniforms. Automobile colors reflected similar themes. The 1948 Chevrolet color chart for 1948 could well have been called Fifty Shades of Gray (and Green), except that there were only ten colors in all. The shades themselves were drab colors in light and dark hues, and one was even called Battleship Gray.

As we have seen, Dior changed the palette for women's fashion in 1948, and automobile colors soon followed. Of course, Kaiser-Frazer led the way with a color palette for 1949 that included a remarkable thirty-seven color codes and no fewer than nine two-tone combinations, among them remarkably vivid shades of Caribbean Coral,

▶ Opposite: During model years 1957, 1958, and 1959, De Soto offered no fewer than seventy-five total paint colors. Many could be two-toned with other colors to offer literally hundreds of possible combinations.

◀ Dupont introduced Lucite Acrylic Lacquer in the late 1950s and caused an explosion of color.

▼ By 1949, Cadillac had moved from postwar drab colors to fashion shades such as chartreuse, paired here with a red leather interior on a convertible from the 1949 brochure.

The Cadillac Convertible—available only in Series Sixty-Two—may be had with either black or tan top. Top, windows and front seat adjustments are hydraulically operated. The interiors are upholstered in leather—available in any one of five attractive colors.

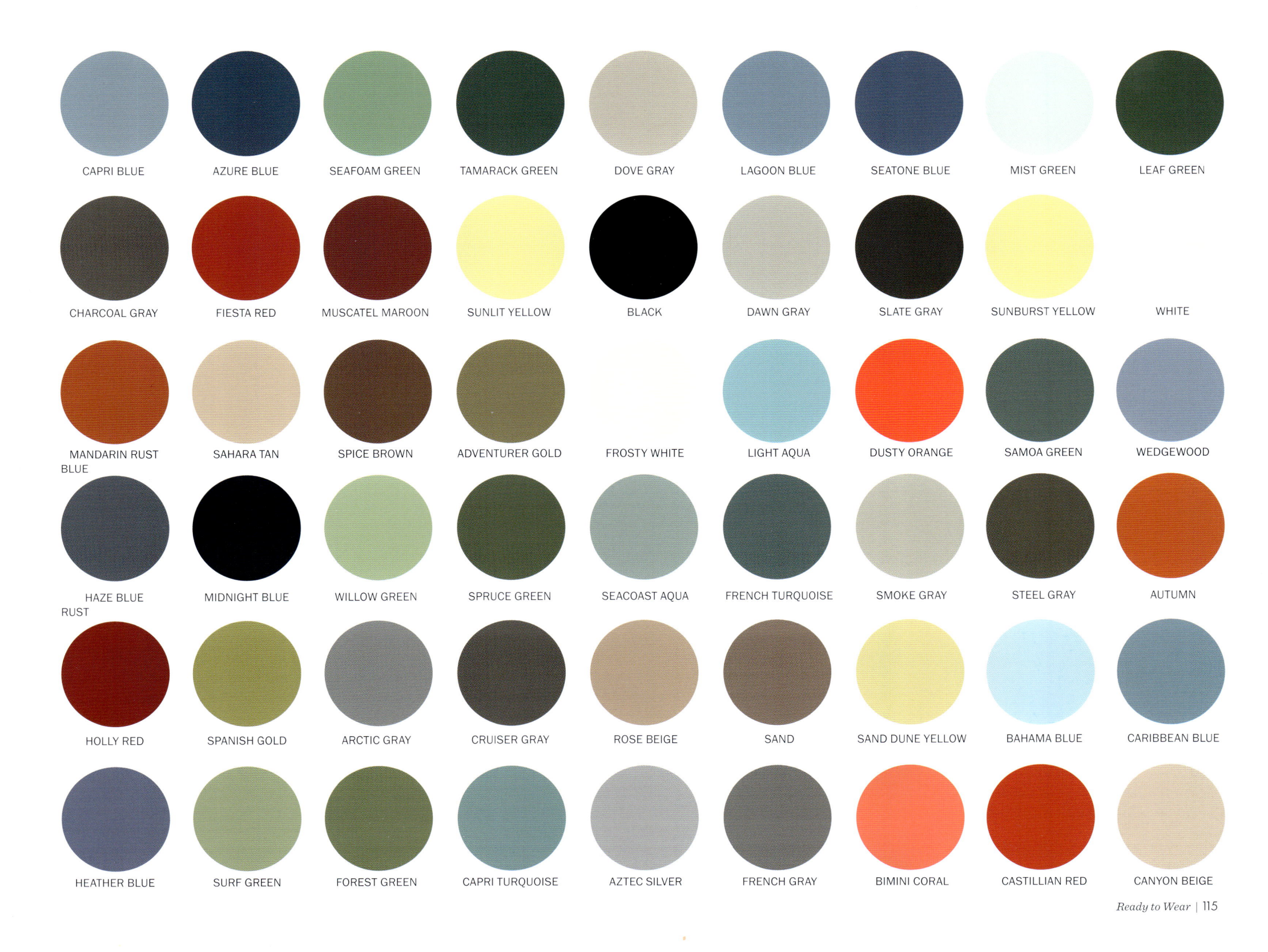

CAPRI BLUE	AZURE BLUE	SEAFOAM GREEN	TAMARACK GREEN	DOVE GRAY	LAGOON BLUE	SEATONE BLUE	MIST GREEN	LEAF GREEN
CHARCOAL GRAY	FIESTA RED	MUSCATEL MAROON	SUNLIT YELLOW	BLACK	DAWN GRAY	SLATE GRAY	SUNBURST YELLOW	WHITE
MANDARIN RUST	SAHARA TAN	SPICE BROWN	ADVENTURER GOLD	FROSTY WHITE	LIGHT AQUA	DUSTY ORANGE	SAMOA GREEN	WEDGEWOOD BLUE
HAZE BLUE	MIDNIGHT BLUE	WILLOW GREEN	SPRUCE GREEN	SEACOAST AQUA	FRENCH TURQUOISE	SMOKE GRAY	STEEL GRAY	AUTUMN RUST
HOLLY RED	SPANISH GOLD	ARCTIC GRAY	CRUISER GRAY	ROSE BEIGE	SAND	SAND DUNE YELLOW	BAHAMA BLUE	CARIBBEAN BLUE
HEATHER BLUE	SURF GREEN	FOREST GREEN	CAPRI TURQUOISE	AZTEC SILVER	FRENCH GRAY	BIMINI CORAL	CASTILLIAN RED	CANYON BEIGE

Ready to Wear

A. Raven Black	M. Corinthian White	G. Silver Mink
N. Diamond Blue	F. Skymist Blue	E. Acapulco Blue
H. Caspian Blue	S. Cascade Green	R. Tucson Yellow
X. Heritage Burgundy	V. Chestnut	J. Rangoon Red
Z. Fieldstone Tan	T. Sandshell Beige	L. Sahara Rose
K. Chalfonte Blue	D. Patrician Green	U. Deep Sea Blue

116 | GLAMOUR ROAD

◀ *1962 Thunderbird colors. In addition to the eighteen standard colors, two-tone paint combinations and vinyl tops were also offered.*

Dubonnet, Teal Blue, and Indian Ceramic. Of course, the industry had to respond, and it was unlikely a coincidence that both Cadillac and Ford had shades of chartreuse in 1949 and 1950, respectively.

And from there, color took off like wildfire. The aforementioned ten colors at Chevrolet expanded to fifteen by 1955 and included brighter shades of Corvette Copper, Autumn Bronze, Gypsy Red, and Coral. The 1955 Bel Air sport coupe shown at the GM Motorama of 1955 was Coral and Shadow Gray with a matching interior. Traditional two-toning of a contrasting roof expanded to contrasting color on the body as well, making both two-tones and three-tones popular by the mid-'50s. And it's not a coincidence that the 1953 Corvette sports car debuted in Polo White—white was actually a new color trend for cars in the early '50s. The palette of the '50s included pinks, corals, yellows, oranges, and more shades of green than were previously known to exist in nature. The decade was awash in vivid color. Only ten years after the death of Henry Ford—famous for his model T in "any color as long as it is black"—the customer could choose a new Ford in Fiesta Red, Peacock Blue, Mandarin Orange, or Sunset Coral and drive it off the showroom floor.

The color scheme had a hierarchy as well—manufacturers could take a single body and use varying paint schemes and trim to create a range of different models. Chrysler Corporation in particular utilized more-elaborate color schemes and tritone finishes to add exclusivity to its higher trim levels—all made out of the same basic body nonetheless—and while it may seem frivolous today, it sold automobiles, and more elaborately equipped ones at that.

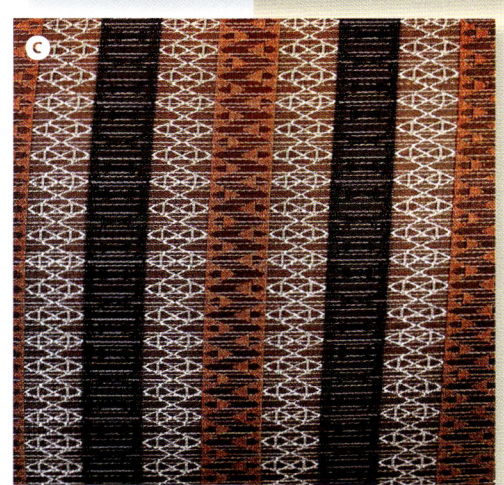

Pattern, trim, and color, along with some well-designed accessories such as clocks, gave medium-priced cars a touch of high style.

A *1960 Dodge Dart upholstery in Dexter fabric*

B *1961 Plymouth clock, looking like a George Nelson design (Chris Menrad)*

C *Detail of 1961 Plymouth Fury upholstery fabric (Chris Menrad)*

D *1960 Dodge Dart interior featuring textured Dakar fabric, highlighted with metallic gold thread*

E *1960 Dodge Dart interior featuring Phoenix vinyl*

F *1961 Buick pedestal clock, elegantly suspended above the dashboard*

Ready to Wear | 117

Say It with Leather

Leather was an upholstery material normally reserved for upscale marques. It was expensive, so it was generally used as bolsters and trim on closed cars—full leather upholstery tended to be reserved for convertible models. Lower- and medium-priced makes used imitation leathers, but in the fifties, leather began to appear on the upper trim levels of medium-priced models. This 1958 advertisement from the Leather Upholstery Group shows the expanded range of models available with colorful leather interiors. Medium-priced cars such as Mercury, Pontiac, and Oldsmobile are shown alongside their more luxurious counterparts. Note also the wide range of color, including bright yellow in the Buick, as well as the extensive use of white leather, which first appeared in automobiles in the fifties.

118 | GLAMOUR ROAD

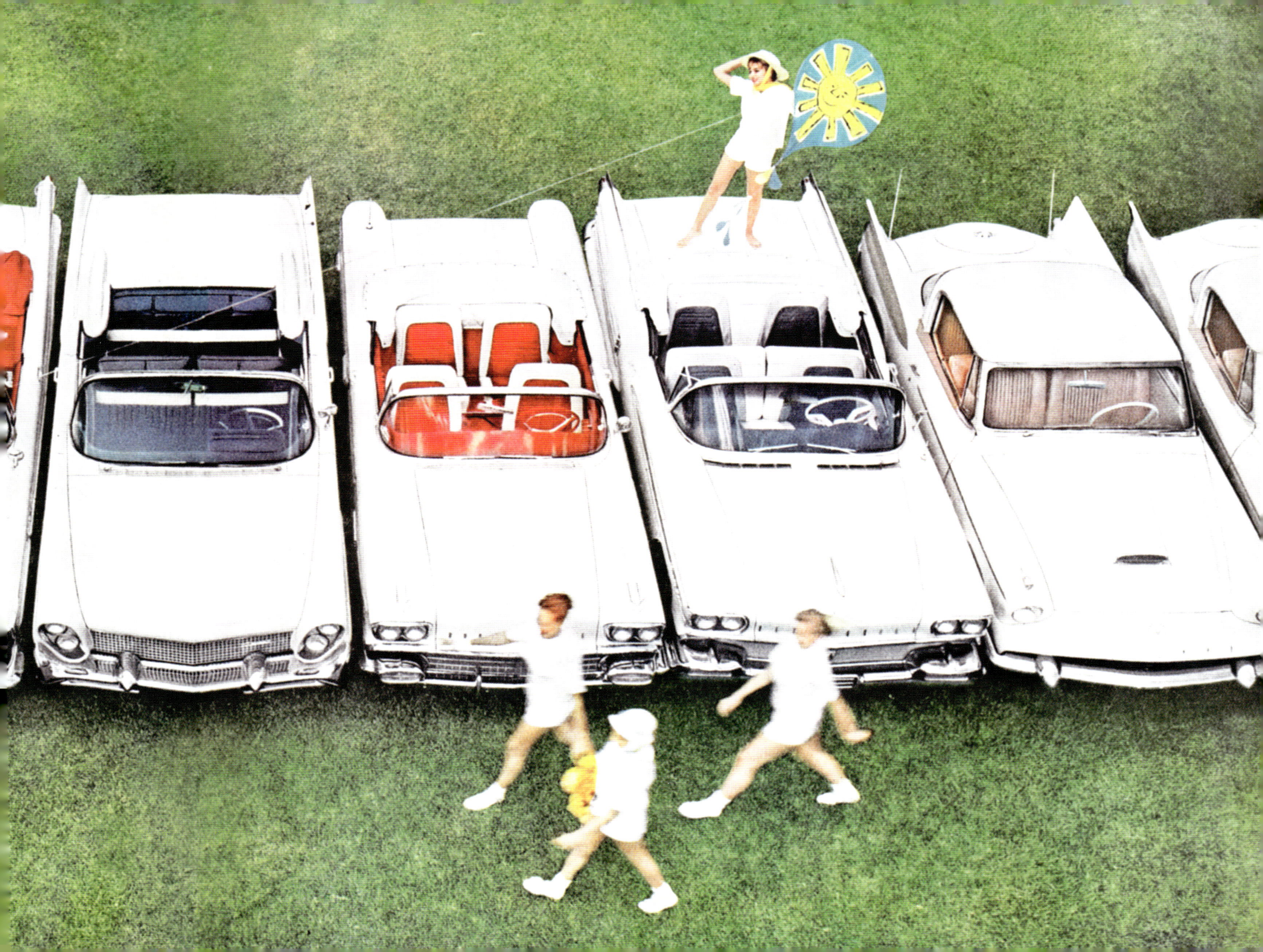

The 1955 Buick Spring Fashion Festival brochure introduced tritone combinations.

The "Spring Special"

Another direct parallel with the fashion industry was the "Spring Special." Just as fashion had a spring line, several manufacturers introduced special spring colors to help boost demand as the snow melted and automobile sales began to thaw out.

Buick made a promotion out of it with a special flyer promoting the Buick Spring Fashion Festival. In 1954, they used the occasion to introduce new col-

120 | GLAMOUR ROAD

ors of Tunis Blue, Malibu Blue, Lido Green, and Gulf Turquoise, the latter of which was available with a red-and-black interior. In 1955, it coincided with the introduction of the four-door hardtop body style and five spring colors, including three greens—Spruce, Nile, and Mist—along with Cadet and Colonial Blue. Five tri-tones were also offered. Interestingly, the three greens reappeared in the spring of 1956, along with the vivid combination of Bittersweet and Apricot, bringing the total number of color choices to twenty, plus two-tone and tritone combinations.

Chrysler took things a step further, producing Spring Special models with unique names, color combinations, special trim, and unique interiors. The most notable of these would perhaps be the De Soto Coronado, which began as a spring special in Cadiz Blue and Sahara Beige with a matching cloth and leather interior in 1954 and was so successful it was repeated for '55 in a tri-tone.

Other examples would be the 1955 Chrysler Windsor "Blue Heron" and "Green Falcon" specials and the 1956 Chrysler Windsor Spring Special, with a unique "Copperglow" of copper-embossed vinyl and special black cloth with black dash and carpets.

Of particular vibrance was the 1959 De Soto Seville Spring Edition, featuring an interior of Nassau Plaid in a "Caribbean Sun" combination of two-tone blue plaid fabric with horizontal stripe of green inset into white bolsters and trim. It's a particularly memorable creation. Of course, these examples are but a handful of many of these limited-run special editions that were helpful to automakers looking to achieve a few incremental sales.

▶ Right, *Spring Special ads, clockwise from top left: 1954 De Soto Coronado, 1955 Chrysler, 1959 De Soto Seville, 1956 Chrysler*

Ready to Wear | 121

▶ Unnamed model makes a fashion statement with 1959 Chevrolet fabric, including the red-striped cloth seen in the brochure opposite. (General Motors Archive)

Chevy Chic

By almost any measure, Chevrolet arrived late to the fashion show. It's not that they weren't good marketers or that they didn't see the value of engaging with women. Chevy had been a pioneer in the new medium of television as early as 1949, when it introduced its iconic theme song before it ever became associated with songstress Dinah Shore. It was Dinah who made the song a legend and made her name and Chevy almost synonymous. Chevrolet signed on to sponsor the *Dinah Shore Show* in 1951, and they remained together under varying show names—including the *Chevy Show* and the *Dinah Shore Chevy Show*—until 1961.

But even though Dinah herself wore glamorous gowns as she showcased the new Chevrolet line, the popular singer wasn't really known as a glamour girl. She had a folksy charm; she was down-home and approachable. Dinah was the girl next door, and Chevy was America's car. Chevy didn't really tie into the concept of fashion until the all-new redesigned Chevrolet of 1955 made its appearance. That year, the Motorama debut car was a Bel Air hardtop coupe in Coral and Shadow Gray, inside and out. When the cantilevered arm swung it across the reflecting pond in the ballroom of the Waldorf, it was unlike any Chevrolet that had come before it. Later that year, another Bel Air hardtop coupe, in Glacier Blue and India Ivory, starred in a Fisher Body ad among a forest of Spanish moss on Sea Island, flanked by a model in a flowered print by Lanvin-Castillo. Perhaps for the first time, Chevy was fashionable. The 1957 Chevy "Color Ideas" selector advertised "466 kinds of beauty for 1957," including sixteen solids, fifteen two-tones, and six Corvette combinations, and only women were depicted in the piece.

Friends Finds Fashion

Chevrolet had published *Friends* magazine back as far as 1940—it was a magazine that Chevy dealers sent to their customers and good prospects. It was 1958 when headlines proclaimed "Chevy Chic!" The text proclaimed "Fashion's glamour is an end in itself" and went on to highlight two ensembles, a ball gown by Simonetta of Rome and a cocktail dress by Antonio del Castillo, both rendered in the colors of new Chevys. And in *Friends* magazine that spring, a three-page section titled "Inspired Fashions" showed Chevrolet-commissioned couture by the aforementioned Simonetta and del Castillo, along with sketches by Guy Laroche, Glen Green, Alberto Fabiani, and Norman Hartnell, and a watercolor by America's reigning queen of sportswear, Claire McCardell herself, in what would have been one of her final designs.

Chevrolet was all new again for 1959—the longest, lowest, and widest Chevy in history, with enormous bat wings and cat's-eye taillights. Chevrolet called the design "Slimline," and ad headlines proclaimed it "Fresh, Fine, and Fashionable." Dinah Shore drove a white Impala convertible and sang about the "Slimline Fresh and Fine Chevy." Other ads called it "Fashion Crafted," and once again, it inspired a fashion collection.

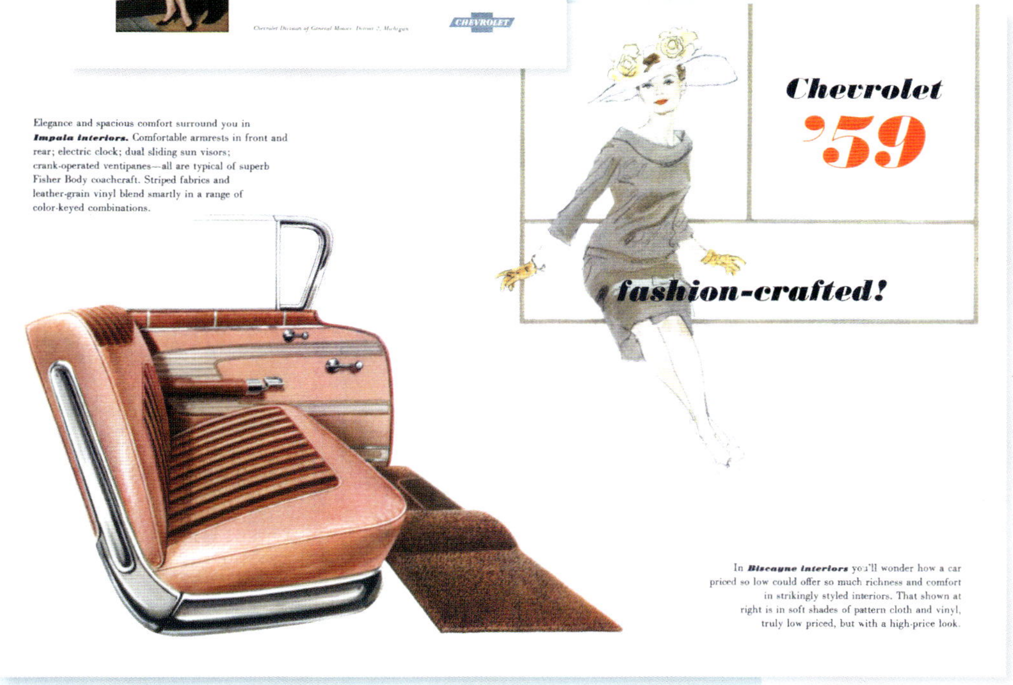

CHEVY CHIC

Fashion's glamor is an end in itself. Rome's

Simonetta and Paris' Castillo have

captured it in these lovely reflections of Chevrolet

style, Chevrolet colors—Simonetta,

with a short silk ball gown

in Chevy's Tropic Turquoise . . .

Castillo, with a daring cocktail dress featuring

billows of Arctic White peau de soie, a silk taffeta

bolero-with-stole in vivid Rio Red.

But in cars, beauty is only as beauty does.

That's why the lovely 1958 Chevrolet

is built to do just as you bid it. You'll

love its effortless steering behavior, its

obedient parking manners. See your

Chevrolet dealer for the key.... Chevrolet Division

of General Motors, Detroit 2, Michigan.

CHEVROLET

▲ Top: 1959 Chevrolet ad—"Cherchez la femme en la Chevy"
▲ Above: Page from the "fashion-crafted" 1959 Chevrolet brochure
▶ 1958 Chevrolet ad promoted Chevy chic.

Ready to Wear | 123

The Slimline Collection

Famous designers all over the world—inspired by the new Slimline accents and contours of the 1959 Chevrolet—used a wide variety of exquisite fabrics and a sweeping range of glamorous colors to create costumes of high fashion

The Slimline Collection was announced in an ad under the headline "Cherchez la femme en la Chevy," which they translated as "Look for the woman in the 1959 Chevrolet—and you'll find a woman in style." A fashionable white Impala sport coupe was shown with a lady in a scarlet-red dress. The ad announced the second fashion collection, this year called the Slimline Collection. The text is worth quoting:

"Here it is, crystallized in couture: that certain inexpressible something about a woman in a new 1959 Chevrolet. For here is one of the new 1959 Slimline fashions—the second annual collection of Chevy-inspired creations from world famous designers (including Hartnell, Fabiani, Plattry, Scaasi, Rodriguez, Laroche, Connolly, Horstman, Castillo and Simonetta).

In this spirited interpretation, Rome's Simonetta ignites wool chiffon excitement with its own flaring halo to create a radiant Simonetta Red cocktail dress . . . and a dazzling lesson in the subtle art of blending evanescent Fashion with elegant eternal style.

It's the same art you will find in each of the sleek, slimlined models that glisten in the Chevrolet showroom near you. It's the art that makes any woman in a Chevy—be she clad in a Hartnell or a housedress, a Scaasi or slacks—a woman in style. Just visit that nearby Chevrolet dealer—you'll see!"

The entire Slimline collection was presented in glamorous full color in the spring 1959 issue of *Friends* magazine. The gowns, coats, and sportswear that composed the collection were shown together with the glamorous new Chevrolets in sparkling ultramodern settings. Unlike some of the other fashion promotions we have seen, there was no information as to where to purchase the fashions, which made the whole undertaking seem much more casual than some of the copromotions from other manufacturers. Still, they were dramatic ads that definitely pointed Chevrolet in the direction of fashion.

Designer Alberto Fabiani of Rome created this formal ball gown and full-length evening coat expressly for the Chevrolet Impala sport sedan. The gown, of pure silk faille in antique gold, is distinctive for its gold-and-silver embroidered yoke finished with gold fringe at the high waistline, and the full skirt, pellon lined, that falls to the floor in graceful folds. The evening coat, in pale buttercup silk faille, has a short, stand-up collar, with revers at the front. The armholes are beneath deep folds set in a shallow yoke across the shoulders.

These new fashions for
daytime and evening,
created by famed designers,
were designed to match
or harmonize with
the distinctive beauty and
Slimline styling of
the 1959 Chevrolet

Parisian designer Antonio Castillo's short cocktail dress of chiffon in Chevrolet's Crown Sapphire (left) has a low, round neck and an accordion-pleated skirt that is gathered at the hemline with an elastic band. Full-flowing panels in the back are draped to the hem. Simonetta of Rome, famed for her exotic and exciting creations, designed the sleeveless red cocktail dress at the right. It is made of a new, soft, wool chiffon, is short and tight, with dramatic draping flowing down from the yoke, which is slit at the front and has a large self bow.

This youthful, three-piece sports outfit by Greta Plattry of New York City has long, slim, apple green pants, with a camisole, tuck-in top of ruffled white cotton lace, and a colorful, hip-length, collarless, lightweight silk print jacket that is lined with silk.

From Spanish designer Pedro Rodriguez of Barcelona comes this afternoon dress in gray and white cotton print (lined with pellon stiffening). It is short and sleeveless, without a waistline, and has two front center pockets.

Daytime designs that are eminently right for the Chevrolet Nomad station wagon are pictured above. At the left is a three-piece, lightweight wool suit with tuck-in blouse of wool print, designed by Laroche of Paris. The short jacket is lined with material matching the blouse. Sybil Connolly of Dublin created the smart suit and coat at the right. Both are of hand-woven tweed, made on looms in fishing villages on the coast of Ireland.

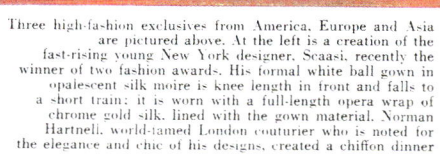

Three high-fashion exclusives from America, Europe and Asia are pictured above. At the left is a creation of the fast-rising young New York designer, Scaasi, recently the winner of two fashion awards. His formal white ball gown in opalescent silk moire is knee length in front and falls to a short train; it is worn with a full-length opera wrap of chrome gold silk, lined with the gown material. Norman Hartnell, world-famed London couturier who is noted for the elegance and chic of his designs, created a chiffon dinner dress (center) in Chevrolet's Harbor Blue, trimmed with matching bugle beads on the neckline yoke. This floor-length dress has pleated chiffon panels which flow from the shoulders to form a blouse at the dropped waistline, then fall loose to the hem. From designer Charlotte Horstmann of Hong Kong comes a formal oriental gown with standing collar and slit skirt. The fitted dress and its matching, chiffon-lined stole are of richly embroidered pure silk—a fabric that is truly rare, for it was hand-woven in Asia 100 years ago.

Ready to Wear | 125

Fabulous by Fisher

Fisher Body, longtime supplier of auto bodies to General Motors, had been a wholly owned subsidiary of the auto giant since all the way back to 1926. Perhaps it's a bit surprising that they advertised at all, but there was probably a budget line left over on the spreadsheet since way back when, and in corporate America, if you have a budget, you spend it. In most years, they advertised features like the all-steel body or flow-through ventilation, but in the early fifties, they took on a more stylish tone.

It was around 1952 that Fisher Body ads went to color photography that showed scenes of wholesome family life, usually depicting an attractive young mother with well-scrubbed small children in the back seat of a GM car, and spoke of the safety and security of Body by Fisher. The signature was a jewelry box that showed the Fisher coach on the lid and all the GM-brand jewels inside. But perhaps it was the influence of the Motorama that turned the ads toward fashion.

Beginning in 1954, they began a series of Gowns and Glamour, where a new GM car was shown in an oh-so-smart location with a glamorous model in a credited designer gown. It had a very upscale feel and showed a rotation of new GM automobiles in full-color photographs. Locale, automobile, and dress designers all were credited, occasionally along with some soft-sell verbiage about the advantages of a Body by Fisher, available only on General Motors cars. It was a visually engaging series that in some ways cribbed on Cadillac—except with photographs of the cars instead of illustrations. Beautiful advertising indeed, although one wonders how many cars it might have sold.

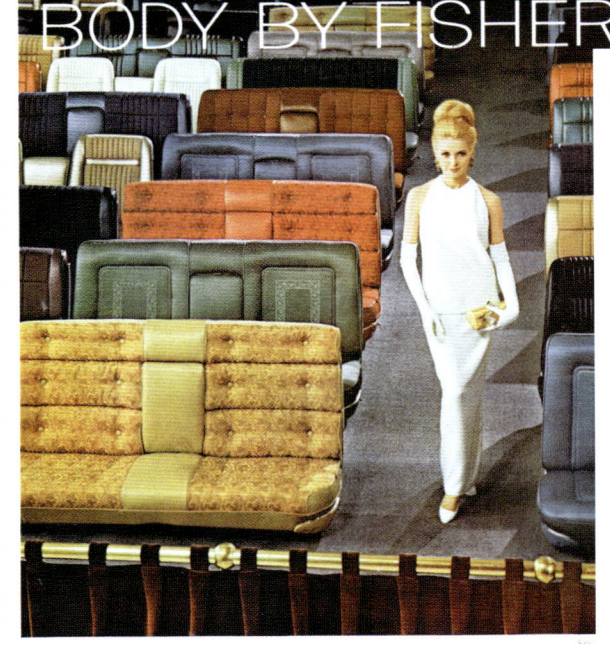

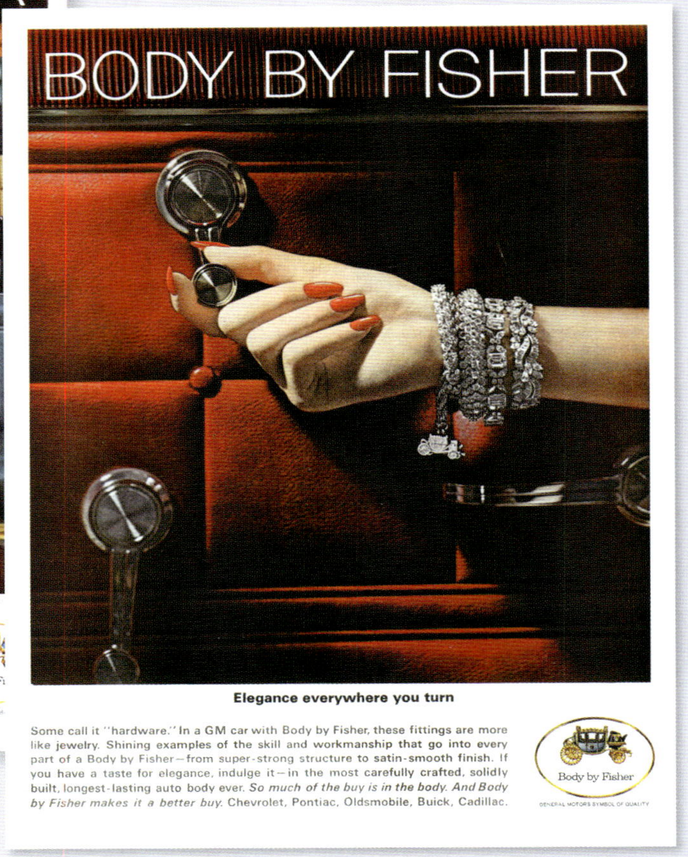

Perhaps they grew weary of being mistaken for divisional advertising, because later in the decade they adopted the flying-car series where a Fisher Body—sans front end, chassis, or wheels—was seen floating through the air at low altitude. It's always been a bit of a mystery what inspired that particular idea—perhaps someone at the agency was a little too obsessed with space travel?

Thankfully those flying-car bodies were grounded after a couple of seasons, and high glamour returned. This time they featured some remarkable photography and focused more on the details of Fisher Body construction, such as a multi-diamond-bracelet-clad hand grasping the finely detailed window crank assembly, or a sufficiently grand and gowned lady strolling through an opera house of new GM seat assemblies, with a headline proclaiming the "Choicest Seats in the House."

The series continued through the decade, in bright color photography and almost exclusively showcasing women. One memorable 1969 ad starred the first female GM studio chief and former Damsel of Design, Suzanne Vanderbilt, behind the wheel of a 1969 Camaro with a wild Pucci-inspired custom interior.

▲ (Above and right) 1967 Body by Fisher ads promote elegance and style.

◀ A Buick Electra flies through space in a 1959 Body by Fisher ad.

▶ Opposite page: 1956 Body by Fisher ad featuring an Oldsmobile Holiday

THERE'S MORE BEHIND THE DOOR / OF AN OLDSMOBILE

More in a host of advantages expressed by the distinguished Fisher Body emblem. A standard of craftsmanship that can only come from the latest tools and techniques, used by people with generations of experience in designing and engineering — a combination of imagination and practicality that has resulted in such innovations as the panoramic windshield and the four-door hardtop.

Arizona Interlude by The Wigwam
The Renoir Ensemble by Mr. John, Inc.
Holiday 2-Door by Oldsmobile

Body by Fisher
found only on *General Motors Cars*

CHEVROLET · PONTIAC · OLDSMOBILE · BUICK · CADILLAC

Ready to Wear | 127

▶ **OFF THE SHOULDER**—Asymmetrical seats were a brief fad in the late '50s. Several manufacturers, including Pontiac, Edsel, and the entire Chrysler Corporation, embraced asymmetrical seats for a time. Pontiac referred to their design as the "Off the Shoulder Look" in this 1957 ad.

▲ **WIDE TRACK**—Pontiac widened the distance between the wheels as part of its total 1959 redesign, and the "Wide Track" look was born. This marked the beginning of Pontiac's revitalized image and led them through a renaissance in the '60s. Note the reference to Wide Track in the 1959 copromotion with Peck and Peck (opposite) and the 1960 ad (above) specifically targeting the security of Pontiac's Wide Track to female motorists.

The *"Off-the-Shoulder" Look*—
just One of the wonderful New Firsts in the
'57 Pontiac

See it **NOV. 9** at Your Pontiac Dealer's

128 | GLAMOUR ROAD

Color is a trademark of Star Chief elegance

No other car built in America today is more justly famous for magnificent colors and interiors—and here you see why. Whatever model you choose, color is a distinctive part of its remarkable luxury. Even from a distance, custom colors in paint immediately set a Star Chief apart from ordinary cars—and you have 92 color schemes to pick from. Inside, these same colors are recaptured perfectly in the soft elegance of Lustrex or leather upholstery. The Sedan offers its own distinguished interiors; the Catalina Sedan and Coupe provide a choice of Lustrex or leather upholstery at no extra cost. The instrument panel is custom tooled and toned to Star Chief luxury—with a hand-assist rail finished in padded Morrokide to match each interior motif.

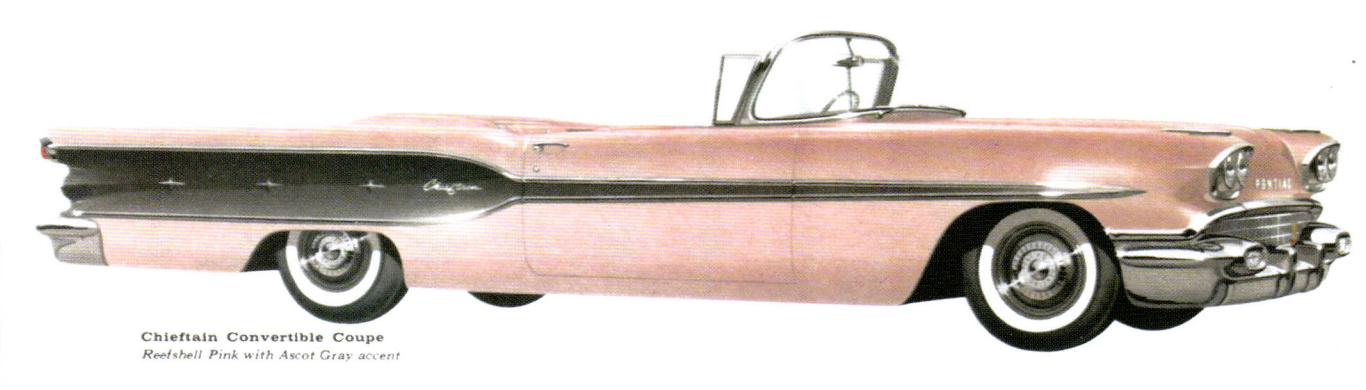

Lustrous new deep-dyed color in top-grain cowhide is achieved by a new process that creates the softest, most elegant leathers you've ever seen in a motor car.

Even from a distance, custom colors in paint immediately set a Star Chief apart from ordinary cars—and you have 92 color schemes to pick from

1958 PONTIAC BROCHURE

Chieftain Convertible Coupe
Reefshell Pink with Ascot Gray accent

Big news in Pontiac's lowest priced line:

CHIEFTAIN '58 CONVERTIBLE!

Here's '58's best news for convertible-loving, but budget-minded, car buyers—a convertible in Pontiac's *lowest priced* line! There's a whole new engineering age under a silhouette less than 4 feet, 8 inches high—and scarcely a yard stick tall at the belt line. The special rear deck lends a sleek custom-car touch ... exclusive Seville-finish Morrokide interiors are color keyed to 66 choices in paint scheme. And for the performance-minded, the fact that both Fuel Injection and famous Tri-Power Carburetion are offered among Pontiac's power plant options for 1958 makes all this news nothing short of sensational!

Touch the automatic control, and a smooth, glossy weatherproof top rises to add colorful beauty to your Chieftain Convertible. White or black top is available with all body colors; special pink, blue or green tones are offered in many color-coordinated choices.

The texture of softest leathers is captured in the new Seville-finish Morrokide shown at left in the special Gray and Pink interior reserved exclusively for the Chieftain Convertible. Offered also are the choices illustrated above: Gray and Silver, two-tone Blue, two-tone Green, all with Ivory accent, and Rangoon Red with Ivory.

▶ Oldsmobile touted their new 1959 styling as the "Linear Look." In this fashion-adjacent illustration from the product brochure, the all-new 1959 Ninety Eight Holiday Sport Sedan sure caught the eye of the window dressers.

▲ In the mid- to late 1950s, Oldsmobile sponsored popular singer Patti Page. Miss Page starred in three different shows for Oldsmobile between the years 1955 and 1959. They sponsored The Patti Page Show in 1955, a syndicated, twice-weekly, fifteen-minute program, followed by The Big Record in the 1957–58 season. Their relationship culminated in The Patti Page Oldsmobile Show, a musical variety program in the 1958–59 season that featured the top acts of the day. Miss Page had a colossal #1 hit record with "The Tennessee Waltz" in 1951 and was the bestselling female vocalist of the '50s.

▲ **Oldsmobility and Mrs. Brady**—One of the guests on both The Big Record and The Patti Page Oldsmobile Show was a young ingenue named Florence Henderson (well before her Brady Bunch days), who paid her bills as a spokesperson for Oldsmobile in commercials, in industrial musicals, and on TV specials for "the Rocket Olds" from 1957 through 1964.

130 | GLAMOUR ROAD

ninety-eight holiday *Sport Sedan*

Skylark   LeSabre   SPECIAL   Riviera

From the 1964 Buick Brochure:

THE FEMININE TOUCH

"We think Buick stylists create the world's most beautiful automobiles, but even they know their limitations when it comes to interior color and fabric selections. Call it '"woman's intuition"' or whatever you will, the ladies have a certain precise, unerring sense in this department that's nothing short of uncanny. That's why in the choice of our interior colors and fabrics we consult not only prominent woman decorators but women who have shown their good taste in the manner in which they decorate their own homes. As you can see on this and other pages our ladies tend to vote for both richness of fabric and bold color schemes. Buick is happy to accommodate them. We think that the interior choices of these discriminating women will make Buick more of a delight when you buy it and more of a joy to own as the years go by."

◀ Automobile companies did a brilliant job of positioning their car models to specific audiences. Through variations in color, trim, accessories—and, of course, extensive marketing—similar cars could have completely different personalities. Here, Buick shows us exactly what type of woman they think each model was designed for.

Ready to Wear

◀ 1952 ad for Motor-Mates to match your Ford. "Mistress and motor are perfect complements in glamorous Candalon fabrics."

Fashion Ford-ward

Ford tantalized its customers throughout the war with a forward-looking ad campaign called "There's a Ford in Your Future," in which a giant crystal ball foreshadowed peaceful poswar relaxation with the glimpse of a Ford car somewhere in the background. Once production resumed, the campaign became "Ford's Out Front" and was a very pedestrian presentation of the new Ford automobiles. It didn't really matter, since they were selling everything they could produce. The first ad directly aimed at women was in 1949, when a pair of green-gloved feminine hands grabbed a giant Ford steering wheel in an ad that demonstrated how easy it was for ladies to drive the Big New Ford.

Ford burst into the world of fashionable motoring in 1952 with the introduction of the Motor-Mates line of car coats, the perfect travel accessory for the smart new Ford Victoria hardtop coupe. The coats were produced of a woven fabric called Kalakina, which was made by the Collins and Aikman company of New York, suppliers of aircraft and automotive fabrics. The two-tone exterior colors of the coat matched the paint colors of the car, and the nylon lining matched the upholstery. Apparently,

134 | GLAMOUR ROAD

1953 and 1954 Ford ads use the fashion industry's focus on seasons to assure women that their new car is the latest fashion—and will surely be out of fashion in a few years.

"Dress Like a Ford" was at least a reasonably popular phenomenon, and they continued the promotion for the 1953 and 1954 seasons.

Ah, seasons. That wonderful fashion term that clearly delineated what was "in" and what was "out." So the Motor-Mates ads from 1953 and 1954 highlighted "The Style Setter of the '53 Season" and "The Best Dressed Beauty of the '54 Season," referring not only to this year's car coat but this year's Ford Victoria, all the while subtly reminding consumers that this year's gleaming new beauty will be hopelessly out of style in about three years.

His and Hers Fords

For those slightly less fashionable (but likely more numerous) than the matching coat-and-car set, Ford also created a series in 1955 and 1956 outlining a brand-new buying habit—Fords by the pair. The goal was to sell a household two new Fords instead of one higher-priced car. It's worth noting that the ads tended to pair a station wagon with a convertible—but the wife is posed behind the wheel of the latter, top down of course. "FORD—Why not own two?"

Ready to Wear | 135

▶ 1959 Thunderbird ads highlight the glamour that owning a Thunderbird promised.

Selling the She-Bird

There was no popularly priced car more glamorous in the fifties than the Thunderbird, hands down. From the first ads in late 1954, they showed the Thunderbird in smart suburban settings, with a high proportion of women in the ads themselves. The launch brochure went so far as to show women behind the wheel in two separate illustrations.

But of course, two-seaters had a limited market in the fifties. General Motors displayed fabulous four-seat dream cars at the annual Motorama car shows, but they never quite got around to building one. The folks at Ford saw the potential of a car with the glamour of Thunderbird and the practicality of a back seat and voilà—an instant classic was born.

So when the restyled four-seat version made its debut in 1958, it was only natural to promote it to upscale women. Ads touted the ease of entry and exit, the easier handling and parking compared to the full-sized car, and of course the glamour, headlining it as "America's Most Becoming Car."

One 1959 ad showed Ann Cole of Cole of California Swimwear praising the flair of Thunderbird and inviting women to see how they look in a Thunderbird. Another showed the versatility of Thunderbird by showing different outfits, for casual, business, and evening wear—and noting how flawlessly each would look inside a new Thunderbird. No car sold sizzle and style quite like the Thunderbird.

"America's most becoming car"
(and it's just right for you...in every way!)

Like a bit of flattery? Flattery is what you'll get in your new Ford Thunderbird. This jewel of a car has an unmistakable *éclat* that sets it—and you—quite apart. And, joy of joys, it's just right for you . . . in every way. It's your size! It seats four people in the most elegant comfort, yet it handles and parks with far greater ease than other luxury cars. Thunderbird is, in fact, the *only* luxury car a woman can really call her own. And it costs *far less* than other luxury cars. See the new Thunderbird at your Ford dealer's. And be sure to drive it, too.

FORD THUNDERBIRD

SO MUCH EASIER TO GET IN AND OUT
Because the Thunderbird's doors are extraordinarily wide—and the front seat folds all the way down. Getting in and out is as easy as going from one room to another!

SO MUCH EASIER TO HANDLE AND PARK
Naturally—the Thunderbird is so beautifully compact, you're completely at ease in it. You never felt so much in command, so *comfortable*, so much at home in any car before!

AND IT MAKES YOU LOOK— OH! SO GLAMOROUS!
All eyes are on you in your new Ford Thunderbird—"America's most becoming car"—the car *every* woman would love to own!

The car that's all the things you are...
THE NEW FORD THUNDERBIRD

It's you stepping out—
Your new Thunderbird might have been specially designed for gala evenings: it has a flair and distinctive elegance all its own. And its doors are so wide you can sweep in and out with bouffant gown unruffled—and your poise intact!

It's you in your play mood—
Smart, original, versatile... your new Thunderbird is in the mood for fun when you are. This car is always *fun* to drive because, bless its heart, *it's just your size!* It's roomy yet compact, a joy to handle ... and so easy to park!

It's you, the Leader—
You set the style, you set the pace wherever you go, driving the prestige car *every* woman would love to own. Yet the 1959 Thunderbird actually costs *far less* than other luxury cars. See your Ford dealer. *Drive this jewel of a car!*

America's most becoming car!

Anne Cole tells...
Why women love the new Thunderbird

The young and vivacious Vice-President of Cole of California commutes to her office (and crosses the country!) in her new Thunderbird

Anne Cole is one of the youngest, prettiest and most successful executives in the world of fashion. Her name and her swimsuits are known to fashion-conscious women all over the country. One of the rewards of success for Miss Cole is her new Thunderbird.

"It's a wonderful car," says Miss Cole. "When I'm in Los Angeles, I drive from my home to my office every day. It's only 20 miles—but you know L.A. traffic! Even so, I handle my T-bird as though I were the world's greatest driver, which I'm not. It's just that it's so easy to handle. It's so easy, in fact, that I drive from the Coast to New York twice a year. That's really traveling!

"What I mean is that other cars I've driven seem to have 'FOR MEN ONLY' signs on them. My Thunderbird says, 'ANNE COLE.' It's *my* car and I love it.

"My Thunderbird has flair!"

"It's a black convertible with a white top and it's beautiful. Personally, I think it's the smartest car on the road, with simple, classic understatement. If you don't like clutter, if you don't like busyness ... you'll like the Thunderbird. But, as you know, I *do* like flair in design and the Thunderbird has great flair!

"The Thunderbird is so luxurious, too. Contoured seats add such a nice touch. They're wide and deep and couldn't be more comfortable. You don't feel as though you're sitting on the floor when you sit in a Thunderbird! And I like having the service console separating the seats. Very smart. And *practical*.

"I like the wide doors. No matter what I'm wearing, I can get in and out with no effort at all. A blessing!

"But do you know what I like best of all? The way I *look* in my Thunderbird! It makes me look *glamorous*. I *feel* glamorous in it. It's that kind of car. And let's face it—a car is an accessory these days. And accessories must be smart."

See how *you* look in a Thunderbird

Next time you look at cars with your husband, let him see how you look in a Thunderbird. Let him see how he *feels* in a Thunderbird. Let him drive it around the corner—just once will do it—and he'll buy it for you. You'll have a Thunderbird all your own!

Your Ford dealer invites you to compare luxury cars for beauty, comfort and glamour. Do this and you'll agree with Anne Cole that the new Thunderbird is "the smartest car on the road." Yet the 1959 Thunderbird costs *far less* than other luxury cars!

FORD DIVISION, *Ford Motor Company,*

"My Thunderbird *fits* me," rejoices Miss Cole. "It's just my size. This makes so much difference in how you feel at the wheel. And how you handle yourself—and the car."

America's most becoming car!

Ready to Wear | 137

There are a list of reasons why the Edsel bombed in 1958, but its ill-fated positioning as a car for the young executive on the way up led to overtly masculine—and decidedly unglamorous—marketing materials.

Most manufacturers emphasized push-button convenience as a female-friendly feature, but Edsel chose a suited man's hands to demonstrate the push-button transmission on the steering wheel.

Edsel Was a Drag

Of all of the Ford Follies in the fifties, none are as noteworthy or so spectacular a fall from grace as the Edsel. The poor car was cursed from the start—ill-timed, disadvantageously priced, dubiously styled, oddly named, and scorned by its own sister divisions, who were envious of any chance of its success. Thankfully for them, there *wasn't* much of a chance of that.

Ford had taken its sister Mercury, in a similar price point with eighteen years of business on the books, and given it a complete makeover in 1957, a unique look inside and out with no panels shared with the Ford—and the "Big M" laid a Big Egg. The fully restyled '57 touting "Dream Car Design" sold fewer copies than the Ford-derived '56, and it was going to be the basis of the upper Edsel range. The car just wasn't going to sell in the Eisenhower recession.

The marketing campaign for the all-new car was decidedly pedestrian. They positioned Edsel as "the car for the young executive on the way up," which is such a great idea that Pontiac, Buick, Oldsmobile, De Soto, Nash, and Studebaker were already playing in that crowded arena. The campaign not only consciously didn't focus on women, it all but ignored their existence, with only two noted exceptions.

Finless and Fashionable

When Edsel Division planned for their press introduction in Dearborn in the summer of 1957, they made a point to invite the wives of the auto writers. This was highly unusual and was designed to increase attendance at the event (and possibly decrease the bar bill at the same time). But it meant that over 240 ladies had to be entertained during the day. For the first day, they were taken to the Ford Rotunda, where the center court had been transformed into an outdoor café complete with reflecting pond, white Citation convertible, and runway. Joie Harrison of *Harper's Bazaar* hosted a fashion show of her own selections from venerable Detroit department store J. L. Hudson. Miss Harrison wore a black Dior suit and white feathered cap (feathers were all the rage in 1957).

To quote *the Detroit News* from the day following, it was quite the affair:

"240 wives, daughters and fiancées of press men were serenaded by a choir of violins. Models in 1958 fashions from top New York designers pranced down an all-white runway that bridged a reflecting pool set in a flower garden... A white Citation convertible, finless and fashionable was a striking backdrop for models as they descended the runway stairs. It drew a second look from at least 75 wives, whose husbands would be driving green and white Edsels to dealers in their home towns today." [1]

During the reception, photographers took pictures of the wives to send to the society sections back home. It is noted that the photographer waited while cocktails were removed from the tables first. While subsequent Edsel promotions featured scale-model cars and even live ponies, there's no record of subsequent fashion shows.

Detroit Free Press, August 28, 1957

138 | GLAMOUR ROAD

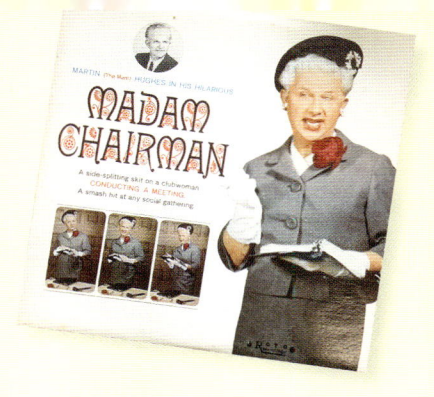

Ladies Who Lunch

The second incident worth noting also took place at the national press introduction in August 1957. The story takes place on the final morning of the introduction, when all the men were taken to the Ford headquarters for a press conference and the wives attended a luncheon at the Dearborn Inn.

They were treated to a lecture called "Style and Adventure," by Miss Gayle Hastings, who was billed as a fashion designer from London. Miss Hastings was said to be en route to Hollywood to design costumes for an upcoming yet-unnamed MGM musical. She was not. In fact, the woman speaking to the wives about her harrowing travel adventures was actually fifty-two-year-old Martin Hughes of Barrington, Illinois. Mr. Hughes, who later released a 1966 comedy album called Madam Chairman, was engaged by Edsel PR director C. Gayle Warnock and was recounted in his 1980 book *The Edsel Affair*. Warnock noted that after Miss Hastings completed narrating her adventures, she challenged the audience about the difference between perception and reality. She noted that none of the attendees could prove that the story she had just told was true, that her name was really Gayle Hastings, or that she was even really a woman. "As a matter of fact, I'm not," Mr. Hughes said as he pulled off his wig, to a stunned and ultimately loudly applauding house. If only any other facet of Edsel marketing has been quite so memorable.

Perhaps the inclusion of Miss Hastings was prophetic. Many people have claimed over the years that the Edsel was just a Ford in drag. Perhaps Mr. Warnock decided to celebrate that fact in a most memorable way.

Even in its last model year (which lasted only a few months), the 1960 Edsel offered a dazzling array of colors and fabrics, but the marketing almost totally ignored women.

Ready to Wear | 139

▲ The tone-deaf 1956 Dodge La Femme was offered only in "distinctly feminine" Regal Orchid and Misty Orchid two-tone. It was a trim package offered on the Custom Royal Lancer.

▼ Chrysler ad from 1955, featuring seven well-known fashion designers testifying in favor of the new Forward Look cars

THE *FORWARD* LOOK

"7 top fashion designers find Chrysler Corporation's 1955 cars a stimulating new concept of good design."

L. L. Colbert, President

Left to right: Tom Brigance • Anne Fogarty • Clare Potter • Lily Daché • Nettie Rosenstein • Pauline Trigère • Claire McCardell

At a special advance showing in New York, the celebrated fashion designers, above, saw a line of motor cars that was bright and alive and *wholly new*. And what they saw, you can see soon!

They saw Chrysler Corporation's new 1955 cars—Plymouth, Dodge, De Soto, Chrysler, Imperial—the cars with the all-new concept of style we call THE FORWARD LOOK.

These experts found THE FORWARD LOOK a design that matches the moods, needs and attitudes of today's motor car owners... and does it in a fresh and imaginative way.

They admired the all-new contemporary design, the *long, low lines* that America's motorists have been eager for. They were struck by the *look of motion* these cars give even when they are standing still.

The beauty and astonishing visibility offered by the New-Horizon windshields delighted them—for these are the only fully swept-back, fully wrapped-around windshields on any car.

They were attracted to the *rich fabrics* and the compelling new *colors*. They found wonderful convenience in the unique new position of the PowerFlite Range Selector.

THE FORWARD LOOK that intrigued these famous designers will no doubt intrigue you, too. We believe you will find in these cars just what you've wanted, just what you've asked for and hoped for in your next motor car. In a few days, you'll be able to see THE FORWARD LOOK. Don't miss it!

On Display November 17! The 1955 PLYMOUTH • DODGE • DE SOTO • CHRYSLER • IMPERIAL

CHRYSLER CORPORATION ▷ **THE *FORWARD* LOOK**

See Chrysler Corporation's great new full-hour TV Shows—"Shower of Stars" every 4th Thursday... "Climax!" the 3 intervening Thursdays. CBS-TV, 8:30-9:30 P.M., EST.

140 | GLAMOUR ROAD

◀ *Page from the 1956 Plymouth brochure, photographed by Irving Penn*

▼ *1956 Chrysler Corporation ad with designer testimonials*

Mopar Mod

Chrysler Corporation had a rocky path into the world of fashion. At the top of the Pentastar, as we have seen, the Imperial Fashion Shows—featuring designs from Tom Brigance, Anne Fogarty, Clair Potter, Nettie Rosenstein, Pauline Trigère, and Claire McCardell—were very successful and well attended. But not all points of the star shone equally bright.

Dodge Division had a more uneven time. It's clear that the 1955 Dodge La Femme, a Heather Rose and White two-door offering to "Her Majesty, The American Woman," did not receive universal acclaim. And while the car—which came complete with raincoat, umbrella, and pink leather purse among its accoutrements—somehow managed to remain in production through 1956, it did not in fact make much of a blip on the radar. In truth it has achieved much more notoriety today—for being a colossal failure—than when it was in the marketplace vying for attention.

On the other hand, Chrysler Corporation was one of the early winners in the transition to color photography. They began to utilize it to a large degree beginning in 1953 and ran a great series of corporate-wide ads featuring well-dressed women, and positioned Chrysler products as smart and stylish. Then they took it up a notch with dramatic ads photographed by Irving Penn.

Tail of the Pup

This look was very different from traditional automobile ads. The traditional pose is the left-front three-quarter view showing the driver. Penn took a radically different view, using a wide-angle lens and capturing a series of rear views from down low to accentuate the tailfins. He did this

Ready to Wear | 141

Designers have achieved the ultimate in new DE SOTO INTERIOR ELEGANCE

This year De Soto has fashioned and created anew, rich, durable fabrics, vinyls and leathers . . . striking weaves and sculptured patterns, into a rainbow of color schemes that blend delightfully and beautifully with exterior color combinations. 39 gay-colored trim combinations are available. Add to this . . . bright, colorful, textured headlinings . . . handsome, sponge-rubber-backed nylon carpeting . . . a new instrument panel . . . glistening modern hardware fashioned to enhance the overall styling theme . . . and you have a stylish, comfortable interior treatment carried out in *perfect* taste.

*World famous fashion authority, Anne Fogarty, says:
"This is definitely a stylish interior.
Fabrics are lovely . . . colors superb."*

successfully with both Dodge and Plymouth and created dramatic rear shots of the Plymouth tailfins that were used in advertising and product brochures. This well may mark the first time the rear view ever graced the cover of an automobile brochure. One photo of the series—a yellow-and-black Belvedere hardtop—was used in an ad with an aircraft designer, a speedboat designer, and fashion designer Anne Fogarty (of Imperial Collection fame) to emphasize the beauty and smartness of the design, even on the lowest priced of the company's offerings.

Beauty and the Budget

Indeed, the style and value for money became a theme for Plymouth advertising. One ad placed an ermine-wrapped woman in the front seat of a new Plymouth alongside a top hat, implying a glamorous night on the town was in the offing. Another placed a mink-clad woman in the back alongside a liveried chauffeur, arms full of packages. The headline said, "Mrs. Mitchell's last car cost more than $6,000," implying that Plymouth was in fact an appropriate alternative to a car twice its price. The theme was a repeating one, with other headlines in the series including "We're not the richest people in town—we're the proudest" and "It's a rich man's kind of car—but my kind of price."

This was a daring proposition. Plymouth was of course the entry-level model, and it was unusual for the bottom rung of the ladder to compare itself to the top—after all, Imperial was a profit maker, and it's a bit surprising that Plymouth got away with it.

Billing itself as the star of the Forward Look, Plymouth also sponsored the unconquerable Betty White on television in *Date with the Angels* and *The Betty White Show*, in which she did on-air testimonials to the brand. They were also involved in fashion copromotions, such as

▲ *The connection to fashion and interior design couldn't be more obvious in these pages from the 1955 De Soto brochure— "a stylish, comfortable interior treatment carried out in perfect taste."*

▶ *Opposite page: Two ads in a series (top, 1954; below, 1956) make the case for Chrysler cars to smart women of style.*

Far right: Even low-price Plymouth was smart enough to go from jeans to fur.

142 | GLAMOUR ROAD

THIS IS THE STYLE FOR YOU! These are the cars that streak long and low, yet handle lightly and softly as silk. These are the cars... the Plymouth, the Dodge, De Soto, Chrysler and Imperial... that put a woman in her place—just the height, exactly the vision and position which make her supremely comfortable behind the wheel. These are the cars that surround you with safety—lavish you with a hundred little luxuries—convince you, in a few delightful days, that you'll never drive anything else!

CHRYSLER CORPORATION
STARRING IN STYLE
PLYMOUTH • DODGE • DE SOTO • CHRYSLER • IMPERIAL

THE SMARTER YOU ARE ... the more you belong in one of these very special cars: Plymouth, Dodge, De Soto, Chrysler or Imperial. Not only because of their cool, assured good looks, their lovely colors and lavish interiors. But because of what they do for you, so willingly and wonderfully. Because they enfold you in a warm sense of security. Because they provide the smoothest ride going. Because they make every trip, long or short, restful and easy—for this glittering steel handles so beautifully it's like putty in your hands!

CHRYSLER CORPORATION
STARRING IN STYLE
PLYMOUTH • DODGE • DE SOTO • CHRYSLER • IMPERIAL

Unretouched photograph of Plymouth Belvedere 4-door Sedan. Jewels by Van Cleef & Arpels, furs by Maximilian.

WITH BLUE JEANS OR ERMINE...IT'S WONDERFUL!

Let's face it. A car leads many lives. Daytimes it takes children to school, wives shopping, husbands to work. But on that Big Night Out, you look for glamor, too. How abundantly it awaits you in the all-new 1955 Plymouth!

Amid the glowing, sumptuous appointments of this big car, any woman will feel like a jewel in a jewel box. Fabrics are rich, varied, colorful. All the spacious interior—biggest in the low-price group—is Color-Tuned to this long, massive car's outer beauty.

Yet Plymouth interiors are *sturdy*—made for the romping of children as well as admiration of friends. This year, of all years, *look at all 3*. Allied with Plymouth beauty, you will find such superior engineering and craftsmanship that you will take great satisfaction in making Plymouth *your* reasoned choice.

PowerFlite and all Power Driving Aids available at low extra cost
Enjoy "SHOWER OF STARS" and "CLIMAX!" on CBS-TV

ALL-NEW PLYMOUTH '55

See it...drive it...today at your Plymouth dealer's...a great new car for the YOUNG IN HEART

Ready to Wear | 143

Mrs. Mitchell's last car cost more than $6,000

Like many other people who can afford *any* car at *any* price, Mrs. Mitchell is one of the most enthusiastic owners of the 1960-new Plymouth.

Yet Plymouth is right in the low-price 3! Why does it appeal so strongly to those used to more expensive cars?

Well, until the new Plymouth dazzled the market you *had* to pay thousands more ... perhaps go to a costly custom job ... to get even a few of the advances that Plymouth offers. You couldn't get them *all* at *any* price! Take just a few—

The utter luxury of the astounding new "floating" Torsion-Aire Ride that floats you over *every* road ... the astounding safety and sureness of sports-car handling ... the tremendous, comforting power for safety of the new Fury V-800, super-powered to 290 hp ... the rangy, roomy grace of Flight-Sweep Styling—the new shape of motion.

And that's only skimming the surface. Your Plymouth dealer has the rest of the story at his finger tips. See him. *Drive this Plymouth. You really have to try it to believe it!*

When you drive a **Plymouth** *suddenly it's 1960*

◄ *"Style leader of the year . . . regardless of price."* The lowest-priced brand under the Chrysler umbrella, Plymouth appealed to stylish young people on a budget, as represented by these fashion models in Glamour magazine.

the one with *Glamour* magazine in April 1957 showing a new Belvedere convertible and fashions from Hope Reed, Tailored Junior, Sue Reed, and Billy Dee of California. This time—in accordance with Plymouth's status as one of the low-priced three—the fashions depicted were priced between $10.98 and $19.98.

Chrysler's other television sponsorship featured a different kind of glamour. Dodge began sponsoring *Lawrence Welk and His Champagne Music* in 1955. The show, originally billed as the *Dodge Dancing Party*, originated from the Aragon Ballroom on the Santa Monica pier and was broadcast coast to coast. Over the balance of the decade, Dodge alternated sponsorship with Plymouth. While it may have seemed folksy to the coastal elites, for much of middle America, it was as close to glamour as they were ever going to get, and they thought Welk was wunnerful, wunnerful. Petticoated champagne lady Alice Lon drove a Dodge La Femme, and Welk himself not only appeared in innumerable Dodge commercials but was loyal to Dodge for putting him on the air and drove Dodges until the end of his life.

▲ Betty White with her 1958 Plymouth Fury, a special model in Buckskin Beige with gold anodized aluminum trim. Plymouth sponsored Betty White on television in *Date with the Angels* and *The Betty White Show*.

Ready to Wear | 145

Room for the whole darn tribe!

▲ Above: *The 1958 DeSoto Fireflite Shopper wagon had more style than its medium price range would indicate.*

Top: *Ford's 1958 range of Ford, Mercury, and Edsel wagons offered gobs of style (and Di-Noc simulated wood paneling) across the board.*

Wagons Ho!

Perhaps no automobile underwent as thorough a transformation in the postwar era as the station wagon. Its transformation from the darling of the show horse crowd to the workhorse of the suburban family is pretty remarkable.

Wagons of the thirties and forties were very different—they were wood bodied, and the bodies themselves were made by specialty manufacturers. As a result, they were expensive and had the same basic maintenance needs as a fine wooden sailing yacht. So while they were a common sight on large country estates and among the carriage trade, they didn't sell in volume.

That changed after the war. The introduction of the steel-bodied wagon in the late forties was a watershed moment. The Willys Jeep was introduced as a steel-bodied wagon in 1946, and the rest soon followed. The all-steel Plymouth Suburban made its debut in 1949 with nary a scrap of wood on board. Chevrolet and Pontiac introduced all steel wagons that year, but they hedged their bets—the wagons featured simulated wood appliques. Ford's all-steel Ranch Wagon first appeared in 1952.

Now that the high cost and extra care requirements were conquered, wagon sales soared, and they soon became a staple of the newly minted suburban set. And then something funny happened—the show pony turned workhorse became a show pony again.

With the increased presence of wagons in the marketplace, it only made sense to expand the range of offerings at the upper end of the spectrum. Chevrolet showed a glamor-

146 | GLAMOUR ROAD

ous show wagon with Corvette styling called the Nomad at the Motorama in 1953—the production two-door hardtop Nomad wagon (and its sister companion, the Pontiac Safari) entered production in 1955. Ford responded with a two-door Parklane wagon in 1956 with so much bright trim it looked like it had been dipped in chrome.

Newly minted American Motors carved out a niche for themselves with Rambler Cross Country wagons—they were the favorite of the collegiate crowd before the advent of the Volkswagen and made little AMC into a profitable specialty automaker. In the late '50s, Rambler sold more wagons as a percentage of production than anyone else.

The upscale makes responded too—Chrysler's Town and Country name went from a wood-bodied convertible in the late forties to a top-of-the-line wagon in the fifties. Many upscale wagons offered pillarless hardtop styling for the ultimate fad within a fad moment—both Mercury and Chrysler offered pillarless wagons along with the Oldsmobile Fiesta and the Buick

▼ *The 1960 Mercury Colony Park, in four-door hardtop styling and chrome-detailed simulated wood siding, could move easily from hauling zinnias to making a suitably elegant entrance at the club.*

Caballero. The Mercury Colony Park debuted in 1957 and soon became the cream of the crop, establishing itself in a prominent position where it would remain into the early '90s.

The prestige was an important part of the charm. When Sky King and Penny weren't flying around in the Songbird, they tooled around in a Chrysler New Yorker wagon. So it was a big publicity win for Buick when they got them into a new 1959 Buick Estate Wagon. Bette Davis also chose a new Estate Wagon (a '64) for her lone appearance on *Perry Mason*.

▲ *Chrysler New Yorker Town and Country station wagons, like this 1963, were top-of-the-line luxury vehicles.*

▲ *The two-door 1955 Chevy Nomad and Pontiac Safari wagons were based on a 1953 Motorama show car.*

Got Wood?

It's perhaps a function of fashion that the very thing that made wagons expensive and needy—the wood trim—also made them prestigious. Of course the steel body was much more practical, but what to do about the lost glamour? This caused some luxury wagons to delay the transition as long as possible—the lavish Buick Roadmaster Estate Wagon remained wood bodied through 1953.

The obvious answer, of course, was simulated wood. 3M created a product called Di-Noc vinyl that allowed wagons to retain their luxurious wood appearance while still being durable enough to conquer an automatic car wash. Chevrolet and Pontiac had attempted to mirror the look of structural wood in their 1949 steel-bodied wagons, but that wasn't really successful—glamorous wood side paneling was the look that struck gold.

Ford was first to market with their wood-sided Country Squire in 1952. The nameplate had originally been attached to their two-door wood-and-steel wagon, but when it became a four-door, steel-bodied wagon in 1952, it took off in sales. The upscale companion Mercury Colony Park made its appearance in 1957 with four-door hardtop styling, tailfins, and simulated woodgrain. The Colony Park was Queen of the Hop and was marketed as the closest thing to a Lincoln station wagon.

It's been strongly rumored that Ford entered into a ten-year exclusive deal around 1957 with 3M for their Di-Noc vinyl. It seems likely because, aside from Rambler offering wood on their top-of-the-line Cross Country wagons in 1956 and 1957, no other domestic wagons other than Ford Motor Company products offered wood-grain siding until 1966. Was there something sneaky in the way Henry Ford II got wood? There's no smoking gun, but it certainly added allure to the Ford wagon lineup.

Ready to Wear | 147

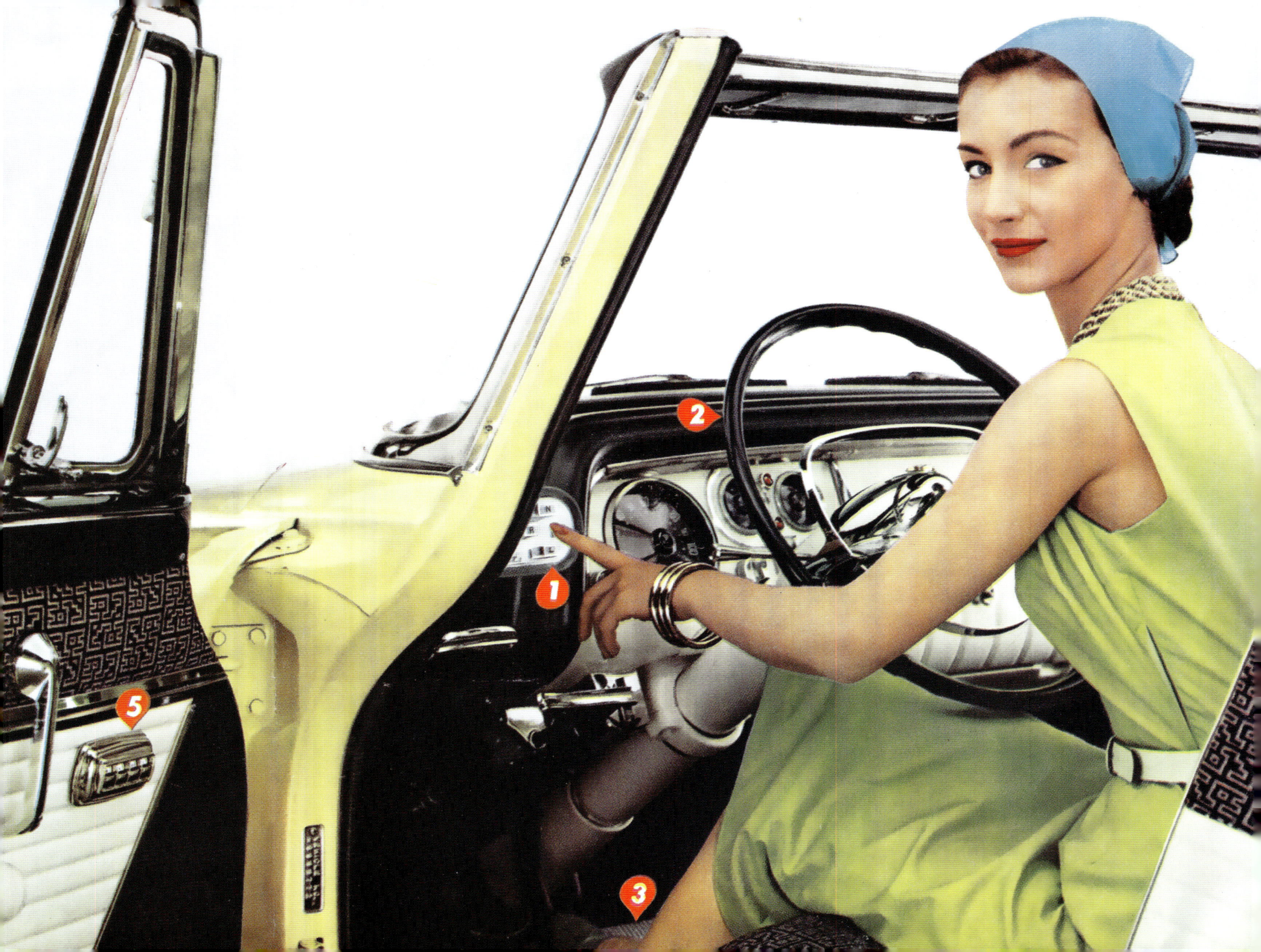
2
1
5
3

Chapter Seven

A WOMAN'S PLACE

THE INDUSTRY STRUGGLES TO ADAPT TO WOMEN'S NEEDS

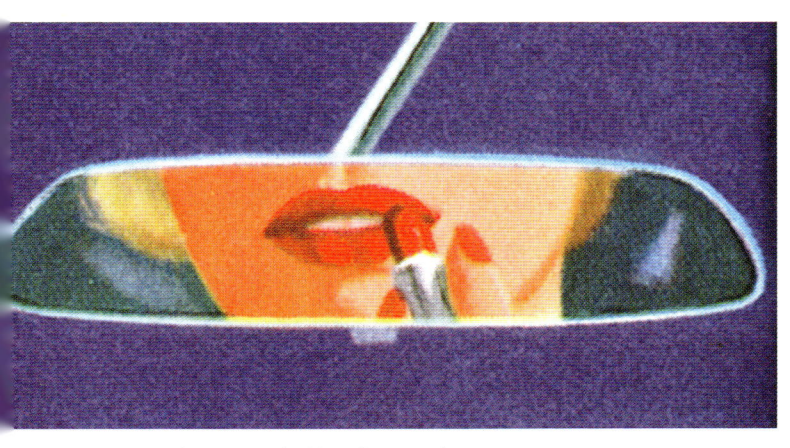

▲ *The 1960 Edsel brochure makes it clear that the rearview mirror is there to apply lipstick.*

◄ *The 1956 Plymouth brochure highlights the power conveniences that female customers would appreciate.*

The postwar automobile underwent a transformation as dramatic as anything Dior might have imagined. To paraphrase Phyllis Diller, *it had work done*. Several things were converging. Roads themselves were being improved, including new highways and turnpikes financed by the Interstate Highway System in 1956. These new roads would allow for higher sustained speeds than the prewar cars could handle. Also the competitive nature of the market would return by the late '40s, and with that came the natural pressure for product innovation. Further, the oil companies were tasked with developing better fuels to support the more powerful engines.

Beginning with the Oldsmobile Rocket V-8 of 1949, all of the manufacturers rushed to develop high-compression V-8 engines. They basically became the price of entry in the marketplace by the midfifties, much to the peril of some of the independents, who couldn't afford to develop them. GM's cash cow Chevrolet, whose reputation was made on the reliable and economical Stovebolt Six, entered the modern age with a V-8 in 1955. Market pressure had really left them no other option. Even economy leader Rambler introduced a V-8 in 1956.

Escaping the Clutches

If automakers were going to sell cars to women, especially more-powerful ones, they had to do two things—they had to make them easier to operate, and they had to *tell* them that they were easier to operate. Call it the "Power Princess Package" of the postwar car, but three inventions came together, and the result was what amounted to a revolution in automobile control systems.

They had already begun before the war. After a couple of false starts, the Hydra-Matic Division of General Motors introduced the first successful automatic transmission on the 1940 Oldsmobile, creating a major innovation in driving ease. The introductory brochure touted the advantages of "A Completely Automatic System of Control," advising that "There Are No Gears to Shift" and "There Is No Clutch to Press."

The Hydra-Matic Drive was a hit. It appeared as an option on Cadillac the following year and led the trend toward automatic transmissions across the industry. But it was an expensive path, and frankly, not all manufacturers could afford to follow it.

Chrysler Corporation came halfway with the introduction of Fluid Drive in 1940. It was a semiautomatic

A Woman's Place | 149

Labor-saving features like power steering allowed women to feel more comfortable behind the wheel—and allowed Detroit to make cars bigger and heavier, yet easily controlled.

transmission that shifted automatically from low to high but still required the operation of a clutch pedal—which was pretty much the whole thing they were hoping to do away with. After several iterations of the semiautomatic transmission, they introduced a two-speed fully automatic transmission called PowerFlite in 1954.

It would be after the war that the automatic transmission would reach across the automotive landscape, and there would be a range of solutions—from two speeds to four speeds and even planetary drive in the Buick Dynaflow—but all were designed with the goal of making driving easier and thereby making cars easier to sell. The widespread acceptance of the automatic transmission caused some unusual alliances within the industry, with General Motors selling Hydra-Matics to rivals such as Lincoln, Nash, Hudson, and Kaiser-Frazer.

Power Steering and Brakes

The more powerful engines were welcome, of course, and the automatic transmission meant freedom from the clutches of clutches—but cars were still heavy to steer and difficult to stop. And of course, larger engines require more power to turn them over, especially when warm. So there were still technological challenges to be overcome, chiefly among them power steering and power brakes. Power steering first appeared on Chrysler cars in 1951, reducing steering effort at low speeds by as much as 80%. Now not only could the daintiest driver drive, she could drive a big Imperial limousine. Cadillac offered the system optionally in 1952, but pretty much everyone ordered it, and it was made standard equipment on all Cadillac models in 1954. Power steering caught on rapidly and was popular not only with women—men liked it too. Automakers did as well, not only because it was a profit center but also because it allowed for ever-larger automobiles to be easily controlled.

Power brakes, with a vacuum assist, really weren't new—they were fitted to some of the larger luxury cars of the 1930s, including Pierce-Arrow and Packard, but again they spread like wildfire in the postwar industry. The first appearance of them after the war appears to be Chrysler in 1949, when "Vacu-Ease" power-assisted braking became an option on certain larger Chrysler models. Adoption was fast but uneven, with Packard offering them in 1952 and Buick in 1953, but luxury leader Cadillac not adopting them until 1954. The feature proved so popular that Cadillac even released a retrofit kit for 1950–53 models already on the road.

Power-Assisted Terror

With every new technology comes glitches, little quirks, or teething pains that may cause customer irritation; that is, if they don't kill them outright. One such innova-

1957 De Soto ad

150 | GLAMOUR ROAD

Cadillac demonstrated the effectiveness and ease of operation of its Auxiliary Power Braking system in this brochure photo from 1954.

tion could be power brakes. On the whole, power brakes were a great step forward in automobile control. They utilized engine vacuum to allow the car to be stopped effectively by the daintiest (insert image of ballet slipper here) driver—when they worked.

A great story from my teenage years comes to mind. One of our family friends was June Yankovich, who was at the time the wife of Polka King Frankie Yankovich. She told me the story of her brand-new 1953 Buick Skylark, a $5,000 top-of-the-line glamour convertible that her husband had bought for her, and how beautiful it was—until the day when she was driving it in the Pennsylvania mountains and it lost all brakes. The pedal went to the floor and she was terrified. Somehow she got the car down from the mountain alive and coasted into a small town at the baseline, where she said she scrubbed the wire wheels against a curb until it stopped, then went to a pay phone where she called her husband's road manager and told him of the ordeal. She told him where the car was parked, asked him to come get it, and added that she never wanted to see that car again.

In fact, she never did. The car was towed to a Buick dealer and traded on a standard Roadmaster convertible, which she noted never gave her a bit of trouble. I didn't have the heart to tell her both cars had the exact same braking system, nor did I mention that 20,000 1953 power-brake equipped Buicks had been recalled for that exact issue. A lowly O-ring in the system would fail, and the vacuum would draw all the brake fluid into the engine and burn it. Amazingly, in those pre-Nader days, the owners were not notified—only the dealers—and they kept it strictly hush-hush.

Of course the vast majority of power-braking systems did not try to send their owners sailing off the side of a mountain, and by mid-decade, all three options—power steering, power brakes, and automatic transmissions, the so-called Power Princess Package of the modern automobile—made cars viable for the millions of newly minted motorists.

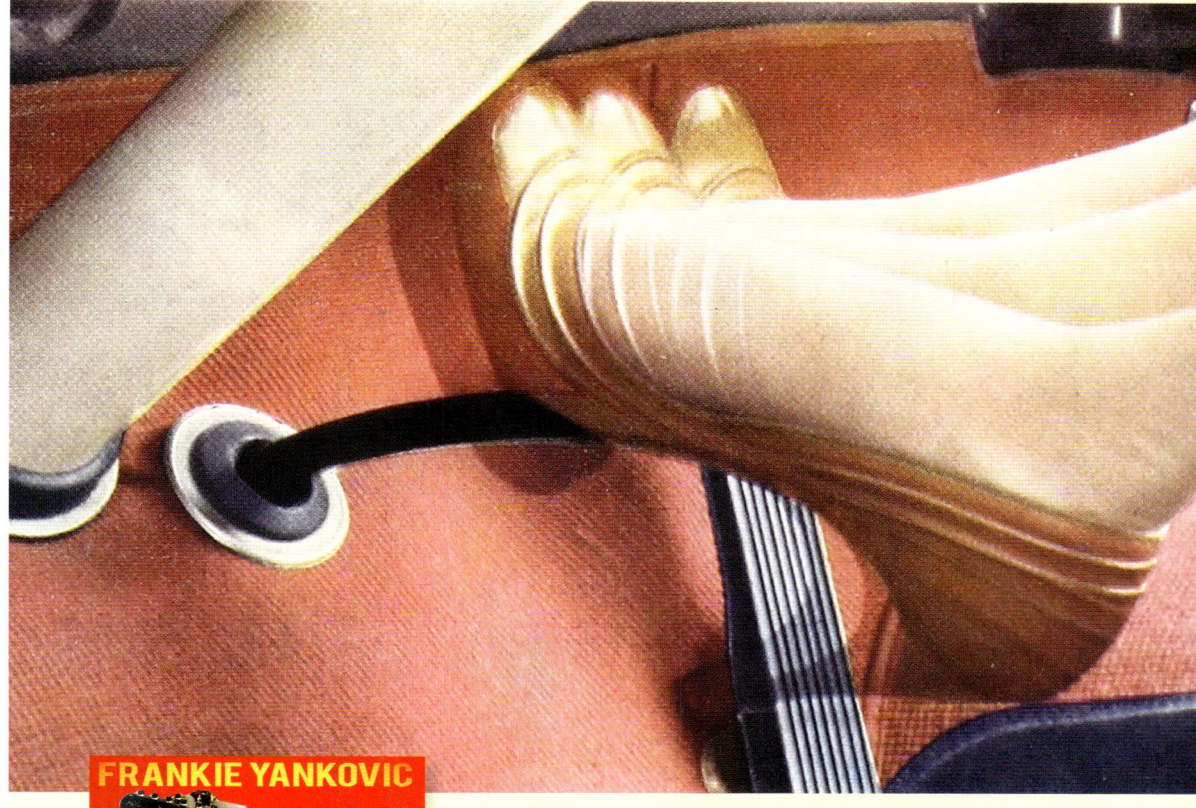

June Yankovich, wife of Polka King Frankie Yankovich, experienced the defect in the 1953 Buick Skylark braking system that led to total brake loss during a harrowing mountain trip in Pennsylvania.

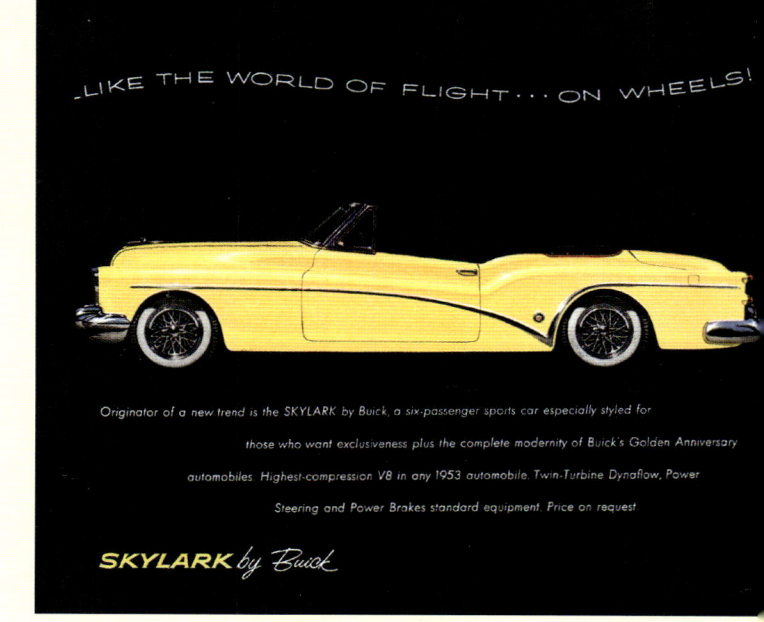

A Woman's Place | 151

◀ The adoption of twelve-volt electrical systems in the mid-'50s allowed cars to be equipped with numerous electrical conveniences—most often pitched to women as driving aids.

▶ This woman is using her time wisely during a traffic jam to reapply makeup—while the battery is charging itself—according to a 1961 Plymouth ad.

Push-Buttons and Swivel Seats

By the middle of the decade, the American automobile had gone through a transformation. The typical new car had a V-8 engine, an automatic transmission, and power steering and brakes. The next big advancement would be electrical—the twelve-volt electrical system. Twelve volts allowed for much-improved starting of those big engines, especially when they were warm, but it also provided voltage to run an array of power accessories that consumers were starting to crave. The result was push-button magic—a plethora of power accessories to pamper the most particular motorist.

Hydraulically operated windows and seats and even hydraulic-power convertible tops already existed on certain luxury cars, but in the wonderful new twelve-volt world, all of these accessories became electric, along with push-button radios (many with power antennas) and even push-button transmission selectors on several makes. Some even added push-button heater and air-conditioner controls to mirror the shifter controls—they looked very space age, but sometimes a confused driver might try to shift into defrost. Power seats became multidirectional with up and down adjustments, and even swing-out pivots on Mopar models.

Mercury created a sensation in 1957 with its Seat-O-Matic electric memory seat, by which a driver could select a fore/aft position of 1–7 and a height from A to E, which the car would recall upon the ignition key being turned. The only other car of the day with a similar system was the Cadillac Eldorado Brougham, the super-luxurious, most prestigious, and most expensive American car of the era, with a base price of $13,074. For that money, one expected a wide array of power accessories, and the Brougham did not disappoint. Some of the more unusual features included a digital clock, a power trunk that fully opened and closed at the turn of the key, self-leveling air suspension, and an automatic restart that automatically restarted the engine if it inadvertently stalled.

And of course, we can't forget air-conditioning, which had first appeared in 1940 but made a dramatic return on the 1953 Cadillac, supported by the new twelve-volt electrical system. Air-conditioning was another miracle of the era and made comfortable and relaxed highway travel into an everyday occurrence. Early systems were somewhat cumbersome, with air-handling systems in the trunk and clear plastic tubes carrying cold air up into the headliner for distribution, but advances came quickly, and by the late '50s, the modern in-dash system debuted, the same basic layout that is still used today. By this point, electrical systems had become quite sophisticated, with many power accessories drawing on them; one final advance at the dawn of the '60s was the alternator, which, unlike the old generator, constantly charged the system, even at idle. This meant no more red GEN lights distracting the driver at traffic lights or air-conditioner fans slowing down at idle.

152 | GLAMOUR ROAD

BLESS DE SOTO
for making seats that let you step out like a lady!

What a relief to step out, instead of having to crawl out of your car. No more hiked-up skirts. No more popping runs. The '59 De Soto's new Sports Swivel Seats let anyone —tall or short—slip in or out in one easy motion.

Being a woman, you'll appreciate De Soto interiors, too. They're as smartly styled as your own living room. And everyone will like De Soto's magnificent ride... roominess... and power. See the fashion leader of the year at your De Soto dealer's today. Try the new Sports Swivel Seats yourself!

The smart way to go places... DE SOTO

◀ *Chrysler offered swivel seats in 1959 to allow women to "step out like a lady!"*

◀◀ *Far left, photo of 1953 Lincoln four-way power seat as seen in the brochure*

▼ *An early forerunner to today's memory seats, Mercury's Seat-O-Matic was offered for 1957–59. "Set Seat-O-Matic dial for your favorite seat position, and then forget it—but the seat won't. When the ignition key is turned off, the seat slides back for easiest entry and exit. Turn the key on again, and the seat automatically returns to your pre-set position."*

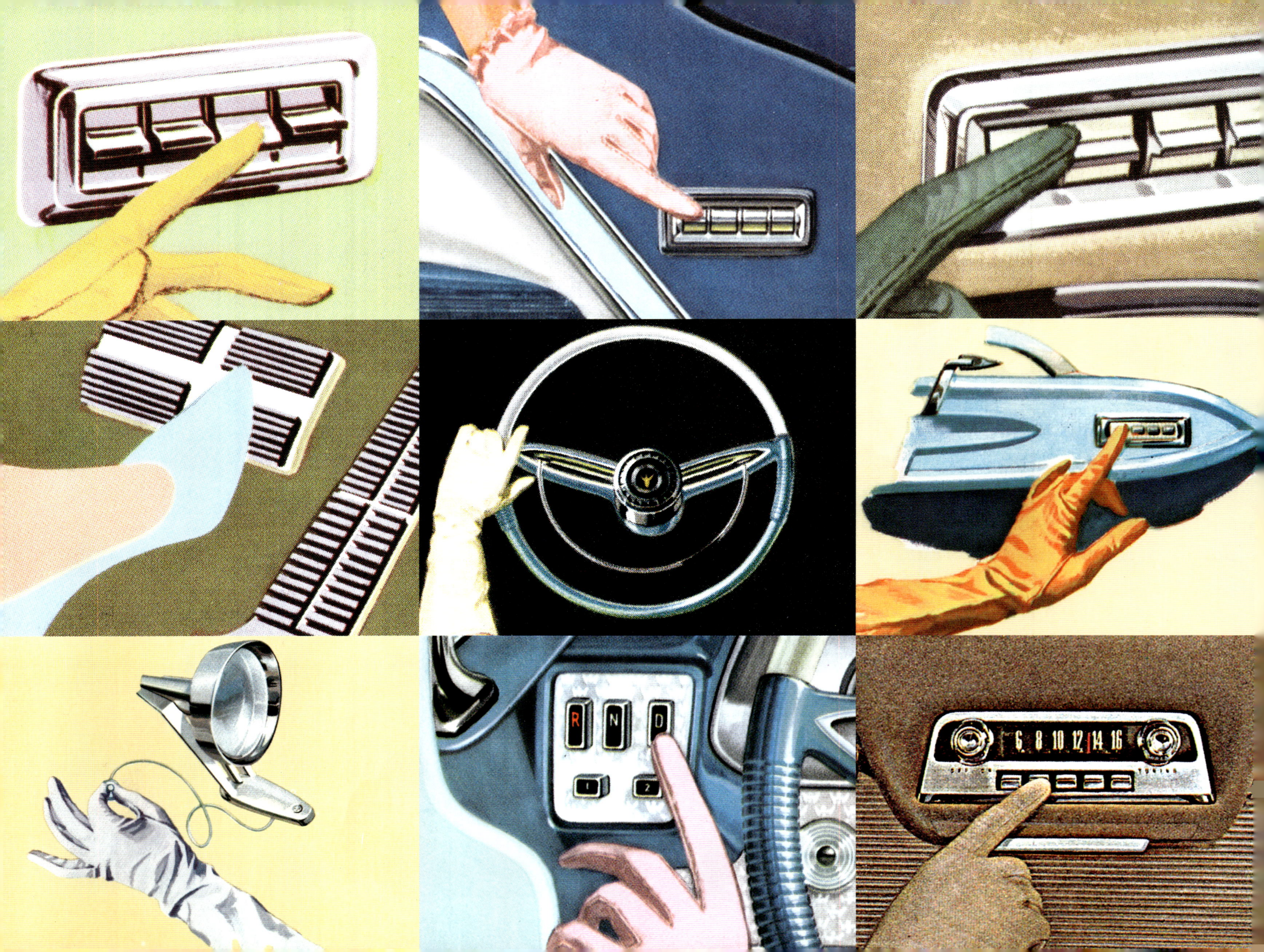
R N D
1 2
6 8 10 12 14 16

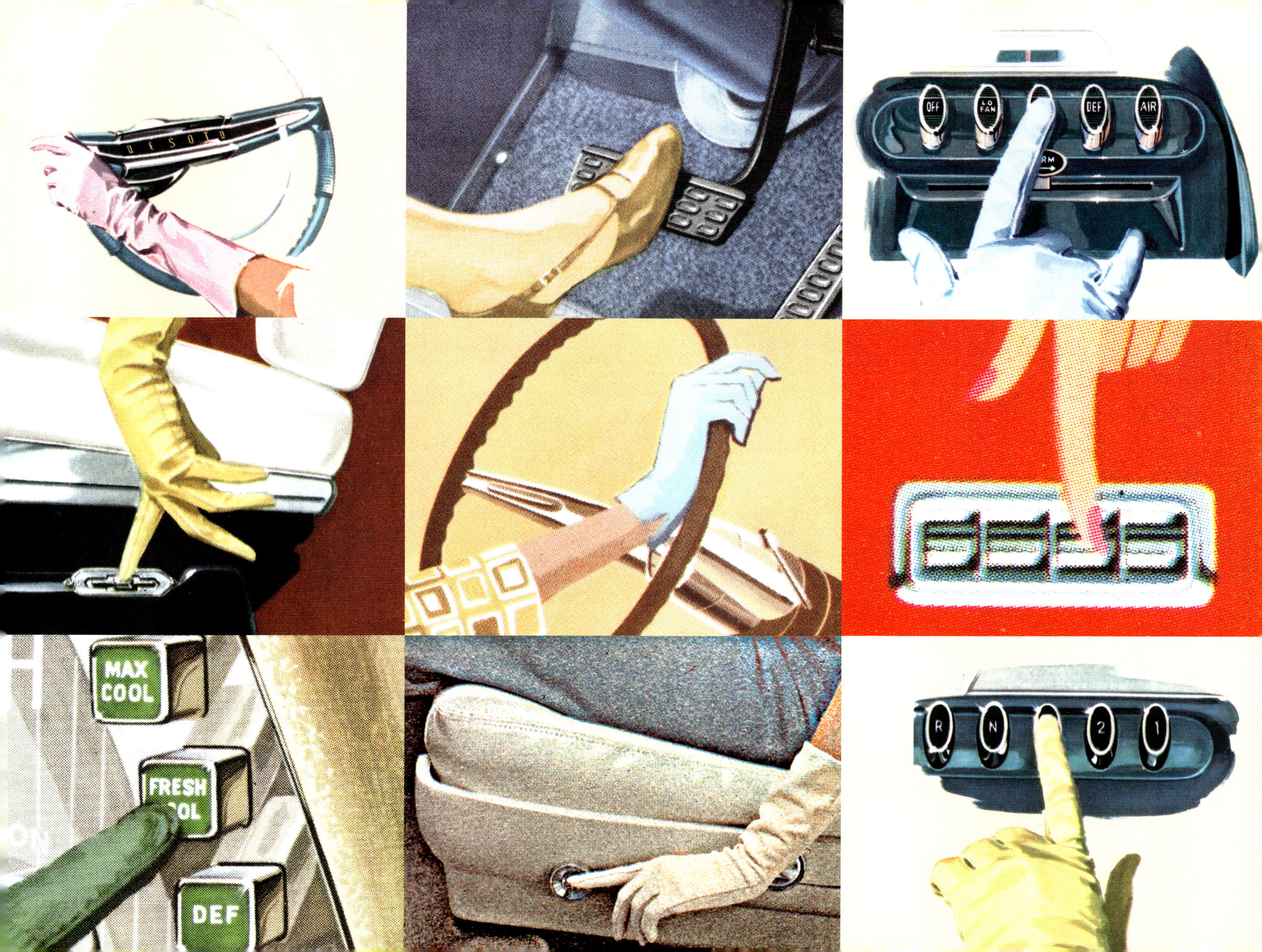

DESOTO
OFF
LO FAN
DEF
AIR
MAX COOL
FRESH
DEF
R
N
2
1

Let's take a look at
FORD'S NEW LIFEGUARD DESIGN

In the '56 Ford you find the first major contribution to added driver and passenger safety in automobile accidents. It is Lifeguard Design—the result of over two years of intensive research. Let's take a look.

Ford's new Lifeguard wheel is part of the story. Drivers are more apt to be injured by the steering post in accidents than by anything else. So, the steering post has been recessed more than three inches. The 3-spoke wheel, with its deep-center construction, is designed to act as a *cushion* under impact.

New Lifeguard seat belts, an optional Lifeguard feature, are designed to keep driver and riders securely in their seats for added safety. Belts are staunchly anchored to the steel floor . . . and are stronger than CAA requirements for airline seat belts.

New Lifeguard padding for control panel and sun visors, also optional, give extra protection against injury should passengers be thrown forward in a collision. Ford's special padding material is five times as shock absorbent as foam rubber!

New Lifeguard door locks help reduce the possibility of riders being thrown from the car in an accident. Conventional door latches, strong as they are, hold in one direction only, like fingers at left, below. Doors may pop open under impact.

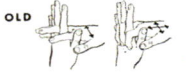

Ford's new Lifeguard door latches have a "double grip" like fingers at right . . . give added protection against doors springing open.

Visit your Ford Dealer soon and see how you and yours are given extra safeguards in the '56 Ford.

Selling Safety

Many of the innovations, especially power steering and brakes and automatic transmissions, were sold as advancements in safety and security to make the vehicle easier to control and more sure-footed in difficult driving situations. But selling collision safety itself was a subject gently trod upon. Ford Motor Company engaged in a notable marketing campaign in 1956 selling Lifeguard Design, which made vehicles safer in an actual collision. The Lifeguard features included a dished steering wheel, stronger door latches to keep doors from flying open, and optional seat belts and padded dashboards. While the format utilized was a soft-sell approach, it no doubt caused many sleepless nights for Ford executives worried about bringing up the subject of automobile crashes. It was something simply not done at the time, and Lifeguard Design was a trailblazing campaign in those pre-Nader days.

Words That Women Understand

As the car reached a point where women could expect to be able to drive it, it fell upon the manufacturers to learn how to talk to women when they came in as prospects to buy it—and that task was accomplished in a very uneven manner.

Pity the poor automobile salesman in the fifties. When demonstrating to a man, he could babble about horsepower and torque curves, and the prospect would just nod. The truth is that there is no automotive-knowledge gene attached to the Y chromosome, so men didn't instinctively understand the mechanical operation of the automobile—but the salesman assumed they did.

Making a presentation to a woman was different, and possibly even intimidating, so manufacturers reached out to help. A well-meaning 1955 Chrysler Corporation salesperson's brochure announced that "Women are people like everyone else."

The piece attempted to teach the salesperson how to talk to this new species of customer, by using words that women use and understand. It hit upon five words—Fashion, Glamour, Line, Decorator, and Practical—and instructed the salesperson in how to use each buzz word. It's worth noting that each of the women depicted is young, attractive, stylishly dressed, and bejeweled.

The salesperson was advised to show how each word was relevant to their presentation of the 1955 Chrysler line. As awkward as these instructions may seem, it's a positive spin that Chrysler instructed them to treat the women as prospects and not just as wives of prospects.

As misguided as it may seem, they do deserve credit for that.

"Women are people like everyone else—

but they sometimes talk a language all their own.

There's nothing really hard to understand about woman talk.

It's just that they respond more readily to certain feminine appeals and words.

The salesman who uses these special appeals and words will sell more cars in '55."

"Here are some words women use and understand"

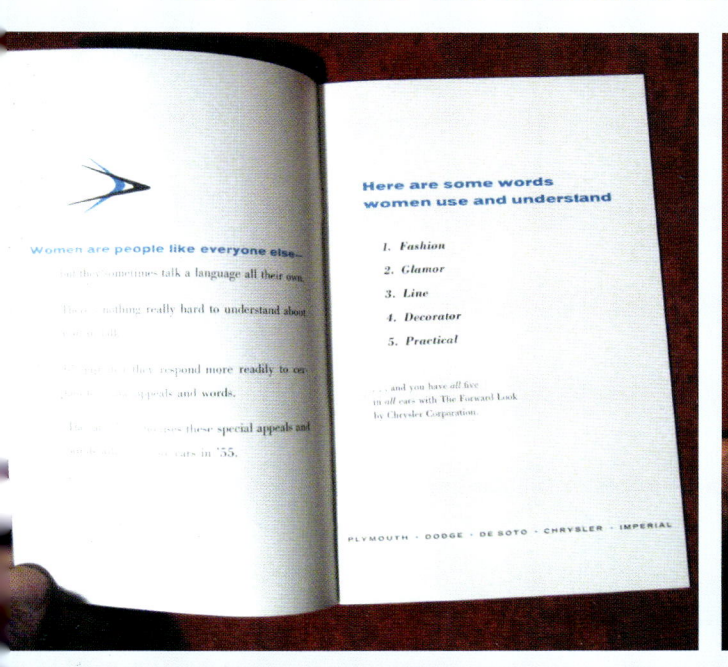

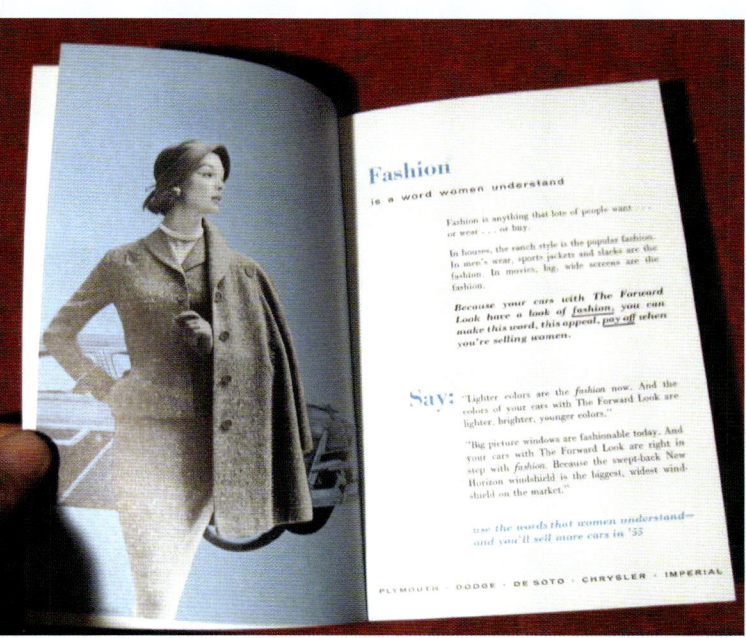

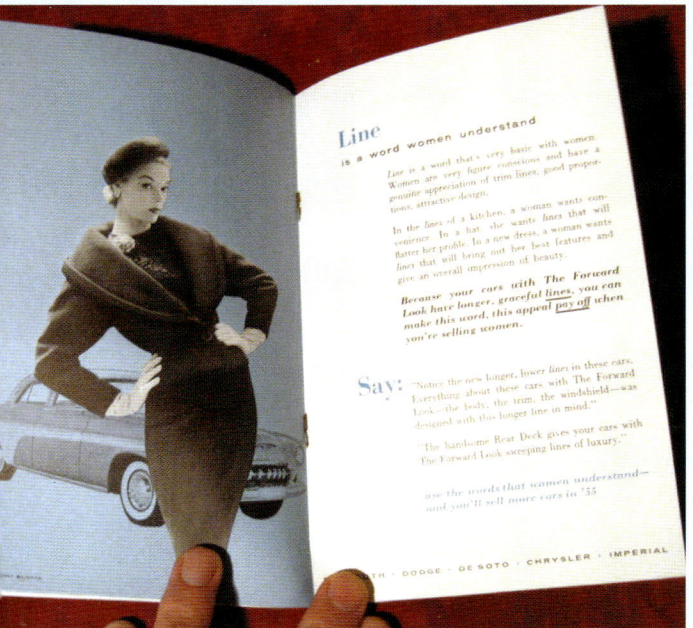

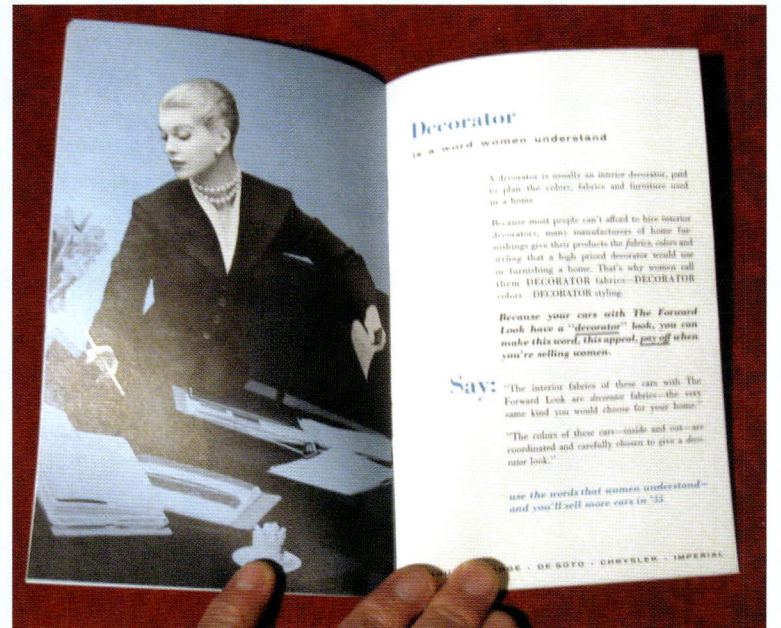

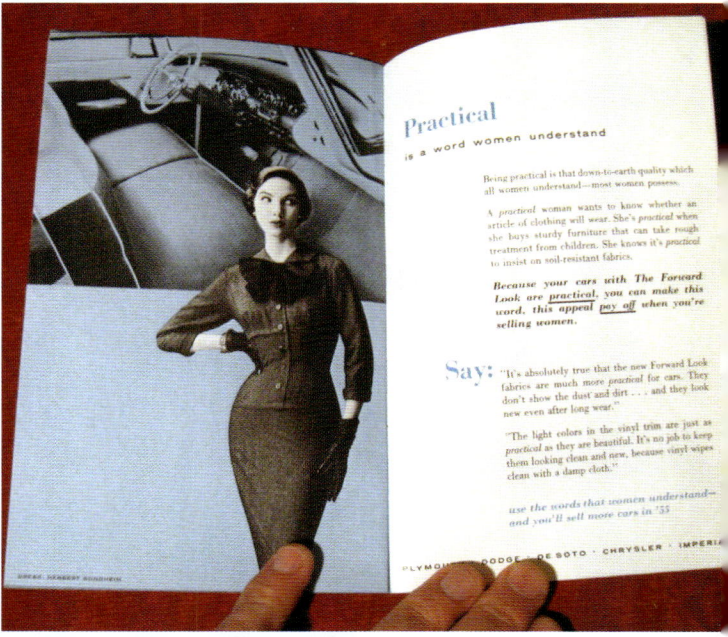

A Woman's Place | 157

Packard's unique "Women's Choice Panel" of 400 housewives, career women, "college girls," and fashion experts was responsible for over 100 improvements in the 1955 Packard due to women's suggestions.

Unsurprisingly, the panel chose "ease of driving" and "dependability" as most important, followed by styling, colors, interiors, and size. Packard produced a special brochure tailored specifically to women, under a grounbreaking headline in which they stated "We Must Give the Women What They Want in a Car, *Not What We Think They Ought to Have.*"

The piece highlighted Packard's power steering and Easamatic power brakes, the four-way power seat, the power windows, and the electronic push-button Ultramatic transmission. They went on to show the decorator interiors of the new Packard and even featured interior designer Mary Ellen Green, who designed the seats of the new 400 and Caribbean models, in a sidebar. All in all, it was a good and sincere effort from Packard. The brochure was mailed out with a pink cover letter signed by the vice president of forward planning and addressed to "Woman Drivers Everywhere."

The sole serious demerit was in the cover headline, "Ask the woman behind the man who owns one," which was a disappointing and dismissive take on their traditional "Ask the man who owns one." They had done a better job with a 1950 ad headline featuring women with their new Ultramatic Packards, in which the world "man" was struck through so the ad read, "Ask the ~~man~~ woman who owns one." Poor noble Packard. Their efforts were sincere, but by the midfifties, the venerable old luxury brand was on its way out.

Packard Asks Women What they Want . . . in Their Husband's Car

Packard did quite a bit better. It was not just that the independent automaker utilized women stylists, but that they convened a "Women's Choice Panel" in 1953 and sought input from 400 women—described as housewives, career women, college girls, and fashion experts—about what they wanted in an automobile. Specifically, they asked the women whether they were most interested in performance, beauty, or comfort; how much say they had in the selection of the family car; how much they drove; and what Packard features they felt needed improvement. They credited the panel with suggesting over 100 improvements in the 1955 Packard line.

158 | GLAMOUR ROAD

"We Must Give the Women What They Want in a Car, Not What We Think They Ought to Have"...

This was one of the first announcements made by James J. Nance when he came to Detroit in 1952 to take over the Presidency of Packard (later to become the Studebaker-Packard Corporation).

Nance believed that women's place is no longer just in the home but also in the automobile! He was also aware of the fact that, when it comes to choosing the family's second biggest purchase—a car—women had become the overwhelming influence, and appeals to eye and ear alone were not enough to "sell" them!

Nance acted immediately by ordering Packard's unique "Women's Choice Panel" set up, and the results of their findings you have been seeing on the *new 1955 Packards**, and will see even more excitingly defined on the *new 1956 models!*

It may be said that Packard is the first automotive concern to give a woman so much of everything *she* wants in a motorcar!

*Over 100 improvements due to women's suggestions—more women's interest items on one car than ever offered before in the industry!

400 Women from Coast-to-Coast...

To determine women's interest in automobiles, Packard set up its unique "Women's Choice Panel" in 1953. Some 400 housewives, career women, college girls and fashion experts set out to find: (1) whether women were most interested in performance, beauty or comfort; (2) how big a say they have in the selection of the family car; (3) how much they drive a car; and (4) in general, what Packard features they liked or thought in need of improvement.

Women chose "ease of driving" and "dependability" first, followed by styling, colors, interiors and size. Packard acted promptly, set up a program carefully designed to give women their ideal in a car.

Influence of the Panel can be seen in Packard's finger-touch controls and improved Power Assists, bigger, easier-to-open doors, lightweight trunk covers, centrally placed glove compartment, ashtrays convenient for driver and passengers, greater variety of untiringly beautiful colors, more luxurious fabrics than ever before used by the auto industry.

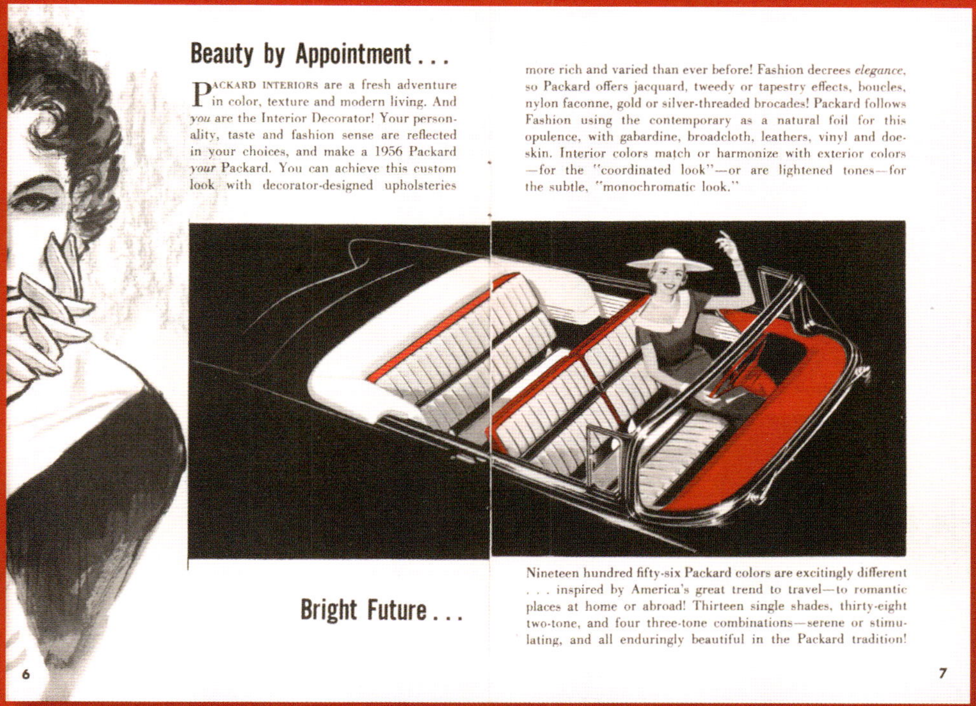

Beauty by Appointment...

PACKARD INTERIORS are a fresh adventure in color, texture and modern living. And *you* are the Interior Decorator! Your personality, taste and fashion sense are reflected in your choices, and make a 1956 Packard *your* Packard. You can achieve this custom look with decorator-designed upholsteries more rich and varied than ever before! Fashion decrees *elegance*, so Packard offers jacquard, tweedy or tapestry effects, boucles, nylon faconne, gold or silver-threaded brocades; Packard follows Fashion using the contemporary as a natural foil for this opulence, with gabardine, broadcloth, leathers, vinyl and doeskin. Interior colors match or harmonize with exterior colors —for the "coordinated look"—or are lightened tones—for the subtle, "monochromatic look."

Bright Future...

Nineteen hundred fifty-six Packard colors are excitingly different ... inspired by America's great trend to travel—to romantic places at home or abroad! Thirteen single shades, thirty-eight two-tone, and four three-tone combinations—serene or stimulating, and all enduringly beautiful in the Packard tradition!

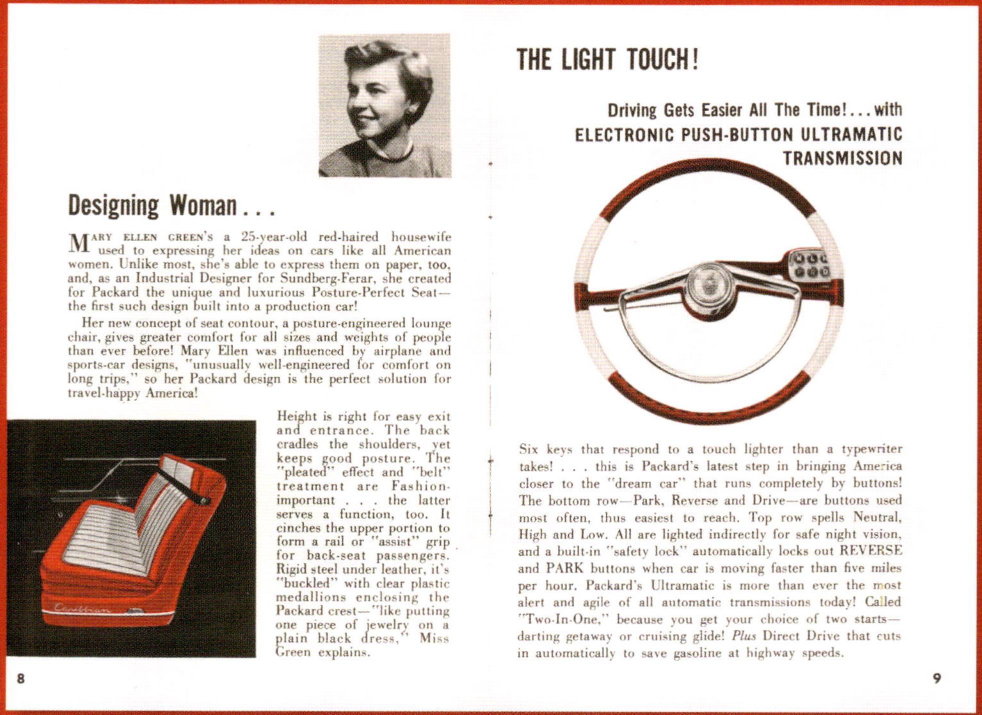

Designing Woman...

MARY ELLEN GREEN's a 25-year-old red-haired housewife used to expressing her ideas on cars like all American women. Unlike most, she's able to express them on paper, too, and, as an Industrial Designer for Sundberg-Ferar, she created for Packard the unique and luxurious Posture-Perfect Seat— the first such design built into a production car!

Her new concept of seat contour, a posture-engineered lounge chair, gives greater comfort for all sizes and weights of people than ever before! Mary Ellen was influenced by airplane and sports-car designs, "unusually well-engineered for comfort on long trips," so her Packard design is the perfect solution for travel-happy America!

Height is right for easy exit and entrance. The back cradles the shoulders, yet keeps good posture. The "pleated" effect and "belt" treatment are Fashion-important . . . the latter serves a function, too. It cinches the upper portion to form a rail or "assist" grip for back-seat passengers. Rigid steel under leather, it's "buckled" with clear plastic medallions enclosing the Packard crest—"like putting one piece of jewelry on a plain black dress," Miss Green explains.

THE LIGHT TOUCH!

Driving Gets Easier All The Time!...with ELECTRONIC PUSH-BUTTON ULTRAMATIC TRANSMISSION

Six keys that respond to a touch lighter than a typewriter takes! . . . this is Packard's latest step in bringing America closer to the "dream car" that runs completely by buttons! The bottom row—Park, Reverse and Drive—are buttons used most often, thus easiest to reach. Top row spells Neutral, High and Low. All are lighted indirectly for safe night vision, and a built-in "safety lock" automatically locks out REVERSE and PARK buttons when car is moving faster than five miles per hour. Packard's Ultramatic is more than ever the most alert and agile of all automatic transmissions today! Called "Two-In-One," because you get your choice of two starts— darting getaway or cruising glide! *Plus* Direct Drive that cuts in automatically to save gasoline at highway speeds.

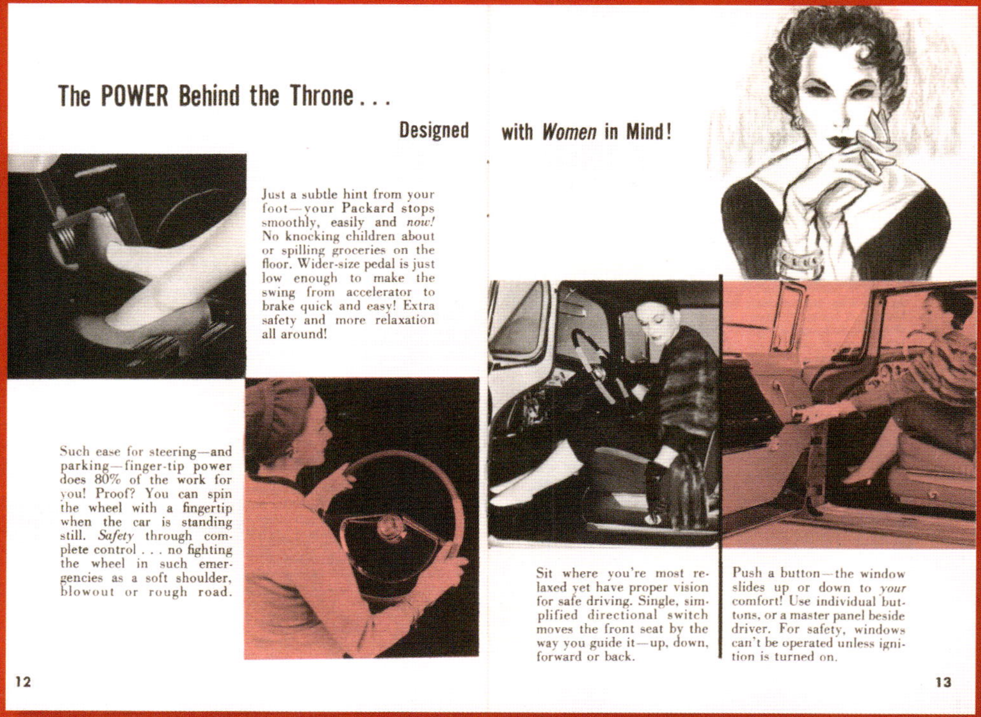

The POWER Behind the Throne...
Designed with *Women* in Mind!

Just a subtle hint from your foot—your Packard stops smoothly, easily and *now!* No knocking children about or spilling groceries on the floor. Wider-size pedal is just low enough to make the swing from accelerator to brake quick and easy! Extra safety and more relaxation all around!

Such ease for steering—and parking—finger-tip power does 80% of the work for you! Proof? You can spin the wheel with a fingertip when the car is standing still. *Safety* through complete control . . . no fighting the wheel in such emergencies as a soft shoulder, blowout or rough road.

Sit where you're most relaxed yet have proper vision for safe driving. Single, simplified directional switch moves the front seat by the way you guide it—up, down, forward or back.

Push a button—the window slides up or down to *your* comfort! Use individual buttons, or a master panel beside driver. For safety, windows can't be operated unless ignition is turned on.

A Woman's Place | 159

Going Steady with Studie

by Bernice Fitz-Gibbon

CURBSIDE BUMPER TIFFS

Studebaker Talks "Girl to Girl"

Chrysler swung and missed, and Packard gave a solid effort. And then there's Studebaker. If there were comedy awards for automotive marketing to women, the hands-down winner would be Studebaker and their 1964 "Going Steady with Studie" pamphlet for women motorists. The pamphlet would have been considered condescending if it had been written by a man. But it wasn't.

"Going Steady with Studie" was the creation of Bernice Fitz-Gibbon, a then-seventy-year-old female advertising executive who had been the publicity director at Gimbel's for many years before opening her own consulting business in 1954. She was renowned for her "Fitzkreigs," described as "a blitz of words springing from the rapier-sharp and highly imaginative brain of Miss Fitz-Gibbon." She was number sixty-two of one hundred people of the twentieth century by *Advertising Age* and was inducted into the American Advertising Hall of Fame in 1982.

It was a wildly creative piece, with a lot of feminist philosophy under all that sass. Instead of teaching a woman how to change a tire, it advised her to freshen her lipstick, flag down a man, and "Look helpless and feminine." Instead of teaching her to be a mechanic, it encouraged her to use the automobile for the pursuit of freedom, and "happiness is a thing called Studebaker."

"I've often said and I really believe that a car is among a woman's most important possessions. It gives her so much more than 'just transportation.' It lifts her whole level of living, widens her world. A woman without a car is like a bird in a gilded cage. She needs a car to give her 'wings.' She needs the most care-free, dependable, smart and economical of all cars—The Lark!"

Miss Fitz-Gibbon created three pamphlets for Studebaker, all in a witty, wildly exaggerated, and sassy style. She started out with "Alice in Lark Land" in 1962, followed by 1963's "Girl Meets Lark" and "Going Steady with Studie." Her short biography on the last page notes that "Bernice Fitz-Gibbon has never changed a tire but has changed the way America looks at women." It closes with two more of her Fitzkriegs:

"An automobile is good for what ails you. It un-jangles your nerves, vamooses your neuroses, gives you a more useful, exuberant, adventurous life."

"Without a car, a woman is a prisoner in her own home. All dressed up and no way to go."

MEN LOVE THE HARD-BOILED DETAILS

YOU'RE A GET-OUT-AND-LIVE GIRL

IF YOU'RE IN A STUDEBAKER... WAVE!

Because now you're a full-fledged Member of the Club. You're a girl with a G O A L. (Meaning you're a *Get-Out-And-Live* girl!)

With your car you're on your own, free as a bird. You've suddenly discovered that parking is a pleasure, traffic is a breeze, turning's no trick at all, and happiness is a thing called Studebaker!

If you have a Wagonaire, you and your passengers will dote on that fresh, airy "whee" feeling you get when you slide open the roof. Kids love that "wide open spaces" feeling, and you'll find it wonderfully handy for loading, hauling, and unloading all sorts of out-sized things—from boats to that lovely old wingback chair you got at the auction (with hubby doing the muscle work, of course!)

SLIP OUT LIKE A MOVIE QUEEN

HOW TO CHANGE A TIRE

It's no fun to change a tire and I hope you never have to. Every woman knows that if there was ever a time when plain unvarnished feminine charm and good old-fashioned "girl appeal" comes in handy, it's that unhappy moment when a tire problem develops on the road.

Here's my advice. Put on some fresh lipstick, fluff up your hairdo, stand in a safe spot *off* the road, wave and look helpless and feminine. If this doesn't do the trick I guess I've over-estimated men, especially truck drivers!

If passing males don't come to the rescue, try to get to the nearest phone and call a service station. If neither of these plans works out, as a last resort, turn to your *Owner's Guide*, which tells you exactly how to change a tire.

Don't get excited, simply follow the rules... just as if you were putting a new needle in your sewing machine. And as you tighten that last lug-nut and snap on the hub cap, you'll feel a wonderful rewarding surge of self-reliance that you *never* felt before!

LOOK HELPLESS AND FEMININE

BETWEEN US DOLLS

Do you tell everything? Of course not. Some of the little details of running the household smoothly, keeping yourself looking beautiful, are little mysteries only you know. Your Studebaker, like a woman, has a few of these girl-type secrets.

For instance, how to drive with windows open and still keep your fascinating new hair-do from getting windblown. The side window vents, plus the ventilators, will cool you without a rumple.

Storing away little necessities presents no problem. It has a wonderful wide glove compartment, and in models with bucket seats you have a console between the front seats with a secret compartment to hide your cologne, library books, Bikini, or whatever!

The glove compartment isn't just for gloves, as we all know, but Studebaker's glove compartment is special! The door opens flat to become a picnic tray with indentations to hold cups. Handy!

BOO... YOU PRETTY THING!

Another Studebaker secret is the "Beauty Vanity". Pull out the tray in the bottom of the glove compartment, lift the cover, and—surprise—a large mirror! This should end for all time the favorite male gripe, "Will you *please* remember to put the rear view mirror back in place?" The vanity tray itself has room to spare for all your beauty needs, plus ample space in the oversize glove compartment for sundry masculine requisities, such as maps, flashlight, pipe tobacco, and the like.

You can lock the doors of your Studie from the outside with a key, from the inside by pushing down the lock buttons. The rear doors have a special safety feature—once the button is pushed down you must pull it up to unlatch the door (prevents youngsters from inadvertently opening the doors!) I always feel it's wiser when a woman is driving alone at night to have all the lock buttons pushed down.

A Woman's Place | 161

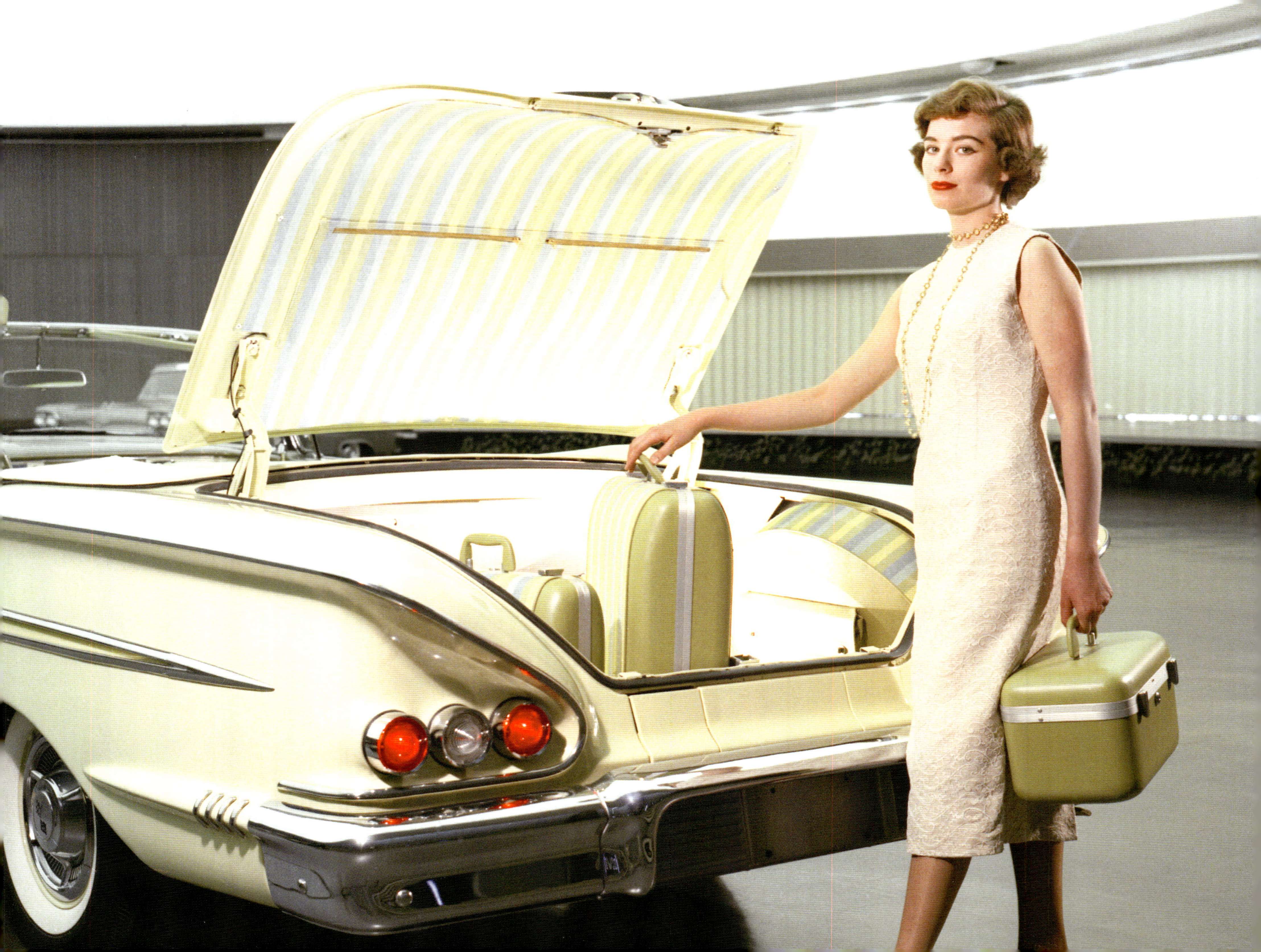

Chapter Eight

DESIGNING WOMEN

THE GLASS CEILING CRACKS AS WOMEN BECOME A VOICE IN THE INDUSTRY

▲ Female designers at GM in the 1950s worked primarily in interiors. (General Motors Archive)

◄ Featured in the 1958 Spring Fashion Festival of Women Designed Cars was Jeanette Linder's Chevrolet Impala "Martinique" convertible in pearlescent yellow and white, with a specially designed four-color fabric seat insert. The same fabric was used to line the trunk and cover a set of custom luggage. (General Motors Archive)

Opportunities for women designers in the auto industry before the war were few and far between. It's known that there were some women in styling at Ford in the '30s under the direction of Edsel Ford, but after his premature passing in 1943, support for the idea was said to wane. Betty Thatcher Oros joined Hudson in 1939 and created a very innovative instrument panel for the 1942 Hudson, but she committed the career-ending sin of marrying—and her new husband was a GM engineer no less—so she was shown the door in 1942.

When iconic industrial designer Raymond Loewy began consulting with Studebaker in 1936, he brought to the task noted illustrator and designer Helen Dryden. Dryden, who was reputedly the highest-paid woman artist in the county at her peak, had a long career creating covers for *Vogue* magazine and costume design before turning to industrial design in the 1920s. Loewy had her initially create interiors for the 1936 Studebaker line. They were apparently pleased with the task, since the advertisements proclaimed, "It's styled by Helen Dryden." Dryden remained with Loewy until 1940.

Audrey Moore Hodges joined Studebaker and Loewy in 1944. She made contributions both to the interior and exterior styling for Studebaker and worked not only on color and trim but also on projects as diverse as front ends, sizes and shapes for exterior lamps, and even a reclining seat. She even won a design contest for a torpedo-inspired hood ornament. Shortly thereafter she went on to Tucker and worked on interior design and fabrics, including a thoughtful recessed storage compartment in the driver's door—the "safety" instrument panel had no glove box. But as important as each of the designers was, they really represented only the slightest crack in the glass ceiling.

Harley Earl Swings and Misses

Harley Earl had a secret weapon, but he fumbled—he kept it too secret.

Harley probably wasn't specifically looking for a female designer in 1942, when he ran an ad in the *New York Times* looking for a "designer of fashioned materials"—he was only looking for a talented designer. And he got one. Her name was Helene Rother.

Her path to Detroit was circuitous. She was born in 1908 in Leipzig, Germany, known at the time as

Designing Women | 163

There is another fact which should not be overlooked. High-pressure advertising has made women very gadget-conscious. It is really surprising how much an American woman expects of an automotive engineer! . . . I will leave it up to the engineers to figure out what a car battery can stand in gadgets! But I am reminding you that it is the gadget that will sell the house or car of tomorrow!

—HELENE ROTHER, IN ADDRESS TO SOCIETY OF AUTOMOTIVE ENGINEERS, 1949

an artists' enclave and home to the Grassi Museum, which featured a Museum of Applied Art. She showed a talent early on for the applied arts and was sent to the Kunstgewerbe School in Hamburg, where she learned metalcraft, goldsmithing, and enamels. She married Erwin Ackernecht in 1932 and had a daughter, Ina, but the rapidly deteriorating political situation in Germany caused them to seek shelter elsewhere. Her husband fled to France around 1934 and she later followed, but they remained separate and ultimately divorced; later she reverted to her maiden name professionally.

Rother opened a design office called the Contempora Studio, where she designed brooches and accessories primarily for the fashion houses of Paris but also for a company called Monocraft in New York. The German invasion of France in 1940 caused her to flee once more, this time with the help of the American-based Emergency Rescue Committee, who got her and Ina to a refugee camp in Morocco and ultimately to New York. Once on US soil, Rother designed textiles and illustrated comic books for Marvel, until one day she saw the aforementioned ad in the *Times*.

The smaller car companies provided more opportunities for women to make an impact.

Earl was impressed with Rother's portfolio and sketches, and soon she moved once more, this time to Detroit. She was tasked with bringing a woman's touch to the interiors for the Buick, Chevrolet, Cadillac, Oldsmobile, and Pontiac divisions, focusing on interior colors and textiles, hardware, and lighting. She was extensively involved in the 1944 Train of Tomorrow concept and did considerable design work on the interior of the all-new 1948 Cadillac, including a daring new instrument panel.

But not all was pretty in the Motor City. As a woman, she complained that she was paid less than the men she was supervising. And as a talented and strong-willed woman, she was likely considered a threat to them, according to an account published by reporter Mary Norris at the *Detroit News*:

"GM officials insisted that designer Rother be kept strictly under cover. The experiment of bringing a woman into this strictly masculine industry was shockingly radical, they explained. The lady might not last out the year. To forestall possible embarrassment for everyone, better to keep the whole matter hush-hush."[1]

No More Hiding

Hush-hush was not a phrase that translated well to Rother. She soon realized that her opportunities lay elsewhere, and left GM in 1947. She opened her offices on the 16th floor of the Fisher Building, directly across the street from GM headquarters. Her first automotive client was Nash Kelvinator, and she had a long and successful relationship with them. Nash had no interest in hiding their involvement with Rother; rather, she became an industry celebrity instead—even to the point of becoming the first woman to address the Society of Automotive Engineers in November 1949, on the subject of "Are we doing a good job with our interiors?" In her address, she pushed not only for color—blaming the grays and tans on the bleak Detroit weather—but also for sophisticated designs and more convenience features, going so far as to suggest baby bottle warmers, as we see here in her own words:

"There is another fact which should not be overlooked. High-pressure advertising has made women very gadget-conscious. It is really surprising how much an American woman expects of an automotive engineer! I have a long list of such gadgets for use in cars, beginning with outlets for heating baby bottles and canned soup, cigarette lighters on springs, umbrella holders, safety belts, and so on. Since this is primarily an engineering problem and only secondly concerns styling, I will leave it up to the engineers to figure out what a car battery can stand in gadgets! But I am reminding you that it is the gadget that will sell the house or car of tomorrow!"[2]

Indeed, there is no doubt that Rother brought her touch to the postwar Nash designs. While the revolutionary Uniscope instrumentation pod of the all-new 1949 Nash Airflyte cannot be tied to her, the Twin Bed folding seats trace directly back to her 1944 Train of Tomorrow, and the dash materials—richly detailed, high-gloss plastics, and dash trim of both metal and vinyl with an identical mottled pattern—all but have her fingerprints on them.

Advocating for Color

Like Carleton Spencer at Kaiser-Frazer, Rother was an advocate of color. Her 1949 Nash interiors included shades of Tampico Brown, Neopolitan Blue, and Sherwood Green. But clearly Spencer's color palette of 1949 made her Sherwood Green with envy, because her redesigned 1951 Nash interior program advertised twenty choices of color and fabric, all of her own design. She used her talents to add upscale interiors to the compact Nash Rambler, a new compact that Nash positioned as an upscale small car and not an economy job.

Nash Kelvinator saw Rother's star power and used it to their advantage. When the 1952 Nash received the

A 1951 Nash interior designed by Helene Rother. "It's true. 20 different interior color and fabric choices! From striking new striped and bar-weave wool cords, to rich diamond-pattern and needlepoint fabrics, you can design your custom interior as you would your living room."

Designing Women | 165

◀ Packard recognized that working women were a viable market, and name-dropped to attract them. Note the suit by Pauline Trigère and decor by Robsjohn Gibbings, two big design names in 1948.

▶ Designer MaryEllen Green, a Pratt alumni who started at GM in 1950, contributed a wonderful Danish modern interior to the 1955 Packard Caribbean luxury convertible.

Jackson Award for Excellence in Design, Rother posed alongside exterior designer Pinin Farina in an advertisement, credited as "Madame Helene Rother, Parisian Interior Stylist." Her contract with Nash ran through 1956, ending only when the merger of Nash and Hudson led to the creation of a new company, American Motors.

She remained busy with her consulting career, which included clients such as Spartan Radio, Mangel Furniture, U. S. Rubber, Stromberg-Carlson, Magnavox, and Elgin. She later designed stained glass for churches and cathedrals but had no additional automobile companies after her contract with Nash ended. As significant as her contributions were, one wonders what she could have accomplished had Harley Earl tried harder to keep her at GM.

It was the early fifties before automakers started to think seriously about how to make their products more appealing to the rapidly expanding number of suburban women. The two-car household had arrived, and that meant a wave of new customers, but with different tastes and needs. By the midfifties, the big question was how to appeal to women, and each manufacturer took a different route to get there.

Fashion-Keyed by Dorothy Draper

Some of the smaller companies provided more opportunity for women to make an impact. Packard hired consultant Dorothy Draper to select fabrics and coordinate interiors for a few years in the early fifties. The 1952 Packard advertisements proudly proclaimed interiors "Fashion-Keyed by Dorothy Draper." Designer MaryEllen Green, a Pratt alumni who started at GM in 1950, was lured away to Packard by Dick Teague and contributed a wonderful Danish modern interior to the 1955 Four Hundred coupe and Caribbean luxury convertible.

166 | GLAMOUR ROAD

PRESENTING PACKARD FOR 1952

with motordom's newest, most exclusive beauty—

Fashion-Keyed
by Dorothy Draper

Here is the newest new automobile idea in over a decade!

Dorothy Draper, internationally famous decorator and color stylist, has touched the 1952 Packards with the magic of her color and fabric genius... *and the result is the most breath-takingly beautiful car of our time!*

From the stunning exterior combinations to the matching interior fabrics and trim, Mrs. Draper's artistic daring and instinctive good taste are in evidence everywhere.

Blendings, harmonies, color complements —one more magnificent than the next—are here... not only to win admiring glances from other motorists and pedestrians, but to suit *your* personality—*your* temperament—*your* taste!

And underneath it all is the brilliance of Packard engineering and precision workmanship: From new Packard Thunderbolt Engines, America's *highest-compression eights*... and Packard's exclusive, *smoother-than-ever* Ultramatic Drive... to revolutionary new Packard Easamatic Power Brakes!

The total effect is definitely something to see—something to drive—something to own!

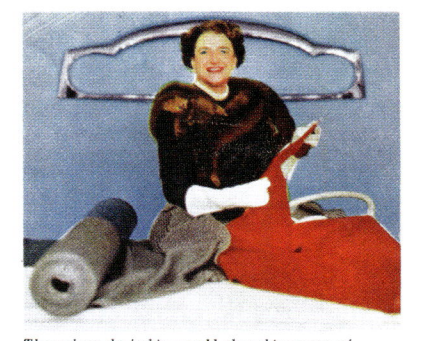

Throughout the fashion world, the achievements of Mrs. Dorothy Draper have long been legendary. Now, for the first time, she has brought her talents to the field of motoring... in the magnificent new 1952 Packard.

It's more than a car—it's a
PACKARD
Ask the man who owns one

Designing Women | 167

DODGE TAKES A WRONG TURN WITH LA FEMME

Auto shows were extremely popular in the 1950s, and many creative concepts were displayed to an enthusiastic public dreaming of the future. The Cadillac Debutante of 1950 featured an interior trimmed in leopard skin. Their Westchester of 1955 had a built-in television set. The Buick Centurion of 1956 featured the first backup camera. The fifty millionth GM car was a Chevrolet Bel Air called the Golden Jubilee, painted in a special gold color with all the brightwork gold-plated inside and out. And the 1951 Kaiser Explorer show car was upholstered in polar bear hides.

So at first glance, the Chrysler La Comtesse (The Countess) wasn't too far out. The show car, based on a New Yorker Newport hardtop coupe for the 1954 season, really barely raised an eyebrow. To quote its introductory press release:

"Chrysler's exotic new plastic top car, presents a gorgeous two-tone exterior of dusty rose with a pigeon gray top. The interior is luxuriously finished in cream and dusty rose leather with seat back inserts of platinum brocatelle fabric. Interior appointments are set off by specially-designed chrome hardware. A long, low note is provided by heavy chrome molding running along the lower body of the car from the front wheel openings to the rear bumper. A continental tire mount and chrome wire wheels add to the car's smart appearance."[3]

But the thing about show cars is that sometimes they really don't belong in the showroom. So when Dodge dealers got the announcement in early 1955 that they would be offering the limited-edition La Femme, it probably set more than a few of them scratching their heads.

Here's the original description from the dealer announcement letter:

"Exterior colour scheme of the car is Heather Rose over Sapphire White, and there is a gold La Femme name plate on each front fender, replacing the Royal Lancer name plate. The interior consists of specially designed Heather Rose Jacquard Fabrics and Heather Rose Cordagrain bolster and trim."

But wait—there's a full list of special accessories to boot:

"Two compartments located on the backs of the front seats are upholstered in Heather Rose Cordagrain. The compartment on the driver's side contains a stylish rain cape, fisherman's style rain hat and umbrella which carry out the Jacquard motif. The other compartment holds a stunning shoulder bag in soft rose leather. It is fitted with compact, lighter, lipstick and cigarette case."

The special midyear announcement brochure was captioned "By Appointment to Her Majesty, the American Woman." The La Femme option added $143.00 to the base price of a Custom Royal Lancer hardtop coupe. Dodge was sufficiently pleased with sales to continue the option into 1956, although the Heather Rose and White combination was replaced by Misty Orchid over Regal Orchid. Her Majesty the American Woman wasn't terribly impressed by either, and only about 2,500 were sold over the two-year period. And while today we may cringe, and rightfully so—at least they didn't upholster it in polar bear.

168 | GLAMOUR ROAD

La Femme By DODGE

...brings to you a brand new world of driving comfort and pleasure

Stunning new interior appointments of richly-woven soft Orchid Jacquard fabric combined beautifully with Gold Cordagrain trim.

Attractively styled rain cape and hat, plus a smart umbrella to match the lovely Orchid Jacquard fabric of the La Femme itself.

Neatly available storage compartments to hold rain apparel—cleverly and conveniently located on the back of front seats.

La Femme now on display at your Dodge Dealer

◀ *This simple sales sheet highlights some of the coordinated accessories included in the 1956 La Femme.*

▼ *1955 La Femme in Heather Rose over Sapphire White*

▶ *Storage compartments in the back of the front seats were designed to hold rain apparel.*

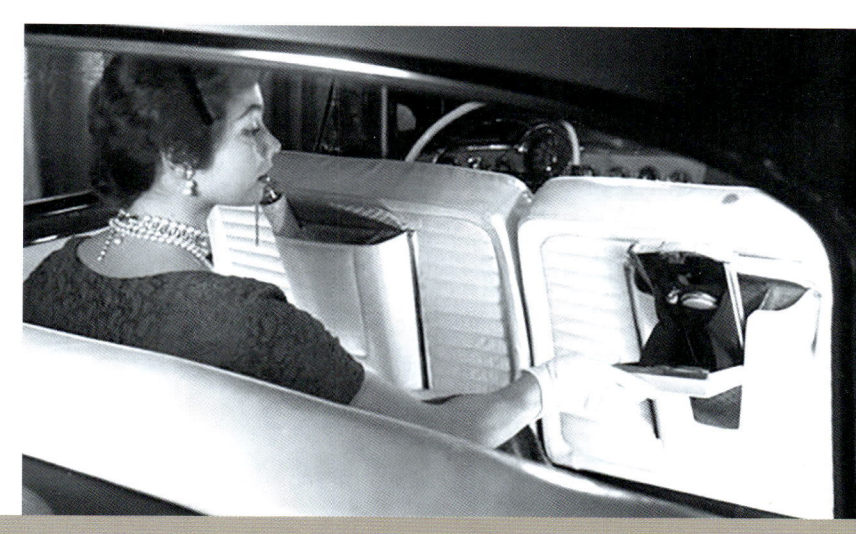

Designing Women | 169

▶ GM designers, clockwise from left, Sue Vanderbilt, Ruth Glennie, styling chief Harley Earl, Jeanette Linder, Peggy Sauer, Sandra Longyear, and Marjorie Ford Pohlman. (General Motors Archive)

▶ Peggy Sauer created the Oldsmobile Fiesta "Carousel" station wagon in a metallic blue with matching interior. "Carousel" was designed around children and featured a magnetic game board on the back of the front seat. (General Motors Archive)

Pauline Trigère Links to the Fashion Industry

Pauline Trigère was everywhere. The French-born couture designer appeared in a Kaiser-Frazer ad campaign in 1948 and supplied car coats to a 1952 Buick Roadmaster ad, evening gowns for the 1955 Oldsmobile and 1964 Fisher Body campaigns, and really many, many clothes for auto advertising images over decades. Her finest hour was dressing supermodel Wilhelmina in a dramatic black gown (with spaceship Emme hat) for the groundbreaking 1967 Buick brochure. She would cap her career by draping a special Mercury Cougar in her signature houndstooth for 1970, but we are getting ahead of the story.

Chrysler Corporation took perhaps a slightly cynical tack to attract women with the Heather Rose–over–Sapphire White 1955 Dodge La Femme, a two-door hardtop coupe with roses woven into the jacquard seat fabric and a matching raincoat, umbrella, and fully fitted-out purse. A pink-and-white advertising brochure was addressed to "Her Majesty, The American Woman." It was a trim package, really, a thorough one at that, but clearly created by men since automatic transmission and power steering still had to be purchased separately. One simply does not imagine Her Majesty double-clutching and grasping the wheel with immense biceps. It was an amusing footnote in automotive history, perhaps, but in reality, women's automotive needs were much broader than one model. And while a petticoated Alice Lon—the first Champagne Lady on Lawrence Welk's Dodge *Dancing Party* TV show—posed proudly with hers, and Dodge dealers ordered demonstrators for their wives, sales were quite limited indeed, although urban legend persists that they were popular with pimps.

The Damsels of Design at GM

Over at GM, Harley Earl had evolved his position. It's quite possible that he came to realize that Helene Rother was a missed opportunity, and that may have led directly to him hiring MaryEllen Green in 1950, but her rapid departure for financially precarious Packard led him to change his approach. He wanted to make his cars more appealing to women by involving them in the design process, but he apparently realized he needed a team of them to stay afloat in the male-dominated GM culture. So in 1955, Earl reached out to Alexander Kostellow at Pratt Institute in Brooklyn to find suitable candidates—there he recruited seven of the nine designers that would become his original "Damsels of Design." Three of the women worked on displays and Frigidaire assignments, and six would work in the automobile interior studios—two at Chevrolet and one each in the other four studios.

The job was really a blend of full-time design and occasional public relations. The women assigned to Frigidaire worked on the "Kitchen of Tomorrow" as well as displays and details for production studios. In the divisions, they were all assigned to interior studios and worked with color and trim and interior detailing. Earl was not hesitant to put the "Damsels" in front of the camera for photo ops and praised the contributions of the feminine eye that made the interior of the car friendlier to women, such as redesigned switches for easier use, the elimination of nylon-snagging

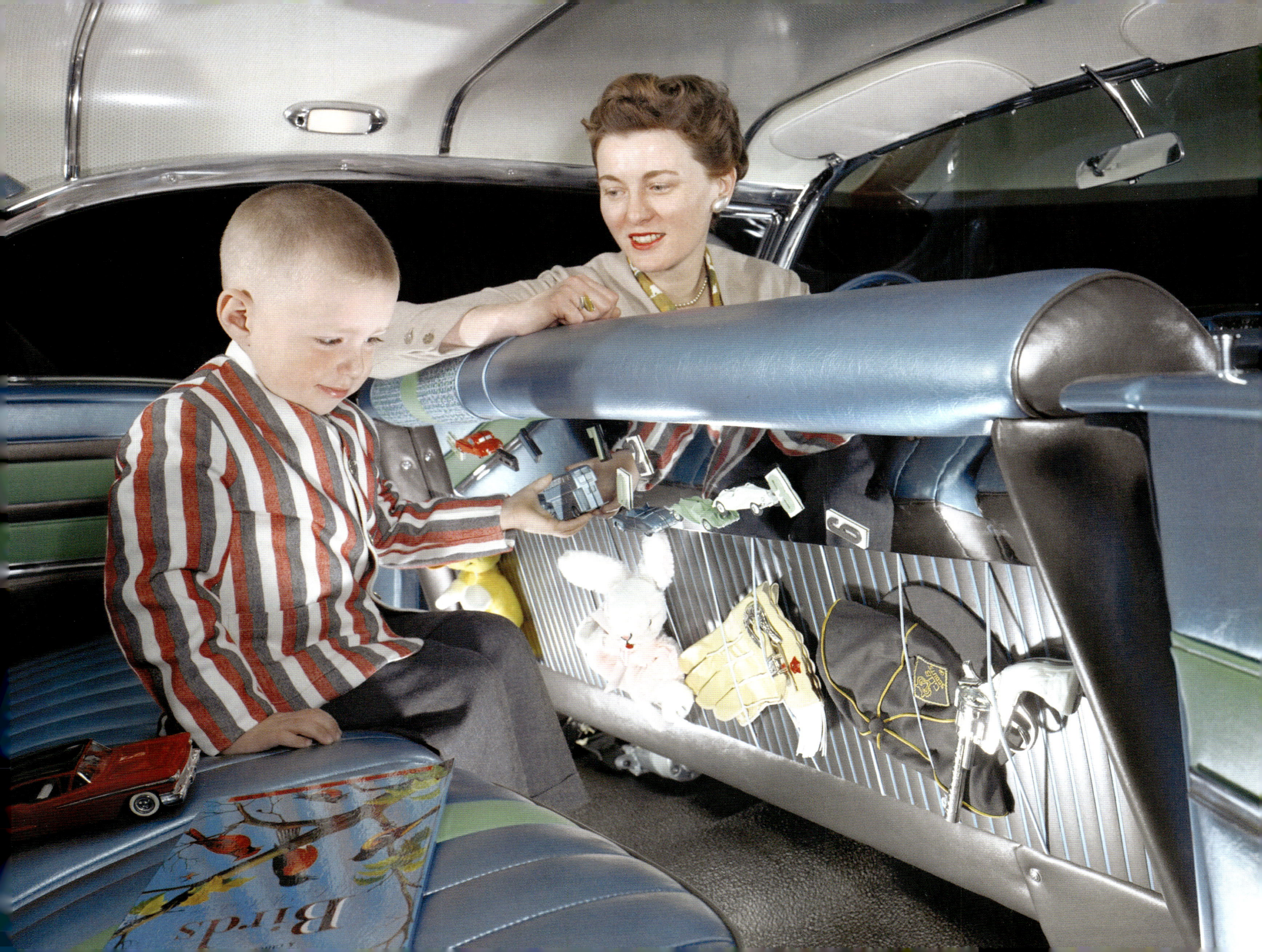
Birds

172 | GLAMOUR ROAD

◀ Marjorie Ford Pohlman created two cars for Buick. The "Shalimar," a top-of-the-line, Limited four-door hardtop painted deep royal purple with an interior of purple and black leather and a special purple cloth, had a swing-out dictaphone in the glove box. (General Motors Archive)

◀ "Shalimar" had a back-seat umbrella that was stored in the seat back, and a front-seat storage armrest. (General Motors Archive)

protrusions, and even their preference for convenience options such as the power seat.

There were also many PR appearances for the Damsels—speeches, television appearances, and endless photo ops. There was attrition as some of the women left for other jobs and others replaced them. Morale among the women was generally high, although they didn't really enjoy being called Damsels—they would have preferred simply to be known as designers and treated on parity with their male counterparts. But at the same time, they realized that they were trailblazers and this was a great opportunity for the advancement of women in the world of design.

1958 Spring Fashion Festival of Women Designed Cars

The Damsels of Design were reaching their pinnacle in the spring of 1958 when Harley came up with the 1958 Spring Fashion Festival of Women Designed Cars. It would be another PR opportunity for Earl but also an unannounced swan song for the Father of GM Styling.

The show was quite unlike any auto show that the nearly new General Motors Styling Dome had yet seen. Six giant red fabric streamers descended from the dome's peak. A trio of cylindrical birdcages 30 feet high were filled with one hundred hired canaries that chirped happily to specially designed lighting. Ten cars were displayed on carpeted circles, two per circle, grouped by make, and each circle was ringed by potted hyacinth plants intended to provide fragrance for the show. But the real surprise was the cars themselves—each of the ten glistening new GM show cars had been customized inside and out by women.

The women had total control over the paint, interior, and special features of the show cars. And while the idea could sound a bit patronizing looking back through modern eyes, there had never been a show of this type in the history of the industry, and the Damsels went all out on the task.

The cars were dazzling. From Chevrolet came Jeanette Linder's Impala "Martinique" convertible in pearlescent yellow and white, with a specially designed four-color fabric seat insert. The same fabric was used to line the trunk and cover a set of custom luggage. Inside, lighted makeup mirrors and a glovebox-mounted vanity were designed to catch a lady's eye.

Ruth Glennie painted her "Fancy Free" Corvette in a metallic silver olive and created a matching interior set off by four sets of seat covers—one for each season. They ranged from a yellow print for summer to black simulated fur for winter warmth. "Fancy Free" was also equipped with a purse storage bin and retractable seat belts, a GM first.

From the Buick studio, Marjorie Ford Pohlman created two cars. Her "Tampico" Special convertible was painted alabaster with a flame-orange interior. It featured bucket seats and a storage console for binoculars and a camera. She also designed the "Shalimar," a top-of-the-line, Limited four-door hardtop painted deep royal purple with an interior of purple and black leather and a special purple cloth. "Shalimar" had a back-seat robe that was stored in the seat back, a front-seat storage armrest, and even a swing-out dictaphone in the glove box.

Peggy Sauer created the Oldsmobile Fiesta "Carousel" station wagon in a metallic blue with matching interior. "Carousel" was designed around children and featured

Designing Women | 173

The women had total control over the show cars—paint, interior, and special features. And while the idea could sound a bit patronizing looking back through modern eyes, there had never been a show of this type in the history of the industry, and the Damsels went all out on the task.

▶ *Marjorie Ford Pohlman's Buick "Tampico" Special convertible was painted alabaster with a flame-orange interior. It featured bucket seats and a storage console for binoculars and a camera. (General Motors Archive)*

In Jeanette Linder's Chevrolet Impala "Martinique" convertible, lighted makeup mirrors and a glovebox-mounted vanity were designed to catch a lady's eye. (General Motors Archive)

a magnetic game board on the back of the front seat. Miss Sauer placed umbrella holders in the front doors and also relocated the rear door openers and window switches to the dashboard. Her "Rendezvous" Ninety-Eight convertible was finished in metallic rose with matching rose leather.

In the Pontiac Studio, Sandra Longyear designed a Star Chief hardtop called the "Bordeaux" in a deep maroon with asymmetrical leather-trimmed seats and a unique system of leather trunk straps to hold groceries. Her Bonneville "Polaris" convertible was finished in a color she called Starfire Blue, and featured two-tone blue leather bucket seats and a storage compartment for a thermos and picnic gear.

Sue Vanderbilt created two Cadillacs. Her "Saxony" convertible was finished in a gray-green metallic with a matching cloth-and-leather-trimmed interior that featured seat-back storage pockets. She also did an Eldorado Seville coupe called the "Baroness" in black with a black vinyl top and a custom black-and-white interior with carpeting and seat trim of black mouton. A storage armrest contained a pencil, notepad, and change dispenser, and the "Baroness" was even fitted with a telephone.

The other feminine contribution to the show was the display itself. The fabric drapes, cages of canaries, and hyacinth-ringed carpet circles were the work of Gere Kavanaugh, one of the Damsels who worked on displays and exhibits.

The cars were exhibited in the Styling Dome for a week, and GM executives from all over the country flew in to see them. After that, the cars were moved to the main exhibit hall of the General Motors Building in Detroit, where they were on public display for two weeks. The attendees were allowed to select their favorite, and top honors went to Jeanette Linder's Impala "Martinique." Ruth Glennie's "Fancy Free" Corvette finished third but somehow managed to withstand the test of time. As the only known survivor of the "Feminine" cars, it has recently been restored to its original condition, seasonal seat covers and all.

And Then They Were Gone

Shortly after the conclusion of the Feminine Auto Show, the Damsels of Design lost their benefactor. Harley Earl retired in 1958, and his successor, Bill Mitchell, did not share Earl's enthusiasm for women designers. Most of the Damsels moved on to other companies—Gere Kavanaugh went to Victor Gruen and then opened her own firm, Ruth Glennie went to Europe with Vauxhall and later joined Sylvania, and Marjorie Ford Pohlman taught advertising at Pratt Institute, the alma mater of most of the Damsels. They were all successful in their subsequent careers—it seems that having Harley Earl as a mentor didn't harm anyone.

And one stayed. Sue Vanderbilt became assistant studio chief at Cadillac and then went on to the Advanced Studio before leaving to earn her MFA at Cranbrook. When she returned, she found herself demoted—starting over as a senior designer at Chevy. Undaunted, she worked her way up to being the first female studio chief at GM, taking control of Chevrolet Interior Studio II in 1971. Sadly, illness forced her early retirement in 1977.

The immediate results of the Feminine Auto Show are minimal. The show cars themselves were sold off to well-connected customers. Buick paid tribute to the "Shalimar" by naming a shade of blue after it in 1959, and the pleated bucket seats of Sandra Longyear's "Polaris" convertible inspired the tritone buckets that appeared in the 1959 Bonneville. But the long lens is more vindicating.

Designing Women | 175

The 1958 Spring Fashion Festival of Women Designed Cars show was quite unlike any auto show that the nearly new General Motors Styling Dome had yet seen. Six giant red fabric streamers descended from the dome's peak. A trio of cylindrical birdcages 30 feet high were filled with a hundred hired canaries that chirped happily to specially designed lighting. Ten cars were displayed on carpeted circles, two per circle, grouped by make, and each circle was ringed by potted hyacinth plants intended to provide fragrance for the show. (B/W photos, General Motors Archive; color photos, Gere Kavanaugh)

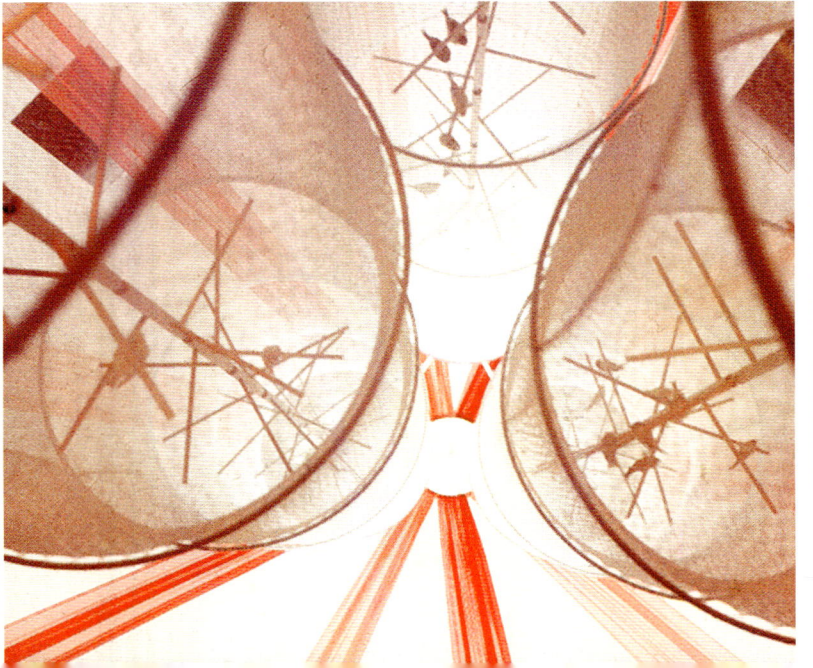

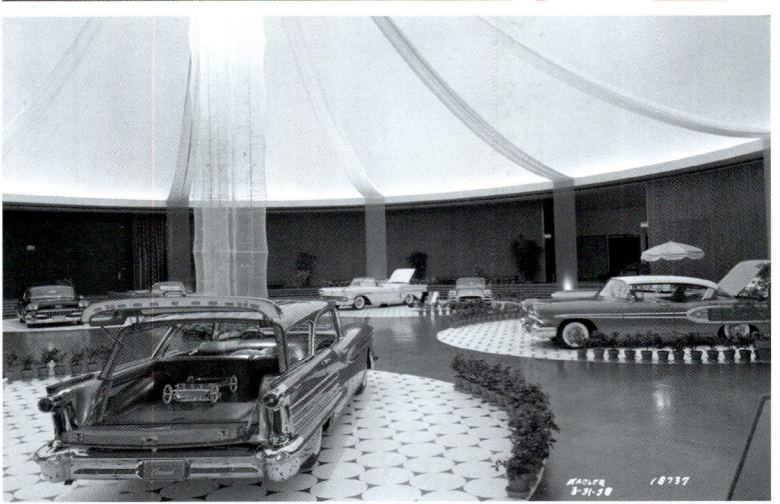

176 | GLAMOUR ROAD

▶ Sue Vanderbilt continued at GM. Here she is seen in a 1969 ad with a Pucci-inspired prototype interior she designed.

Many of the special features that the Damsels included—from retracting seat belts to childproof doors and locks, storage consoles, and makeup mirrors—found their way into modern automobile design. They didn't just choose new colors for the cars, they filled them with useful and desirable features.

"We enjoyed proving to our male counterparts that we are not in the business to add lace doilies to seat backs or rhinestones to the carpets.
—SUE VANDERBILT

Perhaps the whole adventure is best summarized in the words of Sue Vanderbilt, in an address to the Midwest College Placement Association back in the day:

"Not too long ago, management gave the women designers at GM Styling the opportunity to express our viewpoints on cars designed especially for the woman. Each girl was asked to design two cars for the Divisional Studio for which she worked. We were asked to choose new fabrics and exterior colors, and originate new trim design and hardware. These feminine cars caused much comment and were favorably received by corporate management and others. But I think the most significant thing about this program is that the designs were as appealing to the men who saw them as the women. It was a designer's paradise, and we particularly enjoyed proving to our male counterparts that we are not in the business to add lace doilies to seat backs or rhinestones to the carpets, but to make the automobile just as usable and attractive to both men and women as we possibly can."[4]

Who thinks women should help make dream cars practical?

Fisher Body does.

That's why they rely on stylists, like Sue Vanderbilt, to help design GM car interiors. Even when psychedelic fabrics are being experimented with, Sue's right there to make sure that the car seat it covers is contoured and installed at just the right height to accommodate women's smaller frames. She also keeps in mind things like ladylike exits when designing GM's wider-than-ever door panels.

It's this practical approach to pleasing women that can make GM dream cars come true. So much of the buy is in the body. And Body by Fisher makes GM cars a better buy.

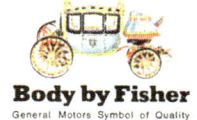

Chevrolet, Pontiac, Oldsmobile, Buick, Cadillac.

Body by Fisher
General Motors Symbol of Quality

Designing Women | 177

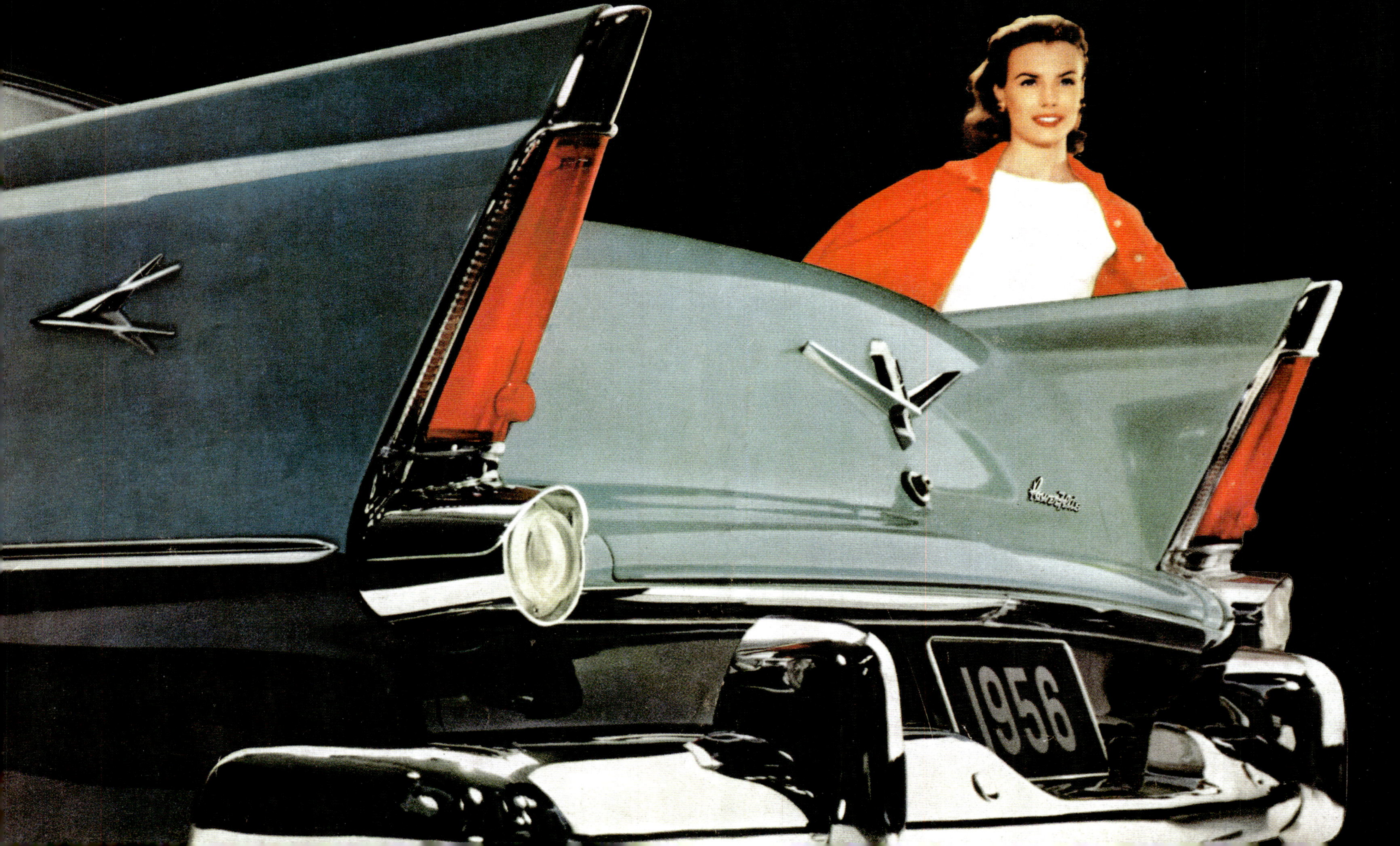
1956

Chapter Nine

STRIKE A POSE

NEW TECHNOLOGIES LEAD TO WIDESPREAD USE OF PHOTOGRAPHY

It should come as no surprise that, shortly after television began its sweep across postwar America, photography began to rival illustration for dominance in the field of advertising. Technological developments as well as changing consumer tastes caused a shift toward photography, with its crisp detail, realistic look, and vivid color palette, including a liberal use of red. It was Damsel of Design Gere Kavanaugh who spoke to me of the color wars of the fifties in a phone interview in 2012. "I'll give you a clue," she said. "Red won!" And whether there was ever a winner declared in the Color Wars, we've all won to the extent that the vivid photographic library illustrates the era for historians. There's no doubt that the use of photography in consumer advertising made huge advances in the postwar economy.

Jim Secreto is a Detroit legend, both as a photographer and as a historian. As a photographer, he was the protégé of GM Photographic's Walter Farnyk and went on to start his own photography studio specializing in automotive advertising. It was Jim who introduced the outdoor light box, that revolutionized automotive photography. As a historian, he is the keeper of Walter Farnyk's archive and a lecturer on the history of automotive advertising photography. We were pleased to sit down with him and discuss the story of photography in automotive advertising in the postwar era.

Jeff Stork: What was the competitive landscape like for renderings versus photography in the immediate postwar era?

Jim Secreto: In the immediate postwar moment, there was an enormous rush to get America "back in business," and that included the auto industry. Practically any new car would sell to a public that had been making do since early 1942. With only a couple of exceptions, McManus and Campbell-Ewald being the most prominent, most of the other agencies handling the auto

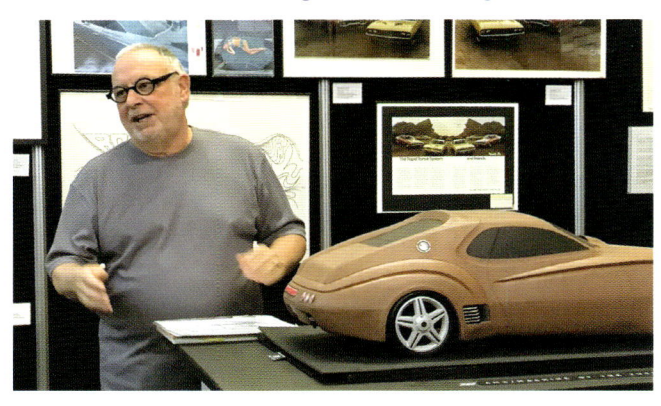

▲ *A behind-the-scenes outtake from the memorable 1958 Lincoln ad campaign photo shoot (Jim Secreto Collection)*

◄ *Strikingly dramatic imagery was created for the 1955 and 1956 Plymouth campaigns by New York fashion photographer Irving Penn, seen here on the cover of the 1956 brochure.*

▶ *Jim Secreto at a 2017 lecture in Royal Oak, Michigan*

Strike a Pose | 179

Bill Johnson, a creative director at Kenyon and Eckhart who handled the Ford Motor Company account, utilized photography to a great extent, starting in 1952 with Lincoln. The same techniques were brought to Mercury, seen here in 1954. The brochures were quite minimal and elegant (above, the glamorous Sun Valley with a transparent roof), but the ad campaign went a bit overboard, with a jam-packed grid of photographs highlighting the car's features.

accounts were New York based and just had satellite offices in the Motor City. The agencies themselves were territorial in nature, and especially at first the New York offices controlled the tone.

The look and technique were very similar to their prwar look—remember, they didn't have to sell at this point, really just casually mention that the production lines were running. The layouts themselves were very similar to other ads for consumer products, varying only by showing a car in place of a refrigerator or a television set, and illustrations (whether in color or black and white) were by far the primary medium.

When did color photography begin to appear in auto ads? Was there a particular company or agency that was innovative?

The competitive environment returned to the auto industry around 1949. The seller's market had cooled off, and the ads had to start becoming more competitive. Color photography began to appear in earnest in the early '50s, around 1953–54. One particular innovator was Kenyon and Eckhart, which handled Ford Motor Company accounts. They had a creative director named Bill Johnson, who was a big advocate of photography. He did some innovative work for Mercury around that time in direct mail, display advertising, and brochures. It was also Bill who made photography prominent in the Lincoln "Modern Living" campaign by rolling into the campaign in 1953. Cadillac began utilizing photography in its direct-mail pieces around 1954.

Were there technological advances that made photography more viable/cost-effective?

Significant improvements were made in the postwar era that included both the film and the camera. Film became faster; the developing process became easier and less expensive. Kodak Kodachrome film dates from 1935, but it was Ektachrome—introduced in the '40s and with much-faster processing time—that was well received by commercial photographers. The cameras themselves underwent transformation as well: thanks to improvements in film and lenses, unwieldy large-format bellows cameras gave way to smaller, easier-to-handle roll film equipment.

Long before ABBA would dream of reaching our shores, and predating even Anita Ekberg and Volvo, Hasselblad became one of the first Swedish brands to conquer America. They entered the US market in 1948 with a series of 2¼- inch square-format cameras, the first of which—the 1600F series—was a beautifully crafted instrument with modular construction, allowing for interchangeable Kodak Ektar lenses and interchangeable film backs. Unfortunately, the 1600F also had more than a few teething pains—problems addressed with the improved 1952 1000F series. As professionals transitioned from flashbulbs to ever-improving electronic flash units, Hasselblad introduced the redesigned 500C series in 1957, which allowed for synchronized electronic flash at all camera speeds—a necessity for studio work. The 500C, in its various iterations, held sway for decades.

Another important development was the dye transfer print, also developed by Kodak. It's best explained by the Museum of Modern Art in New York, which describes it as

"A full-color photographic printing process. In these prints, three layers of dye—cyan, magenta, and yellow—are applied sequentially, by hand, to one emulsion layer. The

A 1957 ad for the original Hasselblad 500 C camera

The 1967 Buick brochure was groundbreaking for its sixty-page magazine-like design and extensive use of celebrities (see chapter 11). On the right is one of the pages in a section with famous male celebrities in various Buick interiors—in this case, actor Lloyd Bridges. What seems like a simple photograph required extensive special lighting effects, including the overhead light panel as seen in the unretouched outtake above. (courtesy Jim Secreto)

Strike a Pose | 181

◀ *Leopard coat, diamond drop earrings, and a 1963 Buick Riviera, photographed for the launch brochure by Bert Stern. Stern was an original "mad man," sought after by Madison Avenue, Hollywood, and the international fashion scene. His celebrity photographs became iconic—Stern shot the last images of Marilyn Monroe six weeks before her death, shortly before the Riviera photos were taken.*

process involves many steps and painstaking alignment of each dye layer, and as a result dye transfers are rare and were seldom made by amateurs. They are very stable, and, when executed correctly, they allow the photographer exceptional control over the final color balance."[1]

The stability lent itself well to the commercial process, allowing for retouching to remove glare and defects in the image. Retouching became a big industry, and retouch artists were in great demand. Retouching also allowed flexibility when shooting new models—grilles and badging could be added later, since final product changes often happened before the assembly lines began to roll. It was even possible to account for unavailable models—you could take the brochure picture of a station wagon and then retouch it into the coupe that wasn't available at the time of the shoot.

How did fashion photographers find themselves involved in auto advertising? Who was the most successful at it?

Again, many of the successful agencies were based in New York and worked extensively with the prominent photographers of the day, especially those used to shooting fashions, so it was relatively easy for them to book them for an automobile shoot. A lot of well-known names ended up doing car shoots in Detroit. Typically, the models would come from New York as well. Irving Penn took an iconic shot of the 1956 Plymouth from behind with a wide-angle lens that accented the tailfins and made the car look a mile wide. He also used white studio lighting to accentuate the shape. Bert Stern did some great work for Buick in the early 1960s, including a launch brochure for the first Riviera that showcased the car in black and silver. Horst Horst shot a series for Ford Thunderbird in the early sixties called "Unique in All the World." Famed fashion photographer Richard Avedon shot ads for Thunderbird as well. John Rawlings, who did new-car sections for *Vogue* each fall,

▲ Richard Avedon is best known for his fashion photography in Harper's Bazaar and Vogue, his celebrity advertising campaigns of the '70s, and his portraiture for the New Yorker, among others. But less known is his commercial work, such as this Thunderbird ad for 1959.

Horst Horst was a German-born American fashion photographer known for his glamorous images of women and fashion. His work for designer Coco Chanel spanned three decades, and he is best known for his surrealist images for Vogue in the 1930s and '40s. As fashion photography changed in the 1960s, he sought other commercial work—here, two ads in a series Horst shot for Thunderbird in 1962.

shot an amazing advertising section for Imperial inside the factory in 1960, with models posed on the assembly line itself; in one shot, a supermodel in couture stands atop the frame and guides the body down onto the chassis.

How do you think the adoption of photography changed the marketing of automobiles?

Perhaps the biggest change was in the early '60s, during the launch of youthful products aimed at baby boomers such as the Corvair Monza and the Mustang. Many agencies felt that illustrations looked stagnant—so photography was brought in for both cars and the lifestyle shots.

Pontiac swung both ways. Of course it was very successful with the legendary Art Fitzpatrick/Van Kaufman illustrations, which began in 1959. So much has been written about Art Fitzpatrick and Van Kaufman that we almost hesitate to mention them here, but there was a very interesting dichotomy upon the introduction of the youthful compact Tempest and Le Mans models in 1962. Art Fitzpatrick is renowned for his beautiful illustrations that accentuated the width of the big "Wide Track" Pontiac, and Van Kaufman's backgrounds were almost exclusively of European settings. Combined they set a classy and upscale tone that dazzled the dads. But for those sporty midyear compacts, Pontiac chose color

Strike a Pose | 183

Pontiac created one of the most successful and iconic automotive-marketing campaigns, using illustrations by the legendary team of Art Fitzpatrick and Van Kaufman throughout the 1960s and into the early '70s. But to promote the youthful compact Tempest and Le Mans models, the longtime Pontiac ad agency Macmanus, John and Adams turned to photography in 1963. For the new luxury-sport Grand Prix coupe, both photography (by Warren Winstanley, seen in the ad below) and illustration (by AF/VK, seen in the main brochure at right) were utilized.

184 | GLAMOUR ROAD

▲ Taking a picture of taking a picture in a 1963 Pontiac Tempest ad

▶ Pages from the 1963 Tempest brochure. Pontiac's transformation from conservative, midpriced cars to sexy performance cars began with the compact Tempest. Photographer Dennis Gripentrog was well regarded for his automotive, lifestyle, and fashion photography—he captured the Tempest as part of a young carefree lifestyle, from surfboards on the beach to barefoot picnics playing the guitar.

photography and youthful models. While the larger Pontiacs were shown in grand illustrations, the smaller ones showed young people in active-lifestyle settings such as the beach or on camping trips. And for the introduction of the iconic Grand Prix—Pontiac's personal luxury sensation—they used both AF/VK illustration and dramatic photography to promote the new glamour coupe to both traditional and youth-leaning audiences.

This dichotomy of larger Pontiacs in illustration and smaller, sportier ones in photography extended to the print ads as well and lasted late into the '60s. Of course, photography lent itself well to the lifestyle shots—which included a lot of bright colors and young people in swimwear frolicking on a beach—that were inset into the brochures.

When did direct mail become popular among auto companies? Was photography utilized more than renderings in direct mail?

It's helpful to start out looking at the role of brochures versus mailers. The brochure was informational in nature, describing various models, trim levels, and options, whereas the mailers could really sell the sizzle. The mailers definitely had greater freedom to try a new product pitch and inherently had more flexibility. Because they were sent to a tailored target versus mass media, there was also more opportunity to try a new approach. The mailer, which could be sent any time during the model year, might also be able to feature a car that simply wasn't available to photograph in time for the brochure. Direct mail was produced on a much more compressed timeline than the traditional fall brochure, so it could respond quickly to market conditions or seasonal promotions.

◀ *Behind-the-scenes contact sheet from the 1958 Lincoln photo shoot (Jim Secreto Collection)*

▶ *Outtake from the 1958 Lincoln photo shoot. The final ad can be seen on page 189. (National Automotive History Collection, Detroit Public Library)*

Lincoln in a Winter Wonderland

To show how automotive photography was accomplished indoors, Jim shared with us these photographs *(left)* from the set of the 1958 Lincoln and Continental ad campaign, which were done by Boulevard Photographic in the summer of 1957. (The large images are from the Boulevard Photographic Collection in the Detroit Public Library.) They rented the Bowen Field House on the campus of Eastern Michigan University in Ypsilanti and staged the shoot there. The Bowen was brand new, having been completed in 1955 at a cost of 1.25 million dollars. The 88,000-square-foot field house was one of the largest buildings of its kind on any campus in the United States at the time and thus lended itself to the elaborate and expansive project.

Ford had great plans for the redesigned Lincoln and Continental. The cars, which varied in trim only, were immense in size and featured unibody construction. They were assembled in a brand-new plant in Wixom, Michigan, which they shared with the new four-place Thunderbird. The cars were longer, lower, and wider than anything on the road, so they didn't need trick camera lenses to make them appear enormous—they already were. But Ford wanted height, so enormously tall backdrops and sets were constructed and all painted in winter white. An enormous portholed wall with a trio of George Nelson lamps, a white staircase to the stars, a curved white wall with white fabric screens, and, you guessed it, white patio table with matching umbrella, a forest of white painted trees. All were constructed inside the Yost field house. Stir in glamorous couples in credited designer gowns and voilà! A striking ad campaign for a car that didn't do particularly well in the marketplace and is largely overlooked today. But these photos remain as a fascinating example of what can be accomplished with an enormous building and a budget to match.

Strike a Pose | 187

188 | GLAMOUR ROAD

All the images in this series of 1958 Lincoln ads were created by Boulevard Photographic at the gigantic set inside the Bowen Field House.

◀ Opposite page: Outtake from the 1958 Lincoln photo shoot. Note the final ad on this page, bottom right. (National Automotive History Collection, Detroit Public Library)

Strike a Pose | 189

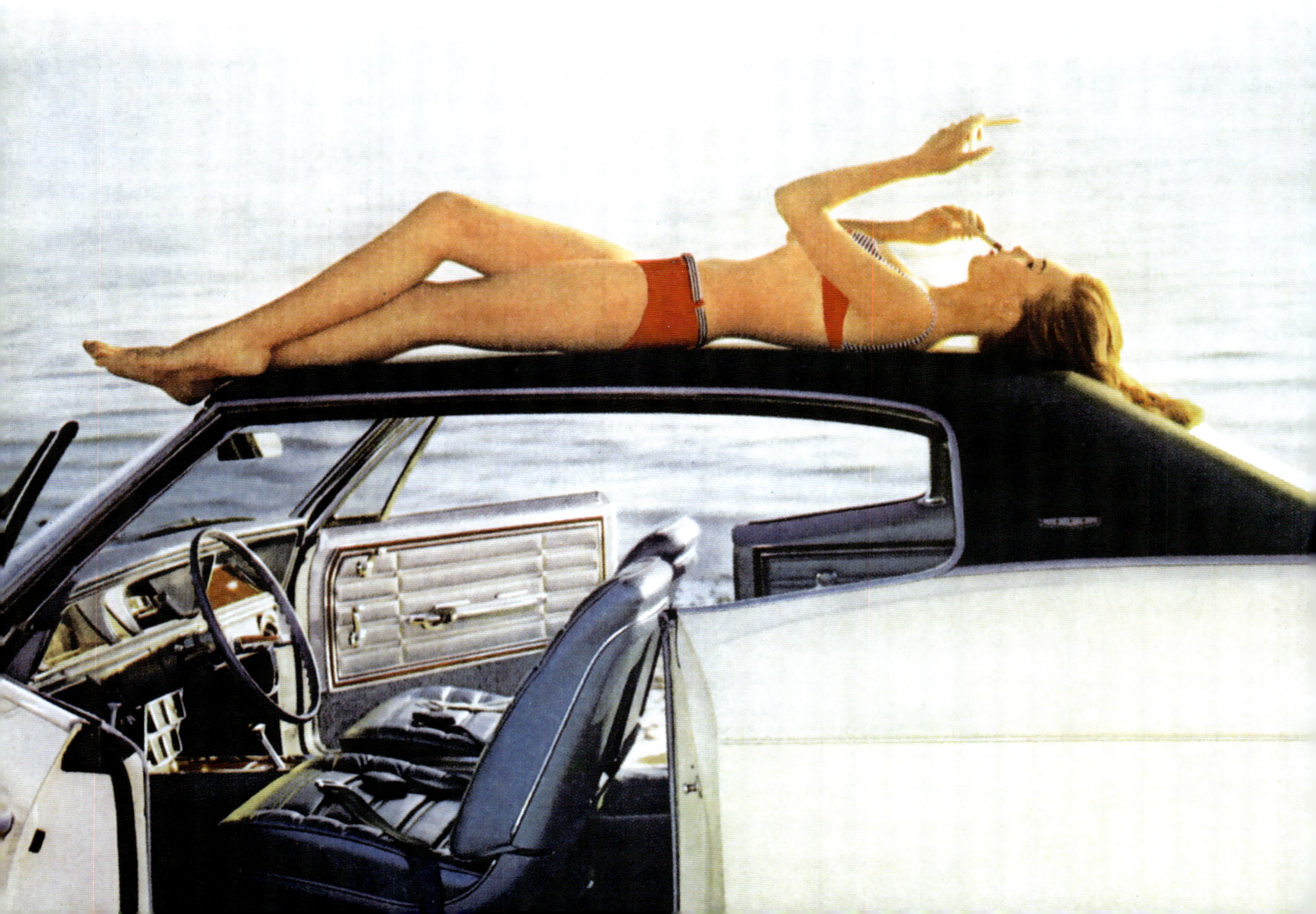

Chapter Ten

BIKINIS & BUCKET SEATS

THE YOUTH MARKET OF THE 1960S CHANGES EVERYTHING

▲ *1967 Dodge Charger joins the Dodge Rebellion.*
◄ *Even traditional full-sized cars like this 1966 Chevrolet Caprice got in on the youth movement by including a bikini-clad woman on a beach in a publicity shot.*

The domestic auto industry entered the sixties with a bad hangover. Collectively, they had spent the waning years of the fifties drunk on tailfins and unnecessary bulk. The crushing Eisenhower recession of 1958 caused sales to tank, and a couple of annoying trends came to their attention—Rambler and the imports.

Rambler, of course, had been introduced as a fashionable Nash compact in 1951, but with the merger of Nash and Hudson in 1955, the name had been applied to a sensibly sized sedan and sturdy station wagon with a roomy interior and reasonably trim exterior, and while the Big Three dismissed it as a college professor's car (which it was), it did very well indeed during the recession years of 1958 and 1959. Enough to make Detroit cast their gaze at smaller cars.

The other splinter in Detroit's eye was the imports. The executives of the Big Three had long commented that small cars weren't profitable and that the entry-level car was a used Chevrolet, but the trouble was the pesky consumers weren't going along with Detroit's plan. By the late '50s, they were buying some imported cars in numbers—big-enough numbers to finally elicit a response.

The Big Three introduced their compacts for 1960. Ford took the most traditional road with the box-on-box Falcon, which looked like a full-sized Ford reduced to three-quarter scale but seated six and delivered respectable economy. Chrysler Corporation's Valiant, sold by Plymouth dealers, also had a traditional front-engine–rear-drive layout. It introduced Chrysler's legendary slant-six engine and again provided bench seating for six. Virgil Exner gave it a more expressive look than the Falcon, styling it after a miniaturized version of an Imperial show car called the d'Elegance.

Corvair Sets the Trend

Chevrolet's Corvair was the trendsetter. It featured a rear-mounted, air-cooled, six-cylinder engine that paid homage to the Porsche (and VW Beetle) of the day. This gave the Corvair flat floors, a roomy front trunk, and a fold-down rear seat for even more storage. All of the new compacts started to sell. The Falcon sold very well indeed—over 300,000 in its first year. There was one problem—none of these economy cars were very profitable. The Falcon sold well, but almost all of its sales took someone out of a

Bikinis & Bucket Seats | 191

Chevrolet interior stylist Blaine Jenkins designed the legendary "Pinky," a handmade pink convertible with pink leather interior and even a pink top, for Sue Earl (wife of Harley Earl, founder of GM's Styling Department). It led to the sporty Corvair Monza.

full-sized Ford with a higher profit margin. Chevrolet had a bigger problem—the Corvair was a money loser. Designer Blaine Jenkins recalls that within a week of Corvair's dealer introduction, he came into the Chevrolet Interior Studio to find a brand-new Ford Falcon. "Clone it," he was told. "And it can't cost a dime more to make."[1]

It seems that Corvair's revolutionary air-cooled engine had missed its cost target by as much as $200, which doesn't sound all that bad—until you consider that the wholesale price of the car was only around $2,000. It was a disaster. Because they were already worried, GM management had kept very tight control of the budget, which meant the cute little car debuted with a very sparse interior—taxicab-style seats, cardboard door panels, and rubber floor mats. The base 500 came with only one sunvisor. It was eminently resistible inside.

At this point, the story takes a turn to the recollections of a then-young Chevrolet interior stylist named Blaine Jenkins. Blaine was in only his third year at General Motors and had worked on the original Corvair interior. He recalls being embarrassed when Tennessee Ernie Ford folded the Corvair cardboard door panel in half on his TV program while promoting the rival Falcon.

Back in those days, it wasn't unusual for a young designer to be asked to work on special cars for very

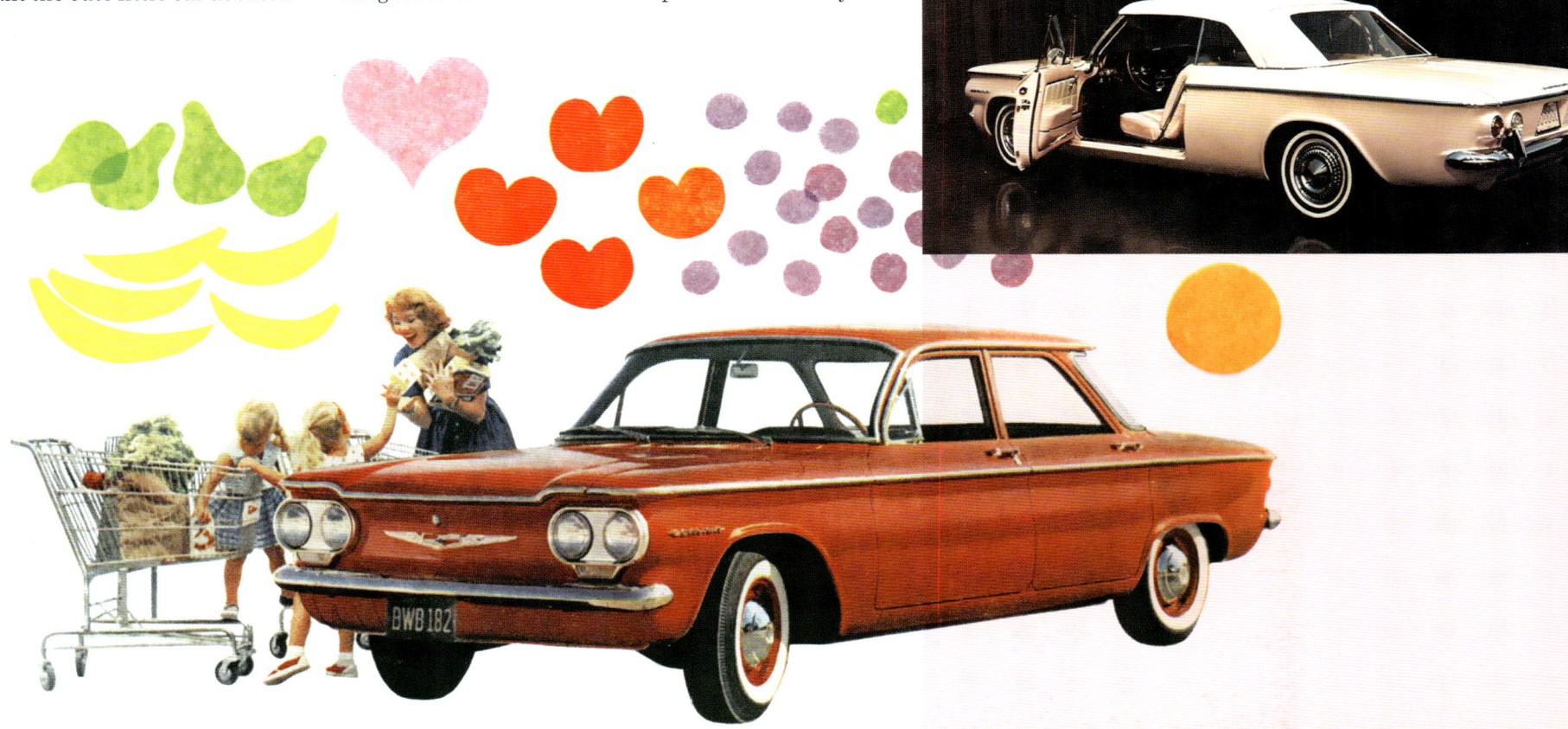

192 | GLAMOUR ROAD

The early Corvair ads, like this illustration from 1960, presented an uncluttered graphic look that made the car seem very fresh, modern— and youthful.

1963 Corvair Monza interior

1961 Corvair 500

Bikinis & Bucket Seats | 193

GO NEW CORVETTE—*IT'S EXCITING!*

GO '63 CORVAIR—*IT'S EXCITING!*

▲ The Corvair was no horsepower champ, but it benefited from the family connection to the Corvette.

▶ It looks like a romantic drive in the country in their 1964 Monza, but the standard four-speed stick shift might get in the way.

194 | GLAMOUR ROAD

About the only thing that can come between a Corvair owner and his Corvair is

his wife

'64 Corvair Monza Club Coupe

important friends of GM, and Blaine was no exception. He recalls it as a two-in-one occasion when he was asked to create two special Corvairs. They would turn out to be very significant indeed.

The two-door Club Coupe model wasn't even on the market yet when Blaine was asked to create a special one for the sixteen-year-old daughter of GM styling chief Bill Mitchell, and a convertible for the wife of Harley Earl, founder of the styling department. Blaine called the coupe the Super Monza and fitted it with a sunroof, wire wheels, and a pleated fabric interior. For Sue Earl, he designed the legendary "Pinky," a handmade pink convertible with pink leather interior and even a pink top. And he fitted them both with bucket seats. And from that the sporty Corvair Monza would spring.

By this time, bucket seats were well known to Americans. American troops in Europe in World War II came home familiar with European compact and sports cars, which pretty much all featured bucket seats and a floor shift. To them, bucket seats meant sportiness. GM had bucket seats in the pricey Corvette and offered them as an option in certain high-line cars like the Cadillac Eldorado and Pontiac Bonneville models, but Blaine's custom Corvairs marked their first application in GM compacts. Chevrolet general manager Ed Cole saw the Super Monza coupe and ordered a production model at once; the Monza Sport Coupe made its debut before the end of the 1960 model year.

The Monza had what the base Corvairs did not—curb appeal. It featured a much more upscale interior with the aforementioned bucket seats, full carpeting, pleated door panels, bright trim on the dash face and bucket seats, a rear folding seat, and even a sporty chrome horn ring. The interior itself came in four colors—bright red, turquoise, blue, and green. Outside, they added full chrome wheel covers and lower body moldings. The result was a handsome small car with a youthful appeal that stood up well against some of the import alternatives. A silk purse, if you will. The Monza was an instant success that would account for the majority of Corvair sales throughout the car's life. And because it sold at a higher price, it was profitable at last. A sporty Monza convertible and a high-performance turbcharged Monza Spyder would join the lineup in mid-'62.

The Monza had not only saved the Corvair program, but it helped change the public's perception of compact cars from sour to sporty.

1960 Corvair

Bikinis & Bucket Seats | 195

Let's throw something in the air! Small convertibles were a potent youthquake symbol of the early '60s—attractive, fun, affordable, and devoid of the heavy-handed styling elements of the 1950s.
Above: 1964 Chevrolet Chevelle.
Right top: 1963 Plymouth Valiant.
Right bottom: 1960 Studebaker Lark.

196 | GLAMOUR ROAD

The Youthquake

It's impossible to understand the sixties without looking at the influence of the baby boomers. The Census Bureau defines baby boomers as those born between 1946 and mid-1965, and it's of note that the midpoint of 1955 breaks the baby boomer population almost perfectly in half, with thirty-eight million in the former half and thirty-seven million in the latter. The implication for marketers is very clear—with seventy-five million customers headed their way, youth is king. People born in 1946 would be eighteen in 1964, and the birth rate peaked in 1949, which made the sixties into a teenage-dominated culture.

It's not a surprise that automotive advertising took a turn toward youthful themes—sun, fun, surf, and sand. Bikinis and bucket seats and smiling young faces of both genders behind the wheel. The product pitch was less gender specific but almost totally youth oriented—less about fuel economy or roomy luggage compartments and

People born in 1946 would be eighteen in 1964, and the birth rate peaked in 1949, which made the sixties into a teenage-dominated culture.

more about bucket seats and driving fun. It was a bright-yellow Studebaker Lark convertible with two young couples inside, the women holding their scarves up in the air. A 1962 Rambler American convertible ad bears the headline of "Sunful—Funful—Wonderful." Even full-sized family sedans like the Chevrolet Impala and the Plymouth Fury used headlines like "Excitement!" and "Alive!" One notable Corvair ad headline walked the line by saying, "It Growls for the men—purrs for the girls."

Left: A college beauty queen and football champ in a 1965 Pontiac LeMans ad. Below: 1962 Plymouth Valiant. Bottom: Bucket seats in a 1967 Dodge Polara.

▲ AMC offered this classic black-and-white houndstooth on their premium Ambassador—it even came with a matching toss pillow!

Above right: Pontiac's 1960 tritone bucket seats featured metallic vinyl and leather.

▶ Pontiac showed three different seat options for its 1966 Grand Prix. The split-back Strato bench seat with fold-down armrest gives the appearance of bucket seats.

198 | GLAMOUR ROAD

▼ Even the sensible 1964 Rambler Cross Country was pitched to youth as a surf wagon.

And sporty cars kept coming. By 1963, Chevrolet had a Super Sport model with bucket seats offered in every series. A plethora of high-line compacts would soon follow—the Buick Skylark, the Pontiac Le Mans and the turbocharged Olds Cutlass, the Plymouth Valiant Signet, the Dodge Dart GT, and a fancy bucket-seated Falcon called the Futura all came to market in rapid succession. Even the Rambler American offered a "400" model with reclining bucket seats.

The success of the Monza and its ilk probably greenlit a project over in Dearborn that would stand the automotive world on its ear.

The sporty cars kept coming. By 1963, Chevrolet had a Super Sport model with bucket seats offered in every series.

▶ Pretty girls in swimwear throwing beach balls in a convertible. This image from a 1964 Dodge Polara ad came to define an era.

Bikinis & Bucket Seats | 199

▶ Right: 1962 Thunderbird Sports Roadster

▼ Below: The elegant 1963 Buick Riviera, seen here in a launch brochure photograph by Burt Stern

Below right: The 1962 Studebaker Avanti, photographed in Palm Springs, where it was designed by Raymond Loewy. It featured a fiberglass body, front disc brakes, and an optional Supercharger.

200 | GLAMOUR ROAD

1963 Lincoln Continental, in a brochure illustration with a backdrop of the Eero Saarinen–designed TWA terminal, which opened in 1962

Slab-Sided Personal Luxury

While much of the industry effort was directed at sporty compacts for younger drivers, a dramatic reshaping of luxury cars was underway as well. The breathtaking 1961 Lincoln Continental, an instant and timeless classic, debuted to rave reviews and changed the look of the luxury car overnight. The car was over a foot smaller and 800 pounds lighter than the behemoth that preceded it, lean and sheer with slab-sided styling and a small greenhouse with curved side glass. And the use of bright trim was kept to a minimum. Production designer John Najjar said, "The Continental should be like an elegant lady in a simple black dress, with her jewelry nothing more than an uncomplicated diamond necklace."[2] The Continental was a breath of fresh air compared to the flamboyant and sometimes bizarre designs of the late fifties, and the designers were no doubt relieved by it and the new trend toward simplicity that it inspired.

The companion Ford Thunderbird was also completely reshaped for 1961. Known to enthusiasts as the Flair Bird, the Thunderbird also featured simplicity in its crisp lines, and minimal bright trim except for the unique large rocket-thrust taillamps. A unique Sports Roadster option was added in mid-1962, with a fiberglass tonneau cover with cove headrests and genuine wire wheels.

Studebaker's last spark of brilliance came to market in mid-1962 as the iconic Avanti. Designed by Raymond Loewy and crew in a hideaway in Palm Springs, California, and utilizing an existing frame from a Lark Convertible, the Avanti offered European flair and seating for four. The fiberglass body included a roll bar, bucket seats, overhead aircraft-style rocker switches, and a glove box with a pop-up makeup mirror for the ladies. A factory supercharger was even an option. It was a brilliant car, but Studebaker's legendary production delays left orders unfilled until it was too late. The design was so unforgettable that a former dealer named Nate Altman brought it back as the Avanti II and built them in small numbers virtually by hand until his death in the 1980s.

General Motors came late to the party, but they arrived ready to rumble with the fabulous Buick Riviera of 1963. It was stunningly low and featured a sharp, razor-edge style that chief GM designer Bill Mitchell called Ferrari-Rolls-Royce. Sporty yet formal at the same time, it was GM's first smash-hit personal luxury car and launched a whole class of wildly profitable personal luxury coupes in the sixties. Amazingly, Buick almost didn't get the car—Mitchell intended it for Cadillac, but GM's luxury leader didn't want it. Buick saw it as just what they were looking for to add youthful flair to their image and lobbied the GM board for the right to build it. They got their wish, and the sporty Riviera turned out to be just what Buick needed.

Bikinis & Bucket Seats | 201

Publicity shot for the new Mustang at the 1964 New York World's Fair introduction

202 | GLAMOUR ROAD

Along Came a Pony

Perhaps no car better captures the mood of the sixties than the Ford Mustang. Introduced at the New York World's Fair via a prime-time television commercial on all three networks, the Mustang took the underpinnings of the reliable compact Falcon and wrapped them in pure magic. A long hood and a short deck, a formal roofline, a sporty interior with bucket seats, a long list of options, and a surprisingly low base price was just the ticket for Ford's new sporty compact.

At first, Ford was reticent. The colossal failure of the Edsel left the company with egg on their faces and a lot of spectacularly embarrassing press. So they started out very slowly with a secret committee called the Fairlane Committee. But this time, Ford had done their homework. They saw the success of the Monza and the Skylark and the other upscale compacts. They introduced their own sporty Falcon Futura in 1962 and added a convertible model a year later. They also looked at the research, which predicted that buyers aged eighteen to thirty-four would account for 50% of the automobile market increase in the '60s. That same research showed younger buyers strongly preferred bucket seats, and a floor-mounted shifter—although most of the respondents preferred an automatic transmission. To quote a Ford press release, "It appeared inevitable that youth would be a potent factor in the marketplace. And research showed that youth would exercise an important influence in shaping car design. Young buyers, it was clear, had definite ideas about style and performance."[3]

It also predicted an increase in the number of multicar households—in 1959, there were one million households with more than one car, but by the Mustang's introduction in 1964 that had grown to thirteen million, and by 1967, there were two million households with three cars. Of course, by 1967, a lot of them included Mustangs.

Six and the single girl.

What makes a quiet, sensible girl like Joan fall in love with a Mustang? Not simply Mustang's steely good looks or smooth, racy lines. Not even the hard-to-resist features like adjustable bucket seats, wall-to-wall carpeting, sports steering wheel, and floor-mounted shift.

What really broke down Joan's reserve was the solid practicality of Mustang's deep breathing Six. She knew she could trust this husky, suave brute of an engine to squire her around town, drive her to the mountains for a weekend, even drop her off for dinner with the girls (who will never guess how little Mustang costs her to own and run). Extraordinarily considerate of a girl's feelings...and her pocketbook.

Take a test drive and see if you should give in to Mustang because of sheer Six appeal. Smart girls do.

MUSTANG
A PRODUCT OF Ford

Bikinis & Bucket Seats | 203

The design itself was groundbreaking. Although it shared many mechanical components with the economical Falcon, it packaged them completely differently. The profile was completely different from other Ford cars of its day, enough so that designer Gale Halderman—whose concept was selected to become the production Mustang—broke no fewer than seventy-seven Ford engineering "rules" when first presented. It was his task to ready the car for production while keeping its spirit intact.

Target: Youth

Mustang was targeted at two groups—the young and the young at heart. The initial sales projection was set at 100,000 units. Ford began to clinic the new car and soon began to wonder if their initial estimates were low. The clinics found a phenomenon that repeated itself over and over—first, that people tended to overestimate the base price by $1,000 or more, and second, that when told the actual price, took a second look at the car and decided it could fit their needs. Thunderbird glamour at a Falcon price was a compelling proposition.

Mustang was introduced from the World's Fair on the night of April 16, 1964, in a commerccial that called it "The car dreams are made of." Twenty-nine million people viewed the new Mustang. Henry Ford II unveiled it to the public the following day at the fair. The Mustang was on the covers of *Time* and *Newsweek*, with editorial copy in *Life, Look, Esquire,* and *US News and World Report*. Ford placed a huge media buy for the announcement day of April 17, with ads in 2,200 newspapers nationwide, as

▲ *The Mustang was introduced at the 1964 New York World's Fair and caused an instant sensation that became a cultural phenomenon.*

Top, in this scene from Thunderball, James Bond gets a ride from deadly gorgeous Fiona Volpe, who speeds him back to town in her Tropical Turquoise Mustang.

well as the top twenty-four magazines. Women's pages were prominent in the buy. Additionally, 100 Holiday Inn lobbies had a Mustang on display. At a press preview four days earlier, 125 reporters were given new Mustangs and set off on a 750-mile trip to Dearborn.

The first appearance of a Mustang on film was in the movie *Goldfinger*. A brand-new white convertible, driven by a beautiful young female would-be assassin named Tilly Masterson (played by Tania Mallet), encounters James Bond in his Aston Martin on the Furka Pass in the Swiss Alps while chasing Auric Goldfinger's Rolls-Royce Phantom III. The following year, another Mustang, this time Tropical Turquoise, made an appearance in *Thunderball*. Pretty lofty company indeed for the little Ford.

The First Customer Is a Perfect Fit

Apparently the first retail customer was female, as well. On April 15, 1964, twenty-two-year-old Gail D. Brown of Chicago had just graduated from teacher's college and was shopping for her first new car with her father. They stopped by Johnson Ford on North Cicero Ave. and were shown a brand-new power-blue convertible, which was in the back under a cover. It was love at first sight for Gail, who said, "It was sporty. It was perfect. It went zoom-zoom. It was a young person's car. I was real happy."[4] She bought the car on the spot for $3,447.50. The dealer, eager to make a sale, ignored the announcement day presale embargo, and so it turned out the first retail customer was a young, college-educated female, precisely in line with Ford's target.

"On the drive home I found out how special this car was because everybody was flagging me down to slow down, and they were waving at me, giving me high-fives," she said. "I felt like a movie star."[5]

▲ The first Mustang was sold to Gail Brown of Chicago, who was twenty-two at the time. After years of everyday service, it sat in her garage for twenty-seven years and was recently fully restored by her husband. (© Kimberly P. Mitchell/Detroit Free Press via ZUMA Wire)

▼ There were plenty of colors and options offered to make your Mustang fit your style.

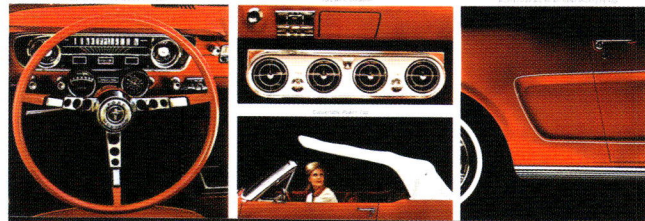

"If they're still waiting for Agnes down at the Willow Lane Whist and Discussion Group, they'll wait a long time."

If they're still waiting for Agnes down at the Willow Lane Whist and Discussion Group, they'll wait a long time. Agnes hasn't been herself since she got her Mustang hardtop (with its racy lines, bucket seats, smooth, optional 3-speed automatic transmission and fire-eating 200 cu. in. Six). Mustang is more car than Willow Lane has seen since the last Stutz Bearcat bit the dust. (And Agnes has a whole new set of hobbies, none of which involves cards.) Why don't you find out if there's any truth in the rumor—Mustangers have more fun?

Best year yet to go Ford
MUSTANG!
MUSTANG!
MUSTANG!

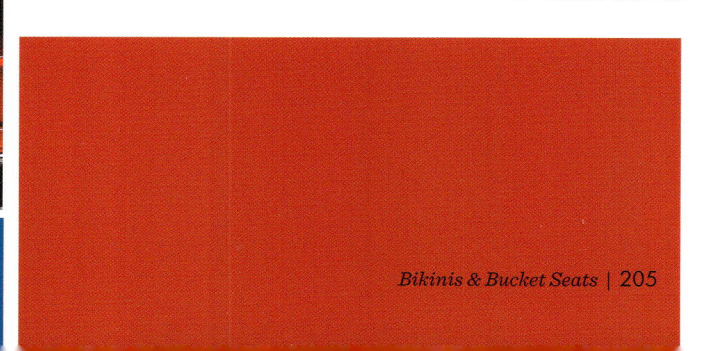

Bikinis & Bucket Seats | 205

Irreverent Advertising Campaign Pays Off

The advertising campaign was particularly playful and targeted at both genders. Ford created a memorable series of Walter Mitty ads—based on the 1939 short story by James Thurber—showing how ordinary people led humdrum lives until they got their new Mustang.

All the ads explained how the subject had their lives thoroughly transformed by the new Ford compact and ended with the slogan "Mustangers have more fun." Mustang targeted directly at young women with headlines such as "6 and the Single Girl" and "Sweetheart of the Supermarket Set." They also made a run at the young-at-heart crowd by showing an elderly couple in a red convertible with the famous George Bernard Shaw quote "Youth is a wonderful thing. What a crime to waste it on children." Clearly, Mustang didn't waste it at all. From the young to the young at heart, Mustang captured the imagination and the checkbook of the public.

I Got You, Babe

And while they weren't quite movie stars in the traditional sense, two of the most visible young Mustang drivers were pop singers Sonny and Cher. Ford shipped two San Jose–built Mustang convertibles with average equipment—289 V-8s, floor shift automatics, power steering and brakes—to legendary Hollywood "King of the Kustomizers" George Barris to create a pair of mild custom show cars for auto shows and publicity. "Sonny and Cher go back a long way with me. They were the hippest young couple I can remember. They dressed way out and wild, and Cher was the most beautiful young woman imaginable," recalled George.[6] His wife, Shirley, assisted the couple in selecting colors and trim.

206 | GLAMOUR ROAD

▶ Pop idols Sonny & Cher both got customized Mustangs by the "King of Kustomizers" George Barris. Shown here are the original finished Mustangs, above, and the stars going over details in their home with Barris and his wife, Shirley, next to the fur-framed original sketches of the Mustangs. Note the airbrushed "fade" highlights on the pearlized paint jobs, not to mention Cher's groovy pantsuit. Cher asked George to paint the car the same color as her nail polish. (Photos by George Barris)

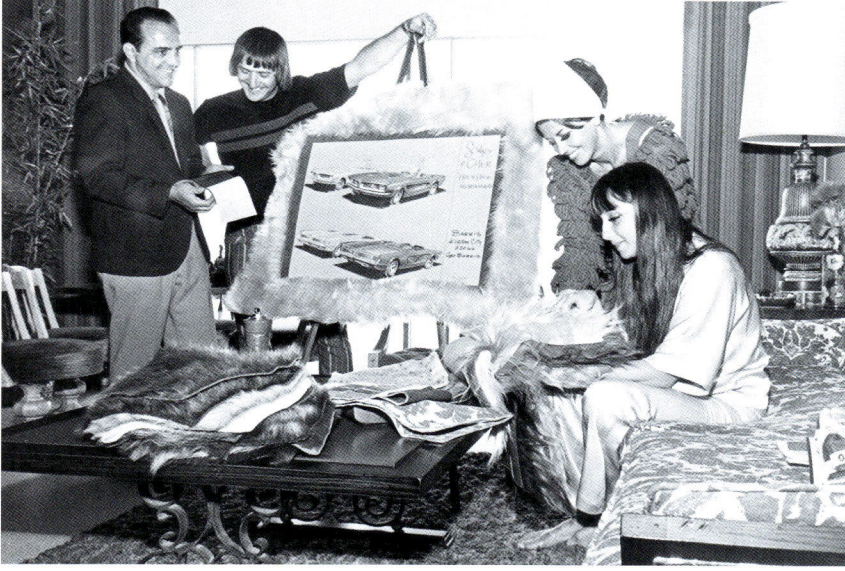

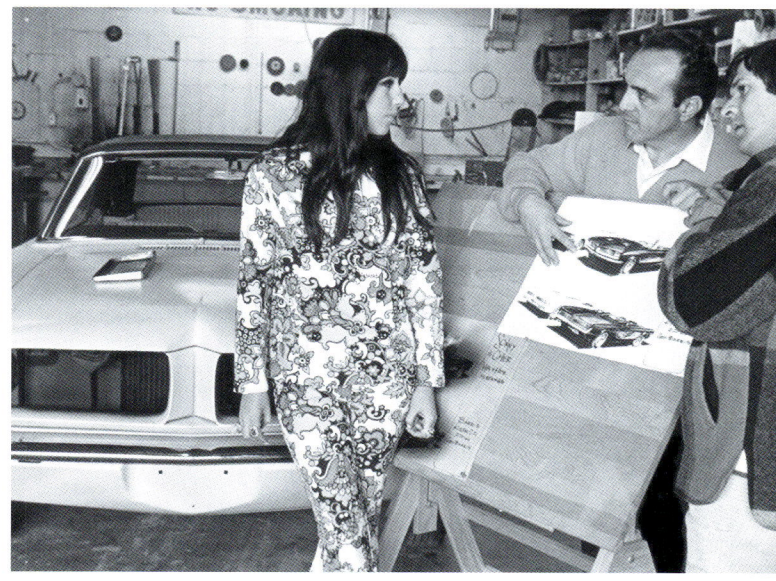

According to a recent Ford press release: "Barris' body mods for both cars were quite similar, including full repaints. The main color for Cher's car is called Hot Candy Pink, and Sonny's is Murano Gold. Barris and company reconfigured both cars' front ends, giving them silver-mesh twin grilles and a bit of a 'beak' in the middle—about where the standard running horse and corrals would normally rest; the stock headlights were also swapped out for Lucas European-style rectangular units, each in their own chrome bezels."

"The interiors of both cars are really over the top, so typical of Barris, and of the era. The seats of Cher's car are stitched of genuine Ermine fur, contrasted by black leather. And Sonny's cabin is done up in a wild combo of bobcat fur, saddle leather and suede; both cars are trimmed in very shaggy faux fur carpeting—you might think of it as "ultrashag."

The Pop Star ponies were used in auto shows and many publicity photo shoots—often still wearing California manufacturer plates, and AMT created models of each for young fans of the duo or the Mustang. But the "I Got You, Babe" couple weren't the only people riding Ford's Pony. It was more than a smash hit—100,000 were sold in the first four months alone—but a true runaway success that became the dominant automotive story of the decade.

Over one million were sold by mid-1966. And it was right on target. The average age of the buyer was thirty-one, with 50% of early purchasers aged twenty to thirty-four. It spawned a whole new class of competitors—called Pony Cars—that included the Camaro, Firebird, Barracuda, Dodge Challenger, Mercury Cougar, and AMC Javelin.

Bikinis & Bucket Seats | 207

BBDO hired a perky young twenty-five-year-old blonde named Pamela Austin, whose screen credits included a couple of Elvis movies and some episodes of 77 Sunset Strip. They put her in white go-go boots and created a multimedia campaign around her called the "Dodge Rebellion."

The Dodge Rebellion wants you!

These Boots Are Made for Sellin'

The Dodge division of Chrysler Corporation needed a breakthrough campaign. They were doing the same sun/surf/sand/bikini commercials as everyone else but had no central theme or even a tagline. They wanted something more commanding. There was a brand-new fastback coming to market called Charger with four bucket seats, dual consoles, hidden headlamps, and a fastback roofline, and they needed a way to introduce it as well as draw attention to the rest of the Dodge lineup. They tasked their ad agency, BBDO, with coming up with something revolutionary.

The agency hired a perky young twenty-five-year-old blonde named Pamela Austin, whose screen credits included a couple of Elvis movies and some episodes of *77 Sunset Strip*. They put her in white go-go boots and created a multimedia campaign around her called the "Dodge Rebellion." The campaign included commercials, print ads, dealer support materials, and even Dodge product brochures. The television commercials were done in a "Perils of Pauline" style.

In each ad, Pamela would find herself in a terrible danger, then the spot pivoted to a product pitch and back to Pamela, who would unexpectedly rescue herself from harm's way and close with the tagline "The Dodge Rebellion wants you." She was tied up next to a bomb, she was chased by a great white shark, she slipped off the roof of a tall chateau, she was pulled out of an airplane, and she even pushed a handcart full of explosives (as one does) as a freight train raced up behind her. In every case, she managed to free herself, but unlike the original Pauline, almost always did so without a man coming to her rescue. It was a distinctive and highly likable campaign.

Sometimes the campaign is just too good. The Dodge Revolution tested very well indeed—research done in late 1966 showed 87% of the respondents correctly identified the campaign with Dodge—but while they had created one of the most recognizable faces in advertising, the sales increase was a modest 5% in 1966 and actually decreased almost 10% for 1967. Dodge executives feared that Pamela was stealing the thunder from the product, so the campaign was changed to Dodge Fever for 1968, and a new model, Joan Anita Parker, was hired for a much more conventional campaign. The Dodge Rebellion had been memorable but short lived.

'66 Dodge Dart

Tired of compacts that put you too close for comfort? Arms too close to the door... legs too close to the floor? Think big, think smart. Get fixed up with the new '66 Dodge Dart GT. With Dart GT, you can insist on size and still economize. Check the price. Check the interior: foam-padded seats, wall-to-wall carpeting, door-to-door luxury. Demand more comfort in your compact—more spirit, more for your money. Step into '66 Dart. Take it on the road. Which way do you want to go, Six or V8? '66 Dodge Dart goes both ways without attacking your budget. If you're fed up with compacts that don't make it in size, styling, and spunk, you've got it made with '66 Dart. The Dodge-sized compact. It's got what you want. The Dodge Rebellion wants you.

CHRYSLER MOTORS CORPORATION

JOIN THE DODGE REBELLION
Avoid the cramped compact squeeze. Stretch out in '66 Dodge Dart.

'67 Dodge Monaco

"Surrender... '67 Monaco has you surrounded with luxury!"

DODGE REBELLION OPERATION '67

Be the big gun on your block. Zero in on the all-new '67 Monaco. It's the biggest Dodge in history, a full half-foot longer than last year. And every inch of that long, luxurious length is loaded. So why settle for less than Monaco's foam-padded seats, plush carpeting, Flow-Through ventilation for hardtops, and padded, completely redesigned instrument panel? Plus a long list of standard safety items that run to over a dozen—from backup lights to retractable front lap belts. Fire up '67 Monaco. Sample the responsive teamwork of its 383-cubic-inch V8 and smooth, optional TorqueFlite automatic transmission. Enjoy the way Monaco's long 122-inch wheelbase smooths out choppy roads. By then, you'll be happy to give up—and admit Monaco is the choice for anyone who demands a full measure of comfort, style and convenience. You'll be able to picture your neighbors snapping to attention when you parade by in a new Monaco. Take a long look at the longer new Monaco today. The Dodge Rebellion wants you.

CHRYSLER MOTORS CORPORATION

'67 Dodge Coronet

"Tired of halfway cars that miss the mark? Aim for Coronet 500!"

DODGE REBELLION OPERATION '67

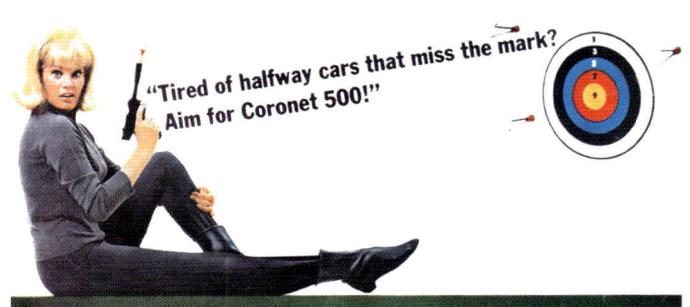

This time, aim high. Set your sights on Coronet's luxury, and distinction, and outstanding performance. And get all you aim for at a very down-to-earth price. Coronet for '67 offers a full line... sedans, wagons, convertibles, hardtops. The Coronet 500 convertible you see here is one. It and its companion Coronet 500 two-door hardtop have these extra touches of luxury, all at the standard price: bucket seats up front, a distinctive grille design, center cushion and pull-down armrest, and plush carpeting wherever your feet touch down. Coronet 500 also offers a choice of five engines—up to a 383-cu.-in. V8. Options include front seat headrests and, on the hardtop, a vinyl-covered roof. So no matter what you want, Coronet's got it. And no matter what Coronet you get, it'll give you a baker's dozen plus of standard safety features that used to cost extra. There's nothing halfway about the exciting, new Coronet. It's right on target. Don't take that old familiar trail to the ho-hum cars again. See your nearby Dodge Dealer for a long, close look at Coronet for '67. If you haven't already enlisted in Dodge Rebellion Operation '67, your time has come.

CHRYSLER MOTORS CORPORATION

Bikinis & Bucket Seats | 209

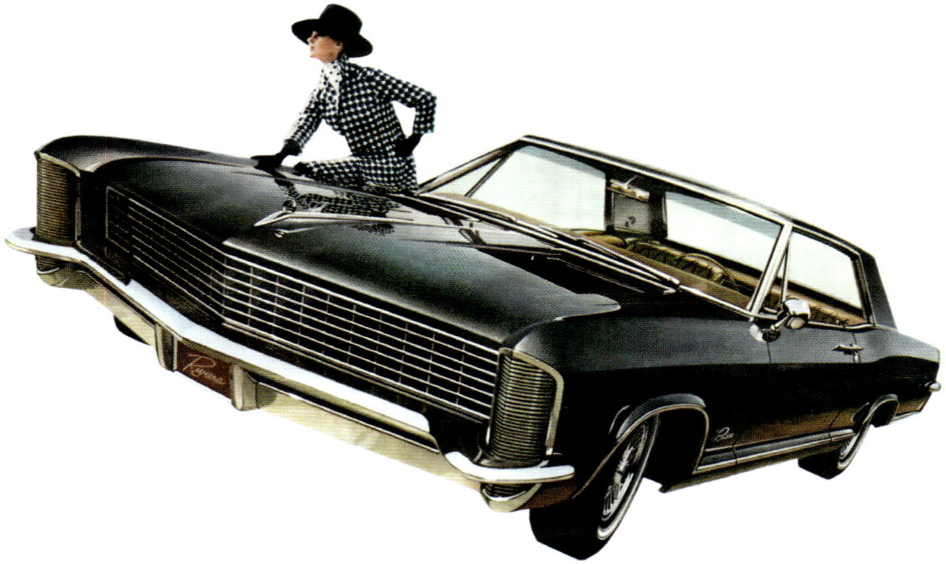

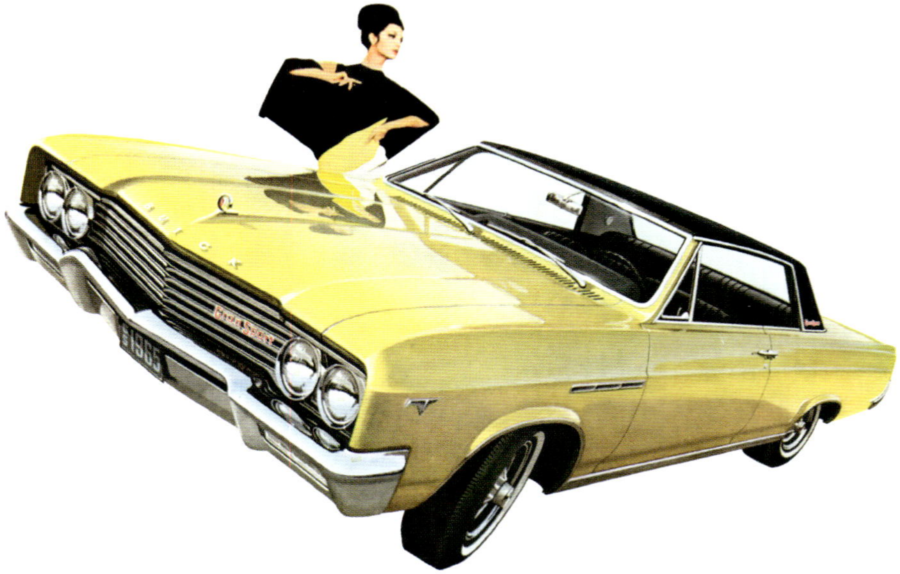
1965

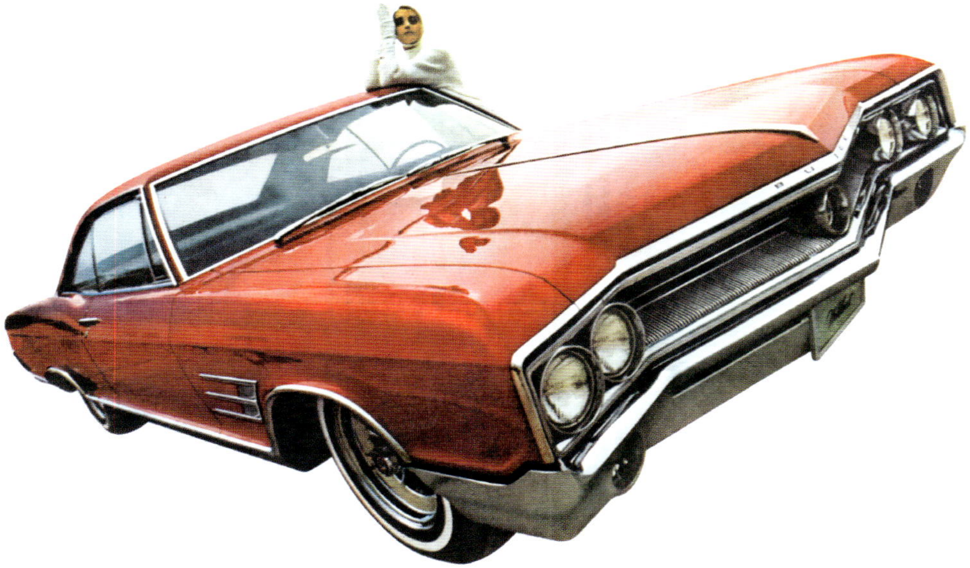

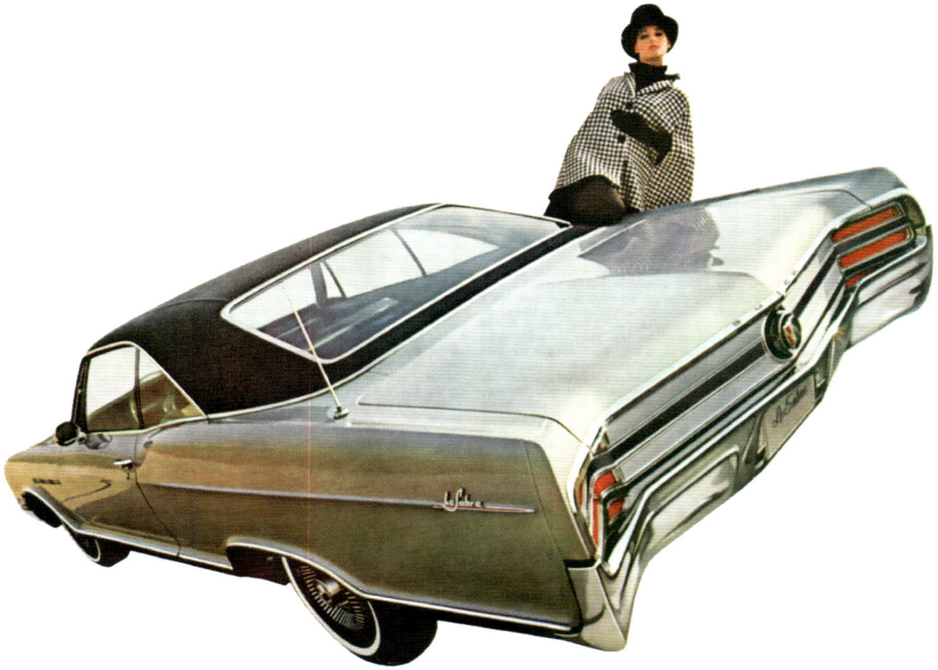

Chapter Eleven

BUICK GOES ALL OUT

"THE MAGAZINE FOR THE IN CROWD" BLOWS MINDS—AND BUDGETS

▲ Bob Cummings shows off a Buick GS400 interior. He was one of fourteen top male actors of the day featured in the 1967 brochure.

◀ As a prelude to the 1967 fashion-obsessed brochure, Buick ran a series of dramatically photographed ads in 1965 featuring models in high fashion.

Automobile dealers have passed out millions of brochures in the last century or so, and while they're fun to collect, most are rather predictable in their layout and ordinary in their production. Only a handful come to mind as truly outstanding or groundbreaking, and none can come close to the Deluxe Buick brochure of 1967. More a lifestyle publication than a sales brochure, it was all but unprecedented and remains a noteworthy piece today.

Billed as "Buick—the Magazine for the In Crowd," it was produced in the style of a magazine—sixty pages with features and articles. And like a great many magazines, it featured not a shiny chrome grill on the cover, but rather a beautiful woman. And not just any woman, mind you—but none other than American supermodel Suzy Parker herself. It was instantly evident that this was no humdrum piece of advertising.

Instead of being arranged by car model like everyone else, it was organized into articles grouped primarily by body style. It opened with a special section for Riviera shot on the California coast, followed by an article called "Convertibles to Put a Song in Your Heart." Each Buick convertible was likened to a musical theme. We learned that Electra was "Bolero in sophistication," Le Sabre was a "Ballad to the girl next door," and the GS-400 was the "Convertible with soul." The section was written in a very flowery lyric and illustrated with watercolor renderings done in a sixties interpretation of an art nouveau style.

Top Fashion Models Add Glamour to Coupes

"The Fashionable Two Doors" was a stunning display of the cutting-edge fashion trends of the time, with the new Buick two-door models as a backdrop. It featured the era's hottest designers and top fashion models and looked like it stepped right out of *Vogue*, including credits for the fashions and hairstyling. A designer friend described it as "A lens on a chic world meant to be traveled only in a 1967 Buick"[1] and noted how amazingly well executed it was—the fashions were at least five years ahead of the mainstream, so we'll try to give it some context as well as a little fashion flair:

The Apple Red Wildcat was shown with the glamorous Dutch-born supermodel Wilhelmina. Willi Cooper was an icon in the industry and opened her own agency, Wilhelmina Models, in 1967. Willi was the height of

Buick Goes All Out | 211

Billed as "Buick—the Magazine for the In Crowd," the 1967 brochure was produced in the style of a magazine—sixty pages, with features and articles. And like a great many magazines, it featured not a shiny chrome grill on the cover, but rather a beautiful woman—none other than American supermodel Suzy Parker herself.

sixties chic, leaning against the hood in her black Pauline Trigère gown and flying-saucer hat by Emme.

Dolores Wettach posed with an Ivory Skylark Sport Coupe, wearing a topknot hairdo and a white, bare-midriff knit top and slacks ensemble by Chuck Howard of Townley. She was a top *Vogue* model who went on to marry American baseball Hall of Fame inductee Ted Williams. Dolores Hawkins, another *Vogue* model, wore a Chuck Howard jumper of lemon yellow and cerise and perched atop a sleek Burgundy Mist Le Sabre coupe.

Pretty young blonde Penny Ashton outshone the Verde Green Special Deluxe coupe in a bodice-fitting dress adorned with pink metallic paillettes by Gayle Kirkpatrick for Fashions of Atelier. Mr. Kirkpatrick won a Coty Fashion Critics award in 1965.

The shoot paid homage to "Swinging London" as well with Jean Shrimpton, the iconic model who is credited with popularizing the miniskirt. She was dressed in a red, white, and blue minidress by Manhattan-based Joan "Tiger" Morse, who specialized in the mini length at her "Teeny Weeny" boutique on Madison Avenue. Silver Capezio shoes and a Turquoise 1967 GS-400 coupe completed Miss Shrimpton's ensemble.

And the Electra 225 Coupe is paired with none other than Suzy Parker herself. Suzy is often referred to as "the first supermodel," and the shoot wouldn't have been complete without her. The tall, statuesque redhead wore a gold Oscar De La Renta gown to match the Gold Mist–painted Electra—along with gold jewelry by J.K.L. There's even a credit for her hairstylist, Ingrid of Kenneth.

212 | GLAMOUR ROAD

CONVERTIBLES TO PUT A SONG IN YOUR HEART

These are the melodies that build our '67 Buick Convertible rhapsody. The soft caress of summer sun...a vaulted roof of stars...the sigh of wind in the trees...the rhythmic chuckle of rolling tires on warm pavement, all are preludes to that certain time when you climb into your new convertible by Buick and drop the top. It's a great, free feeling that must be experienced. It's a feeling that truly puts a song in your heart.

Electra 225...Bolero in sophistication. The subtle throb of power, sparkling embellishments on style, luxury in custom interiors, these are all a part of Electra 225, the ultimate in convertibles. Now, slide into foam-padded comfort. Peel back the top and feel the freedom of the great outside. Touch the array of controls to answer every command. Start it. Drive it. Now you know real roadability...true handling ease. Now you know how it feels to ride under the sun and stars, secure in the knowledge that the 360-hp engine and Super-Turbine transmission will respond to your needs, instantly. This is integrity in a fine automobile. This is cushioned comfort. This is romance on wheels...convertible living set to music. This is Electra 225.

Wildcat...Serenade to people on their way. Wildcat pulses with response and agility on the road in any model. But, put a convertible top on it and you've got light-hearted living with flair. The style and sweeping lines seem to put it in motion even at rest. It's a car for people on the move...for people going places. Take to the road and feel the tickle of 360-hp touch your toes. Catch the evening breeze at the flick of your finger and open the cabin to the star-studded blackness of soft summer nights. Feel the positive control and handling ease as you sweep into a curve on the highway. Sense the soft envelopment of padded cushions, spacious roominess and finger-tip convenience. It's all a part of Wildcat, tuned to perfection...the going-places machine.

LeSabre...Ballad to the girl next door. Popular, all-American beauty arranged with comfort, style and fine taste to reflect quality in every line, this is a LeSabre convertible. Look at the lines. Touch the fine finish. Delight in the sleek accents in steel and chrome. Slip into spacious inner comfort on padded cushions. Put down the top and experience the feeling of youthful freedom. These are magic moments with carpet soft on sand-flecked feet...happy moments with a seabreeze whipping your hair...quiet moments in the dappled shade of tree-lined boulevards. Under it all, rests a spirited 220-hp power plant and Buick integrity. Nowhere else can such full-sized style, comfort and roadability be packaged at the price. You and LeSabre were meant for each other and in her convertible mood you'll love her.

GS-400...Speaks in the language of jazz. Riffs and ripples from a brassy, sassy baby that performs...in spades. Hit a few hot licks and listen to the down-deep, tones of 340 horses under the deceptively simple bonnet. Climb behind the wheel and sink into a bucket seat just made for you. All the keys are at your fingertips so play a little counterpoint with the nimble-footed handling ease and instant response of the controls. Baby, this is life in the great outdoors. This is movin' music. It's music you can feel. This is a machine to take you way out and back again. "It's in." It's the Buick GS-400...the convertible with soul, man.

Skylark...Swing with a swinger. It's the popular Skylark convertible that sets a trend in style, tone, size and performance. The dash and color are all strictly Buick, but the price is less than you'd think. Up to 220 horses in V-8 harness put you right on the road for those moonlight spins. The big surprise is the comfort and ride, so much like the big Buicks. Skylark's fast on her feet, too, with a personality all her own. She'll match your mood whether it's family fun or a quiet ride with your special girl. If you're going to pick a swinger, pick the most popular swinger...Skylark.

BUICK INTERVIEWS MARTA RETZLAFF

Marta Retzlaff, two-time winner of the Mobil Economy Run, talks about her automotive hobby, the men she competes with and of course—other women.

Q. As a two time winner of the Mobil Economy Run Marta you must have gotten off to an early start. Who taught you to drive?

A. Actually I was a very athletic teenager, but hardly what you'd call a tomboy. I believe that girls can and should be feminine regardless of the activity. As for my driving, I owe a lot of credit to my Dad. He taught me control by having me stop at every corner and shift down to low again. I was only 14 at the time.

Q. Do you think that women are emotionally capable of handling emergencies that crop up in everyday driving?

A. Personally I feel that women handle more emergencies daily than men do, particularly with an injured child. Chances are a man will emotionally panic while a woman will calmly take the necessary steps to correct the situation. Emotional panic often comes through lack of knowledge or experience. So given the proper driving experiences, women should certainly be able to cope with driving emergencies as well as men.

Q. Has there been any noticeable male resentment against you because of your wins?

A. It's understandably hard for a man to be bested by a woman in any field or career. But I've found that the men I've been in competition with know what goes into making a win. They're fully aware of the practice and hours necessary to make the right reaction to driving situations come automatically. They have always respected my abilities and training in this area. These men know that to bring in a winner you need a car that's engineered in "economy details". The best driver in the second best car may win but the best car with a properly trained driver has the advantage. To my benefit, Buicks have been finely engineered for economy as well as performance.

Q. Do you think there's any truth to the remarks men make about the hazard of women drivers?

A. Well, there are always a few women, and men, too, who are hazards on the road. From those I know, I'd say women were wonderful drivers. Women often drive under conditions men never encounter. A car full of children and animals can be extremely distracting. But, now, with improved visibility and power assists available on our new cars there's no reason women should be thought "hazardous". The woman who does feel insecure and could become a hazard should get to know her car and adjust her seat for good pedal reach and visibility. Six-way power seats are marvelous for the small woman. High heels can be a problem, too. They throw the foot out of position and create muscle strain. I like to keep soft driving shoes in my car at all times.

Q. What got you started in competition?

A. Several years ago, my husband Jim, who's a Buick dealer, asked me if I'd be interested in the Mobil Economy Run. Since we had relatives living with us at the time, it was easy to get away and leave the children well cared for. To get me started, Buick factory engineers came out to the desert and showed me how to practice for a steady foot. This was in 1959 and I haven't missed a year since.

Q. How time consuming is your driving schedule?

A. When training for the Run I put in a lot of hours getting back in the "saddle". It's quite necessary since I need to build up my endurance to 10 to 12 hours on the road without feeling muscle aches and pains or fatigue. This year I put 7,000 miles on my practice car during the two months before the 3300 mile Run began—four week-end trips out of state over different 100 mile routes we had previously logged for use.

Q. Does this leave you any time for other hobbies or pastimes?

A. Like most American mothers I'm very interested in our public schools and what I can do to promote and protect the system. School board participation has been deeply rewarding and gives me a feeling of real accomplishment. I've also been a Girl Scout leader for the past four years and love to go camping with the girls.

Q. What in your opinion are the major reasons why a woman chooses one car over another? Are they usually different than a man's?

A. Within our own family we do have a difference of opinion as to desirable features in a car. Luckily we're a two car family. My car is always a wagon and Jim's is a beautiful coupe or convertible. Both men and women appreciate beauty equally but practicality comes first with me—like medium tone colors that won't show dirt readily and fabrics that are comfortable and easy to wash. I also like power windows all around so I can control as much as possible from the driver's seat, and the six way seat is a favorite since I'm quite tall and like to change positions.

Q. Would you encourage other women to enter driving competition?

A. Only if they have a real desire to compete. It does take a deep incentive to win—a vast amount of energy and drive. When the going gets rough and the sleep short, you need calm nerves, good humor, patience and the ability to remain alert and keep going.

Q. Do you have any words of advice for a woman who wants to take up competitive driving?

A. No advice really—only "Good Luck."

A Brief Note About Marta

She and her husband Jim live in Barstow, California with their five children—three boys and two girls—age 2 to 10. She won both of her Mobil Economy Runs in Buick LeSabres. The first in 1964 and the second in 1966. Most of her competitors were male.

214 | GLAMOUR ROAD

The revolutionary 1967 Buick brochure is an unforgettable sixty-page, full-color spectacular including just about every graphic style in a glossy-magazine format, featuring the top sports figures, fashion leaders, and Hollywood actors of the day.

Scrapbook for Wagons

From the world of high fashion, it's quite a transition to the family workhorses; namely, station wagons. Buick depicted them in a family photo album, done from the point of view of a young girl living in a horse ranch with two Buick wagons. (And don't all wagon owners live on horse ranches?) All the photos are made to look like snapshots glued into a scrapbook, the captions appear handwritten, and the overall effect is quite charming. In addition, there's an article highlighting Buick safety features and an interview with Martha Ratzlaff, who was a two-time winner of the Mobil Economy Run, which seem tailored to women buyers. There are also two-page sections in the back devoted to colors, options, specifications for each model, and engines.

Top Sports Legends for the Dadmobiles

So the convertibles have their watercolor renderings, the wagons have a photo album, and every Buick coupe comes with a supermodel. But how would Buick add some glamour to the Dadmobiles—the four-door sedans and hardtops that represent the bread and butter of Buick sales? Easy. To broaden the appeal to the Buick-driving Dads everywhere, each of the hardtops is shown with a sports legend. The brochure was called "the Sports Hall of Fame," and it featured golfer Sam Snead with the Electra 225, legendary football player and coach Joe Schmidt with the Wildcat, hockey star Ted Lindsay on the ice with a LeSabre, basketball great Bob Cousy with the Skylark, veteran New York Yankees shortstop Frank Crosetti with the Special Deluxe sedan, and boxing legend Rocky Marciano with a new Special sedan.

Major Hollywood Actors Show Off Interiors

And if you thought that the bankroll had already been blown, you were wrong—Buick saved the best for last and went all out on their giant "67 Premiere of the Buick Interiors" section. Hosted by movie actress Diana Lynn—best known for costarring with Martin and Lewis—Buick showed each model's interior in a sixteen-page spread, with a major Hollywood movie actor of the day seated behind the wheel. The section featured Robert Taylor, Cornell Wilde, Charlton Heston, Cliff Robertson, Gardner McKay, Bill Bixby, Stuart Whitman, Tony Franciosa, Fess Parker, Van Heflin, Robert Cummings, Lloyd Bridges, Robert Lansing, and David Janssen, all black-tie clad and seated in a new Buick, while Miss Lynn commented on the TV or film projects that each star was working on.

And there it is—the revolutionary 1967 brochure, an unforgettable sixty-page, full-color spectacular featuring just about every graphic style of the day in a shockingly different format, featuring the top sports figures, fashion leaders, and Hollywood actors of the day. A classic from the first day, and according to GM insiders, it was the most expensive Buick brochure ever produced.

This Apple Red Wildcat is shown with the glamorous Dutch-born supermodel Wilhelmina. Willi Cooper was an icon in the industry and opened her own agency, Wilhelmina Models, in 1967. Willi was the height of sixties chic, leaning against the hood in her black Pauline Trigère gown and flying-saucer hat by Emme.

216 | GLAMOUR ROAD

FASHIONS BY PAULINE TRIGERE. HAT BY EMME.

The Wildcat & Wilhelmina

"I know cars quite well.
I know what they should be
and what they are.
Buick is a very good car;
it is strong, but quiet.
I can sense its strength and power.
"But what makes Buick
one of the world's best automobiles
is that it is a complete automobile.
It has power, yes.
But it is also luxurious.
It is sporty.
It is elegant.
It is tailored.
"I think American automobiles
have undergone
the same kind of change as fashions
in the last ten years.
They've become very young.
But too often they're showy.
Perhaps this is why
I've always appreciated Buick.
It is very modern.
But it is also very elegant.
When I saw this Wildcat,
I fell madly in love with it."

Buick Goes All Out | 217

The Skylark & Dolores Wettach

"I have an old 1940 Buick.
Right now it's sitting in Vermont
in my sugar orchard.
When I gather maple syrup
in the springtime,
I sit in it to keep warm.
When my father hunts, he uses it, too,
but he thinks I should get rid of it.
I don't want to.
I always like to hang on to things
that mean something to me.
"I've always been very competitive.
I love to win.
I love the winning sense
of strength and power in certain cars.
I can see it in this Buick.
"How would I use this Buick?
I'd put my dog in it and
go for long rides in the country...
anywhere.
Or better yet, I'd use it
to take my mother to Alaska
...she always jokes
about panning gold
and you'd certainly need
a tough car up there."

FASHIONS BY CHUCK HOWARD OF TOWNLEY. SHOES BY CAPEZIO.

Dolores Wettach posed with an Ivory Skylark Sport Coupe, wearing a topknot hairdo and a white, bare-midriff knit top and slacks ensemble by Chuck Howard of Townley. She was a top Vogue model who went on to marry American baseball Hall of Fame inductee Ted Williams.

Pretty young blonde Penny Ashton outshone the Verde Green Special Deluxe coupe in a bodice-fitting dress adorned with pink metallic paillettes by Gayle Kirkpatrick for Fashions of Atelier. Mr. Kirkpatrick won a Coty Fashion Critics award in 1965.

FASHIONS OF ATELIER BY GAYLE KIRKPATRICK.

The Special Deluxe & Penny Ashton

"I think this Buick is a real groove.
It's a sharp car. It's clean.
It's fine. It's smooth.
It's a conservative car,
but in a chic sort of way.
"I like way-out things,
young things, different things.
But I don't like gimmicks.
I like things that are so clean
they're really outstanding.
"When I dress to go out,
I wear plain things,
clothes with beautiful lines and
beautiful cloth, but young clothes.
I think it's more important
that the things you wear
show you off than just
show off themselves.
It's the same with a car.
"A car has to compliment you.
It has to make you look good.
I don't like fads, so I don't worry
about who's wearing what
and who's driving what.
I just want to know that
my clothes and my car fit me.
This Buick Special would
make anyone look good."

Buick Goes All Out | 221

The LeSabre & Dolores Hawkins

"My husband and I
have a farm in New York
near the mountains
with lots of room for our horses.
Can you see what would happen
if I drove up to a horseshow
pulling my trailer
with this chic LeSabre?
"The ideal thing for me would be
to have a Buick station wagon
for the farm
and this LeSabre for going places
and to use in New York.
"I think a woman should always
wear the things that suit her,
not just the things that are in Vogue.
I like simplicity
in everything I wear.
I think that
you have to choose a car
the same way you choose
your clothing
—it should be suited to you.
It should fit you
and the things you like.
The LeSabre's a very special car;
you can see that immediately."

FASHIONS BY CHUCK HOWARD OF TOWNLEY.

222 | GLAMOUR ROAD

Dolores Hawkins, another Vogue model, wears a Chuck Howard jumper of lemon yellow and cerise and is perched atop a sleek Burgundy Mist Le Sabre coupe.

Buick Goes All Out | 223

Jean Shrimpton—the iconic "Swinging London" model who is credited with popularizing the miniskirt—is dressed in a red, white, and blue minidress by Manhattan-based Joan "Tiger" Morse, who specialized in the mini length at her "Teeny Weeny" boutique on Madison Avenue. Silver Capezio shoes and a Turquoise 1967 GS-400 coupe complete Miss Shrimpton's ensemble.

224 | GLAMOUR ROAD

FASHIONS BY TIGER MORSE. SHOES BY CAPEZIO.

The GS 400 & Jean Shrimpton

"In London
 we're used to very small cars.
 The GS 400
 is so much larger,
 so much more comfortable.
 But, you know,
 it still has that sporty look,
 that special flair
 It would get a lot of attention
 in London.
"I'm funny about cars.
 I like cars that look and act
 like they have a lot of power.
 The minute I saw the GS 400
 I liked it.
 You can sense its power.
"In some ways cars are like fashions.
 Some fashions are obviously
 extreme, and some cars
 are built the same way.
 Not so with this Buick.
 Even though it's very fine
 and very young,
 it's quite casual and relaxed
"Perhaps the best way I can think of
 to describe this car
 is . . . it's simply fabulous.
 I'd really love to drive it at home."

Buick Goes All Out | 225

The Electra 225 & Suzy Parker

"When I was in school,
I knew a boy whose name was Buick
... Buick Jackson or Johnson
or something.
Anyway, he was named Buick
because he was born on the way
to the hospital
in the back seat of his father's Buick.
You've got to admit he was lucky.
Buick's a good name.
I've heard Buick Jackson
... or whatever it was ...
is quite a success.
"A woman should think of her car
as a personal accessory
like jewelry.
She doesn't wear just any
piece of jewelry
and she shouldn't
wear just any kind of car.
When you're in a car,
you're really wearing it
and people's opinion of the car
is their opinion of you.
"To me Buick is like a fine piece
of jewelry.
It looks good;
it has fine architectural lines.
But it's even nicer inside.
It's nice to drive,
but it's a lot more fun
just to ride in and enjoy."

FASHIONS BY OSCAR DE LA RENTA. HAIR BY INGRID OF KENNETH. JEWELRY BY J.K.L.

And the Electra 225 Coupe is paired with none other than Suzy Parker herself. Suzy is often referred to as "the first supermodel," and the shoot wouldn't have been complete without her. The tall, statuesque redhead wore a gold Oscar De La Renta gown to match the Gold Mist–painted Electra—along with gold jewelry by J.K.L. There's even a credit for her hairstylist, Ingrid of Kenneth.

DIANA LYNN AND FRIENDS AT THE '67 PREMIERE OF THE BUICK INTERIORS

Guests in order of their appearance:

Robert Taylor
Cornell Wilde
Charlton Heston
Cliff Robertson
Gardner McKay
Bill Bixby
Stuart Whitman
Tony Franciosa
Fess Parker
Van Heflin
Robert Cummings
Lloyd Bridges
Robert Lansing
David Janssen

Diana Lynn steps out of the new Riviera.

228 | GLAMOUR ROAD

THE ELECTRA 225 INTERIORS

The sheer size and comfort of Electra 225 is manifest in the Madrid grain vinyl notchback seats shown above. They're standard equipment in the Custom sport coupe, convertible, and available at no extra cost in the 4-door Custom Electra hardtop and Custom 4-door sedan. Colors are blue, saddle or black in all models plus red in the sport coupe and convertible. Strato bucket seats can also be ordered in the convertible in black. The standard seat in the Custom 225 4-door sedan and hardtop sedan is an unusual combination of two exotic materials. Barcarole for the broader areas and Bard cloth for a tasteful tapestry accent that's as rich as it looks. Available in green, blue, maroon or black.

"The face is familiar but I can't seem to place the name. Let me see. Moses? No. Michelangelo? No. Ben Hur? No. Charlton Heston? Of course. And currently complicating matters even further by playing Chinese Gordon in 'Khartoum', a United Artist release."

"KHARTOUM" IS A JULIAN BLAUSTEIN PRODUCTION

Charleton Heston looks comfortable in the Electra 225 Custom.

Gardner McKay looks dignified in the Electra 225 with base trim.

What a variety of Electra 225 interiors to choose from. Standard 225 trim is Brocatel cloth and beautifully rugged Madrid grain vinyl. Available in the sport coupe, 4-door sedan and 4-door hardtop sedan in blue, black, champagne or aqua. You can also order this same seat in solid Madrid grain vinyl in dove or black in the sport coupe and 4-door hardtop sedan. To give you an idea of just how roomy Electra 225 really is—you get 40 inches of leg room in both front and rear seats, over 38 inches of headroom, and shoulder room that exceeds 60 inches. It's a moving living room

"You sailing fans will remember Gardner McKay from 'Adventures in Paradise.' Well, Gardner can't seem to stay away from adventure. His new TV series (which he also produces and directs) is called 'I Love Adventure'."

Buick Goes All Out | 229

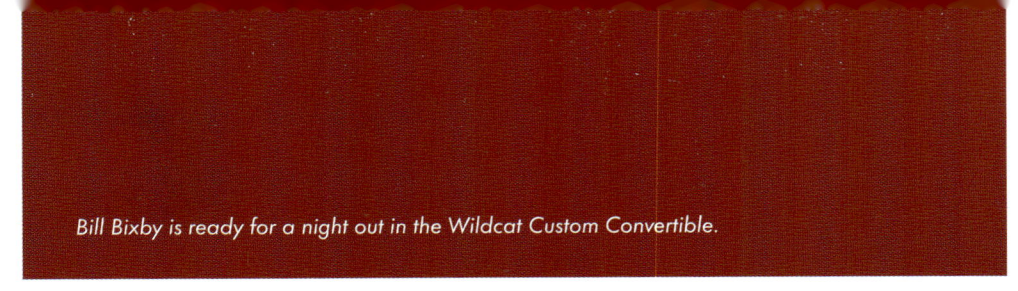

Bill Bixby is ready for a night out in the Wildcat Custom Convertible.

THE WILDCAT INTERIORS

Custom Wildcat interior features Madrid grain vinyl notchback — beautifully contoured for maximum driving comfort. Available in the sport coupe and 4-door hardtop sedan in blue, dove, aqua or black and the convertible in blue, dove, red or black. Other luxury touches are upper and lower door panel moldings of extruded aluminum, a center panel molding of horizontally brushed aluminum and carpeting that covers the lower portion of the door on 2-door models. You can also order Madrid grain vinyl bucket seats in black that recline on the passenger side and a shifting console as optional equipment.

"Know this guy? It's Bill Bixby, star of MGM's Doctor, You've Got To Be Kidding. Bill is best known for his TV role in 'My Favorite Martian' — a logical place to develop a taste for out-of-this world transportation."

MR. BIXBY CAN ALSO BE SEEN IN COLUMBIA PICTURES' "RIDE BEYOND VENGEANCE".

230 | GLAMOUR ROAD

THE SPORTWAGON INTERIORS

Rugged Custom Sportwagon interior with child-proof vinyl is featured throughout as a sensible approach to high style for young families. The exposed stitch seat cushion and back insert area is bordered by a tooled overlay of colored vinyl—a motif that also appears on the upper door panel. The lower portion of the door panel is carpeted for added protection against scuffs. Colors for the three-seat models are green, blue, black or saddle. Two-seat models are available in blue, red, black or saddle.

"That Buick Sportwagon must really be something to seat comfortably the likes of Fess Parker. Why he's as tall as Daniel Boone. As a matter of fact he is 'Daniel Boone' on NBC TV. Fess stars also in a current motion picture, the remake of Will James' 'Smoky', a 20th Century-Fox release."

DANIEL BOONE, 'IS AN ARCOLA FEI/PAR PRODUCTION. SMOKY IS AN ARCOLA PICTURES PRODUCTION.

And Fess Parker does his best Daniel Boone in the western-themed Sportwagon.

Lloyd Bridges picked the wrong week to give up Skylark. (Think about it, Airplane! fans)

THE SKYLARK INTERIORS

"Here's a guy who took to the sea— swimming and diving his way to television fame. Lloyd Bridges can be seen in his latest MGM movie, 'Around the World Under the Sea'."

"AROUND THE WORLD UNDER THE SEA" IS AN IVAN TORS PRODUCTION

Featured above—the standard Skylark interior for Thin Pillar Coupe, and Sport Coupe. A combination of Beaufort body cloth with Brent bolster and vinyl in blue, champagne and black. For convertibles in all-vinyl dove or black. The hardtop sedan features notchback seats in cloth and vinyl in blue, champagne, maroon or black. For an especially plush effect, Madrid grain vinyl notchback seats may be ordered in blue and black for all models, and, in addition, red and saddle for convertibles, dove for hardtop sedans and dove and aqua for Thin Pillar and sport coupes. All-vinyl bucket seats will add a sporty feel to your Skylark. These are available in dove, black and blue for both Coupes and in red, blue and black for convertibles.

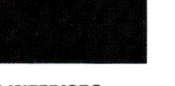

THE RIVIERA INTERIORS

Exquisite styling and tastefully luxurious decor in the Custom Riviera are highlighted by strato bench seat of Barcelle cloth and Madrid grain vinyl in champagne or black. This same seat also comes in solid vinyl in plum, green, black or white. Or if you prefer, strato bucket seats in Madrid grain vinyl are available in blue, saddle, aqua or black. Notice the fold down arm rest between the seat backs in this strato bench design. The seat back reclines on the passenger side, and headrests can be ordered for both driver and passenger. Even the door panels reflect Riviera's custom trim. Jewel-like chrome and deep, durable carpeting that extends part way up the door.

"Oh by the way, the handsome fella who looks like Spangler Arlington Brugh is—you guessed it —Robert Taylor. Bob is currently swapping bullets in MGM's 'Return of the Gunfighter'."

Robert Taylor shows off the Riviera Custom interior.

Buick Goes All Out | 231

*One question remains—
how did they get all of those
celebrities into the interiors?*

The Secret Ledger

One question remains—how did they get all of those celebrities into the interiors?

For the answer, we turn to a worn ledger book, wrapped in duct tape, that was used to keep track of the Buick Los Angeles Zone Office Company cars. The entries were made by Phil Vogel, Buick's longtime company car coordinator. Phil called the notebook his "Buick Bible" and never let it out of his sight.

Each car was logged by model, color, trim, key numbers, license number, delivery date, and driver. A glance through reveals some of the drivers that Buick provided cars for. Jack Entratter owned the Sands Hotel in Las Vegas. Dick Van Dyke and Frank Sinatra you've probably already heard of.

And it's the Buick Bible that unravels the mystery of the celebrities in the 1967 Buick interiors—first one finds company car entries for Robert Lansing and Charleton Heston. Lansing was given an Electra convertible, Heston a Riviera. Both cars were hard plated as opposed to sporting manufacturer's plates.

Continue scrolling and it all falls into place. Cliff Robertson and Van Heflin both got Sportwagons. Fess Parker got a Riviera and David Janssen chose an Electra Convertible. Both Bill Bixby and Lloyd Bridges were furnished with new Rivieras. And now we understand—every celebrity that appeared in the brochure sitting inside a new Buick was *given* a brand-new Buick.

By today's standards, it was a pretty inexpensive way to obtain endorsements. But I'd love to know who approved the budget, and it's no surprise that the 1968 Buick brochure was a far more conventional affair, with nary a supermodel or Hollywood celebrity in sight. But that doesn't in any way delete the magic that was the 1967 piece.

And I can't help but wonder how many of the celebrities still have their free Buicks.

Buick Goes All Out | 233

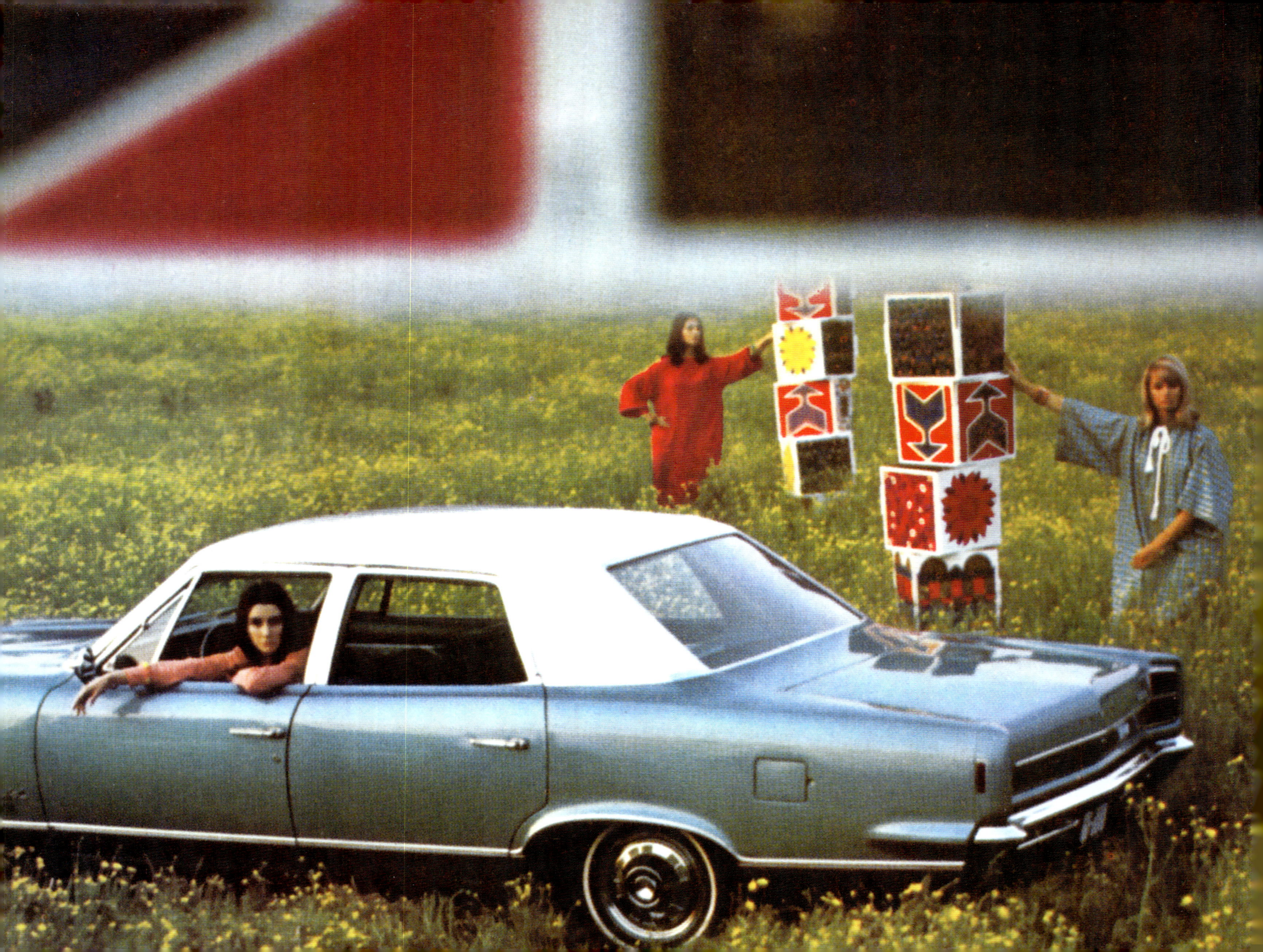

Chapter Twelve

TURN, TURN, TURN

MARY WELLS, POP ART, OP ART, AND PSYCHEDELIA END THE SIXTIES

◀ Mary Wells took over AMC advertising in 1967 and flipped the company from being practical and dowdy to being cool and "with it."

In the mid-sixties, Mary Wells Lawrence was arguably the most powerful woman in the auto industry. And yet she never worked for a car company. It's a great tale involving the Big Three and the Little Fourth.

By the mid-sixties, American Motors was in a world of hurt. Once the profitable niche maker of station wagons and the darling of college professors (in those pre-Volvo days), AMC had made some product blunders. They had tried to go head to head with the Big Three, a game for which they were sorely unprepared. They spent $60 million on a badly needed product update plan, but the bills were rapidly coming due. The chief architect of the expansion, a guy named Roy Abernathy, was forced out over the dire financial position he had put them in. AMC needed a savior, and fast—they decided it would be none other than Mary Wells Lawrence. Mary was the Wonder Woman of Madison Avenue, the woman who painted Braniff planes purple and gave Alka-Seltzer its plop-plop fizz-fizz.

Mary opened the door of her hip, mod ad agency Wells, Rich and Greene one morning in 1966 and found AMC chairman Roy Chapin on his knees begging for help. AMC was on death's door. The agency partners were skeptical—the company was in such dire shape they were afraid they couldn't pay for the ads. She admittedly relished the challenge but agreed to take the account only because she thought the upcoming Javelin was marketable. But first, she had to sell enough '67s that the company could raise the money to even get the Javelin to market.

Mary created a hard-hitting campaign called the NOW Cars. Whether the bold tagline really meant AMC needed money NOW is best left to speculation. The NOW Cars featured bold graphics and colors and bold brass horns. It was undeniably brassy and bold. She positioned AMC as the "Company on Top of Today." The Ambassador was NOW Full-Sized comfort, the American had NOW Typhoon Power in a compact, and the Rebel was NOW the First Excitement Machine in the Intermediate Class.

Her Ambassador commercials literally rolled a red carpet in front of the car to demonstrate ride quality. She added free air-conditioning and compared it to Cadillac and Rolls-Royce. The brand-new intermediate Rebel was placed in the hands of fearless driving instructors to prove its durability. If it can stand up to this, they said, it can stand up to you. The brochure set the cars in fields of wildflowers with young people and Alexander Girard–inspired folk art. Young girls ate watermelon on the bucket

The 1967 AMC brochure is chockful of slightly wacky images that match the youthful antiestablishment zeitgeist of the era.

Mary Wells created a 1967 advertising campaign called the NOW Cars. The bold tagline could have referred to AMC needing money NOW.

seat; bangled hands gripped the steering wheel in the detail shots. It was peace, love, and flower power—and a 180-degree turn from the dowdy Rambler.

And they went all out in '68 for the introduction of the sporty Javelin and its two-seat companion, the AMX. It was a genuine challenge. AMC had about 3% market share, which Mary noted meant 97% of buyers didn't know the cars or what they stood for. She decided the way to introduce it was by comparing it in ads to the Mustang, probably the best-known and most-loved car on the planet. She sold AMC on the campaign by explaining that they never said the Mustang was bad, mind you—just pointed out ways in which the Javelin was better. The result was a bold ad showing both cars with the headline "An Unfair Comparison between the Javelin and the Mustang"—unfair, of course, because the Javelin had so many advantages. It went directly against a long-standing gentleman's agreement among the Big Three not to do direct comparisons, but Mary noted she didn't have the luxury of wearing white gloves—they had to sell Javelins. The television commercials were exceptionally daring—in the launch ad, workers smash a mockup of a Mustang and build the Javelin in its place. Comedian Herb Edelman drove a new Javelin across town and found that at every stoplight, people challenged him to a race. He declined because he had a bowl of goldfish on the seat. When he reached his destination, he gave the car to a parking attendant, and all you heard was the screeching of tires.

Mary noted, *"In that era of anti-authority, American Motors was transformed into the young man's sporty automobile company because we dared. Sledgehammering an icon seemed a wondrous thing to young people."*[1]

The campaign worked. Not only did they sell Javelins, but they improved sales on the other models as well. And the new-owner surveys brought excellent news indeed, since 57% of Javelin buyers were under thirty five and 53% of them were conquests from other brands. Mary reported that the comparison campaign was so effective that she found herself personally uninvited from dinner parties where certain Ford family members would be present. The financial health of the company was restored—for now anyway—and Mary Wells Lawrence sold Ramblers to flower children.

To summarize in her own words, *"It was a love affair for a long time. We enjoyed each other and learned from each other. I learned, for example, that a business based on engineering can be just as romantic in the eyes of its people as the movie business, publishing or advertising... Dick Teague was a sculptor of undulating steel, a Frank Gehry of the auto design business and the Javelin was his Bilbao, his life was filled with grace, every new project was the best one he ever had. Since then I've had my eye out for romantics in business, they are full of ideas, and I am crazy about people who are happy in their work."*[2]

236 | GLAMOUR ROAD

An unfair comparison between the Mustang and the Javelin.

We asked a professional photographer to take a picture of both cars under identical conditions.

Thereby putting the Mustang at a disadvantage.

Our Javelin is equipped with massive contour bumpers.

Unfair to Mustang, because thin blade bumpers don't photograph as well.

Our Javelin is endowed with yards of costly glass. Side windows are all one piece, without vents to break up the line.

Unfair, because Mustang isn't nearly so generous.

Our Javelin has a richer, more polished look. Roof joints are hand-finished.

Unfair, because it is cheaper to make roof joints by machine.

Our Javelin has a bigger displacement and more horsepower in its standard 6-cylinder engine, bigger displacement in its standard V-8.

Unfair.

Our Javelin has more leg room, more head room, the backseat is a good 5 inches wider.

Unfair.

Our Javelin has a bigger gas tank, a roomier trunk, a more powerful battery.

Unfair.

Our Javelin comes with a sophisticated (flow-through) ventilation system, wheel discs, reclining bucket seats and a woodgrain steering wheel.

And, unfairest of all, our Javelin lists for no more than the Mustang.

The preceding comparison was made between a 1968 Javelin SST and a 1967 Mustang Hardtop, only because this year's model was not available from the manufacturer in time for this printing.

We really tried to get one.

American Motors
Ambassador · Rebel · American · And the new Javelin

The 1967 Mustang

The 1968 Javelin SST

Price comparison based on 1968 list prices. Vinyl tops and whitewall tires optional on both cars.

In a bold move, AMC compared itself directly to the most popular car on the road in this 1968 ad.

◀ By the early 1970s, car companies became aware that they needed to include Black models. This outtake from a 1971 photo shoot for Chrysler by Boulevard Photographic has an interesting op-art feel—and perhaps social commentary—with a black-and-white theme. (Courtesy of the National Automotive History Collection, Detroit Public Library)

Ebony Breaks the Color Barrier

There is no doubt that the Black consumer was very important to the auto industry, even if they were reticent about acknowledging it publicly. The reality is that, in less enlightened times when there were red-lined housing tracts and clubs that weren't open to Black consumers, the automobile was one symbol of prosperity that *was* accessible.

Even that didn't come easily. In the 1930s, it was not unusual for a wealthy Black customer to hire a white person to buy a Cadillac for them. It was only when the GM board of directors was seriously considering the idea of discontinuing the Cadillac division that then chief engineer Nicholas Dreystadt told the board that he believed he could save the division if GM would allow dealers to sell to Black customers. They did. Dreystadt was named general manager of the division, and Cadillac ultimately survived the Depression.

Ebony magazine was founded in 1945. It was a lifestyle magazine along the lines of *Life* and *Look* but targeted at Black families. As it became more popular, it had no problem attracting advertisers—including the automobile companies in the postwar years. In the beginning, advertisers simply ran the same ads as in other publications, but as the sixties dawned, things changed. There are PR photos of 1958 Plymouths alongside Black models, but the first car ads with Black models that we have found appeared in late 1959 for the Studebaker Lark. There was a whole series of ads showing an attractive couple with their new Larks, including a convertible in front of an aircraft hangar and a private plane, and two young couples standing around a Lark sedan on their patio, as one did back in the day.

More ads followed, and manufacturers were not shy about showing off their more expensive, high-end cars. In the November 1961 issue, they had a whole editorial section called "New Cars for 1962—Mechanical improvements prevail over drastic style changes." The section was a full five and a half pages long and mostly in color, showing a wide range of models from Corvair to Cadillac and Falcon to Thunderbird, with Imperial and Lincoln Continental given prominence as well. The photos shown were standard PR shots with no models at all, but two of the accompanying ads—for Dodge and Buick—clearly showed Black models. By the late '60s, racially integrated

▲ These 1960 ads for the Studebaker Lark, which ran exclusively in Ebony magazine, were among the first car ads to include Black models.

▶ These two ads—for the Dodge Dart and Buick Invicta—appeared in the November 1961 issue of Ebony.

ads were not only common in *Ebony*, but the ads crossed over to mainstream publications as well. And by the dawn of the '70s it became a common sight.

Soon Black models would also appear in new-product brochure photography. The last Pontiac brochure to utilize the watercolor renderings of Art Fitzpatrick and Van Kaufman in 1971 was also the first to include a Black couple, posing proudly with their new lime-green Bonneville.

And Cadillac, which first internally acknowledged the importance of the Black community to its bottom line back in the 1930s, finally broke through the color barrier some four decades later with a racially integrated product brochure in 1977.

Turn, Turn, Turn | 239

By the late 1960s, more car companies included Black models portrayed as car owners in photo shoots—and they weren't afraid to feature their premium cars in Ebony magazine. Below left, 1970 Mercury Marquis; right, 1970 Pontiac Bonneville; far right, 1970 Dodge Charger.

▶ *Opposite: the general-market car brochures were slower to include nonwhite models. This full-page illustration by Art Fitzpatrick and Van Kaufman in the 1971 Pontiac brochure was one of the first.*

240 | GLAMOUR ROAD

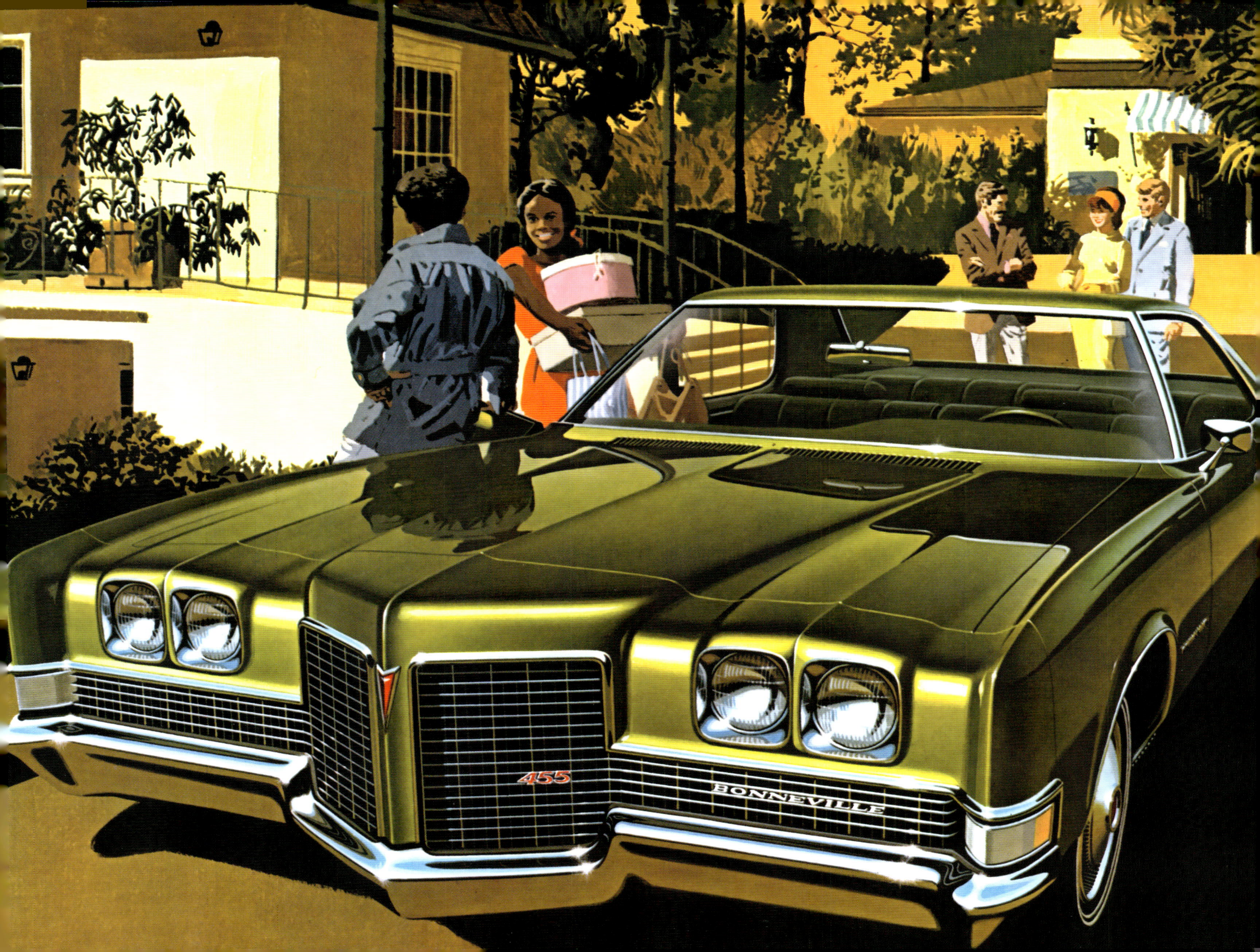
455
BONNEVILLE

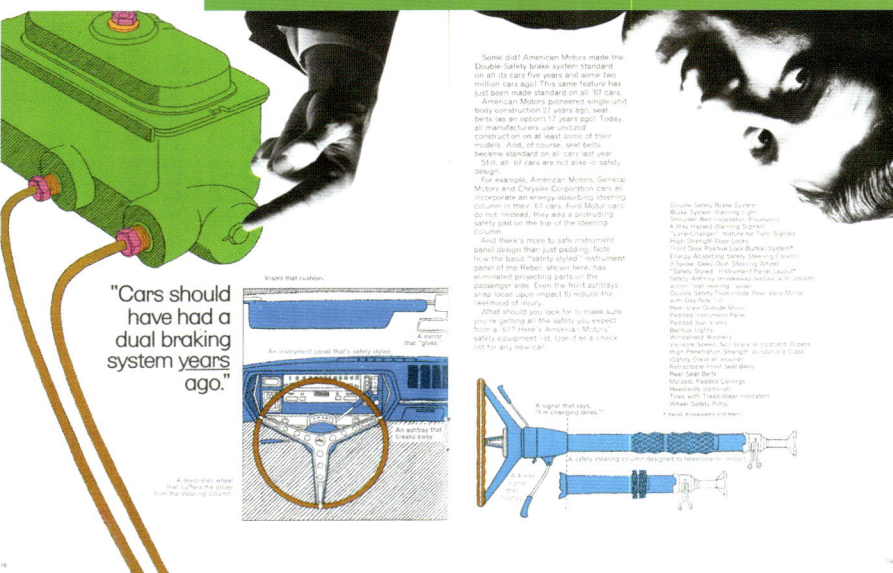

▲ AMC produced an "X-Ray" brochure every year to provide the technical details of their cars (and would often compare them to the competition). This brochure from 1967 adopted the pop-art graphics of the era.

242 | GLAMOUR ROAD

The pop-art graphic style combined bold colors, posterized images, overlaps, and an irreverent attitude that matched the mood of the era.

▲ The 1965 Marlin was a halo car for AMC, with a sporty look and distinctive styling to reach a younger audience. The bold, graphic art direction for this ad featured black-and-white op-art graphics.

there are five ways to Let yourself go... Plymouth in '66

Pop Art and Op Art

The pop-art movement started in Britain in the 1950s but reached its height of popularity during the 1960s. Artists such as Andy Warhol, James Rosenquist, and Claes Oldenburg used common popular imagery, much of it pulled from mass media and consumer culture, and utilized mechanical techniques such as silkscreen to give it a sharp, colorful, and optimistic look. Off-register printing was a favorite of Andy Warhol's, and the 1966 Plymouth brochure seen here proudly displays that technique. It's brash, modern, and young and reflects the definitive style of the mid-'60s.

In 1965, *The Responsive Eye* exhibition was held at New York's Museum of Modern Art and immediately raised interest in the concept of op art, a perceptual experience of color relationships and the illusion of movement. Op art gained favor with fashion and interior designers, since it often involved patterning in striking color combinations—most notably black and white. Verner Panton created radical and psychedelic interiors of his curved furniture, wall upholstery, textiles, and lighting. His designs endured and are still in production today. In the fashion sphere, Yves Saint Laurent, Mary Quant, and André Courrèges all incorporated op art in their fashion lines. Pierre Cardin went further and created fashions, furniture, and entire lifestyle environments with his futuristic graphic designs—and even a fabulous interior for the AMC Javelin in 1972.

Both pop art and op art became synonymous with the youth culture of the 1960s. Although the car companies were hesitant to go too radical with their car designs, pop/op art did become an effective way to make their cars seem "with it!" Case in point—the 1966 Ford Fairlane brochure seen on the following pages.

Turn, Turn, Turn

The 1966 Ford Fairlane brochure goes op art!

244 | GLAMOUR ROAD

Turn, Turn, Turn | 245

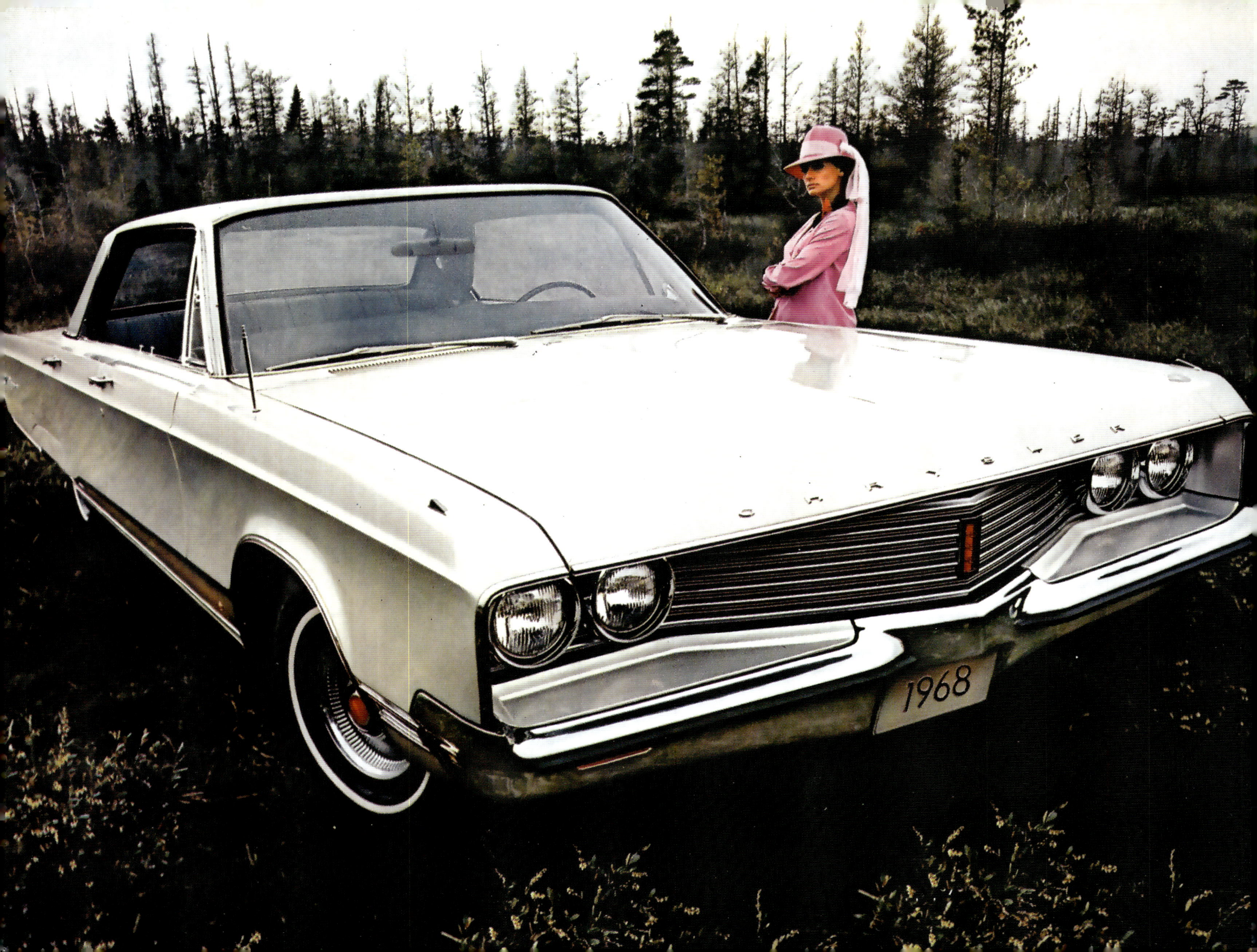
1968

Driving through the Glamorous Apocalypse

Enough with the flower children and optimism! Although the film *Mad Max* was eleven years away, Chrysler decided to give us a preview of that postapocalyptic world to showcase their new lineup for the 1968 brochure. Solitary figures with blank expressions, cars assertively positioned in the middle of nowhere (Did they location-scout the moon?), the barren landscapes (Is that morning fog, or are the trees smoldering?), and cars that all seem to be shot in black and white give us a cheerless look at that year's lightly restyled vehicles.

Of course, the late '60s was a turbulent period, and maybe Chrysler's art directors were going for the mood of the times as assassinations, riots, and the Vietnam War consumed the news cycles. But it makes you wonder—did the caftan-clad model with shovel in hand *(left)* just bury a few bodies, transported in the back of her elegant Town & Country wagon?

Turn, Turn, Turn | 247

▶ 1970 Plymouth ad featuring psychedelic cartoons of their performance lineup

Psychedelia Hits the Showroom

It's doubtful any car manufacturer wanted to conjure an acid trip when you walked into their showroom circa 1968, but they were always agreeable to co-opting a trend. After the Summer of Love in 1967, the prevailing youth style quickly transitioned from the slick graphics of pop art to the edgy, cartoonish, and slightly hallucinogenic style of psychedelia. That was reflected in ads for mostly performance cars, especially from Plymouth and Dodge.

"Today's car blossoms with flowered tops, bold stripes and colors that are mixed to order 'like prescriptions,' as one paint company executive put it," from the story "Colors Enhance, Sell Cars" in the December 1, 1968, *Detroit Free Press*. "'And tastes are getting wilder, especially among buyers of performance cars,' Bill Brownlie, chief stylist of Dodge studios, said."

Starting in 1968, bold, saturated colors were offered for sporty cars with names like Competition Orange, Grabber Green, Big Bad Blue, and Daytona Yellow. Striping and graphics got more aggressive too. By the end of the decade, these color trends filtered down to popular cars and continued into the early '70's.

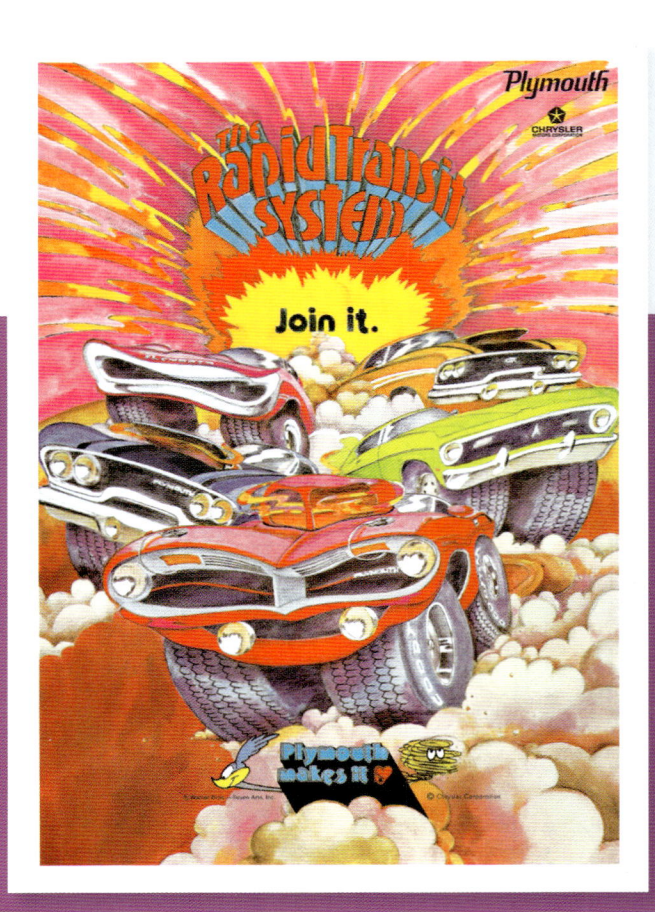

Two ads for 1968 Plymouths

▶ Opposite: 1968 Oldsmobile 442 ad with a model in full bohemian Woodstock attire, down to the eccentric sandals and enormous braided ponytail

248 | GLAMOUR ROAD

Turn, Turn, Turn | 249

The Wildcat & Wilhelmina

'I know cars quite well.
I know what they should be
and what they are.
Buick is a very good car;
it is strong, but quiet.
I can sense its strength and power.
"But what makes Buick
one of the world's best automobiles
is that it is a complete automobile.
It has power, yes.
But it is also luxurious.
It is sporty.
It is elegant.
It is tailored.
"I think American automobiles
have undergone
the same kind of change as fashions
in the last ten years.
They've become very young.
But too often they're showy.
Perhaps this is why
I've always appreciated Buick.
It is very modern.
But it is also very elegant.
When I saw this Wildcat,
I fell madly in love with it."

An Ode to Pauline Trigère

The old adage that the two things likeliest to survive nuclear holocaust are cockroaches and Cher has gotten around so much that it's even appeared in the *Washington Post*. And while we have no reason to doubt its wisdom, we will pause only to add that if it were to happen, she would probably appear in a gown by Pauline Trigère.

Yes, Pauline Trigère, the Parisian-born fashion designer and the Energizer Bunny of fashion for automobile advertising, whose affiliation with the industry dates back to the Kaiser-Frazer ads of the late 1940s and who kept going well into the 1980s. She has the somewhat dubious honor of having outlasted many of the brands she designed clothes for.

She flanked a new 1947 Kaiser with a summer dinner dress of Chinese silk, created fashions for the Imperial Fashion Show of 1955, dressed a young lady in a floral print dress with matching parasol alongside a new 1956 Oldsmobile on a bluff in Pebble Beach, and created custom gowns out of Fisher Body upholstery material in the 1960s. She even dressed legendary fashion model Wilhelmina in a black crepe gown for the breakout 1967 Buick brochure.

And now in late 1969, in the very last moments of the timeline of this book, she hitched her wagon to a car. Not any car, mind you, but the very smart Mercury Cougar Houndstooth Edition, which featured a houndstooth check, full-vinyl roof with matching cloth inserts on the "hi-back" bucket seats. She even designed a houndstooth cape to match and was credited by name in the advertisement. So after twenty-five years dressing models standing next to a car, she finally got to design the car itself. And while she was at it, she almost created the designer car fad to boot—but that was still a couple years off and will have to be a story for another day.

250 | GLAMOUR ROAD

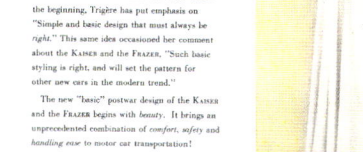

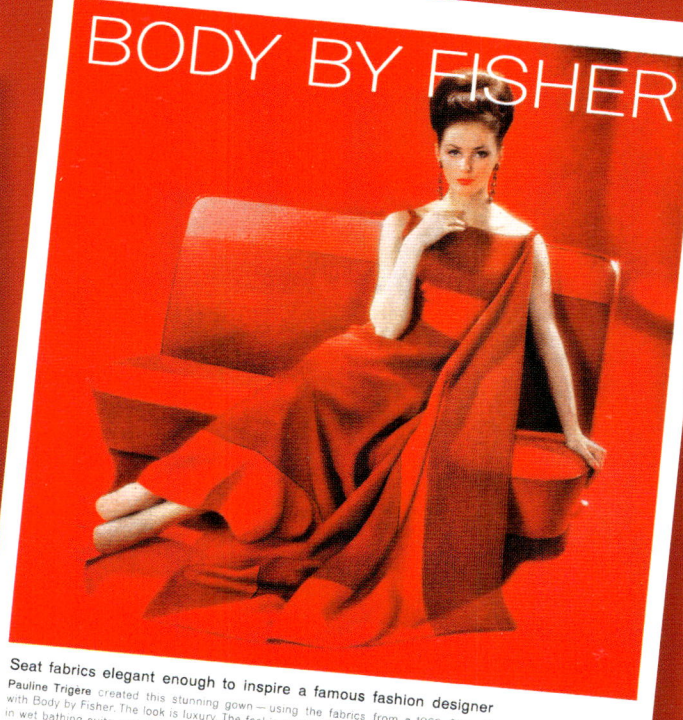

paulinetrigère

View by Pebble Beach · *Flowered Print by* Pauline Trigère · *Holiday 98 by* Oldsmobile · *Body by* Fisher

Bold, beautiful trend-of-tomorrow design! Excitingly, exclusively yours in Bodies by Fisher — whose solid excellence of structure and exactness of fit evidence the many millions of dollars devoted to advanced construction techniques. For commanding style, greater safety and lasting value it is good common sense to choose a car with Body by Fisher.

"Be careful...drive safely"

BODY by FISHER

GM on cars only: **CHEVROLET · PONTIAC · OLDSMOBILE · BUICK · CADILLAC**

1954 Oldsmobile in a Fisher Body ad

▶ 1970 Mercury Cougar, with houndstooth top, upholstery, and matching cape by Pauline Trigère

252 | GLAMOUR ROAD

Introducing the Houndstooth Cougar... with a little something to match by Pauline Trigère.

It's wild. It's sophisticated. It's elegant. The sporty look of houndstooth for spring. Cougar sets the trend with houndstooth check vinyl roof and hi-back cloth-and-vinyl buckets. Designer Pauline Trigère comes up with a swaggering houndstooth cape to match. Cougar... far more than just a sporty car. It's styled with European flair. Lean and sculptured, with concealed headlamps and sequential rear turn signals. Powered by a restless 351 cubic-inch V-8. It's the best equipped luxury-sports car in its class. Cougar. Definitely the top cat for spring... now dressed in houndstooth. Ask about it at the sign of the cat: your Lincoln-Mercury dealer.

Inside: deep, foam-padded, hi-back buckets in optional houndstooth check cloth and vinyl.

Outside: optional houndstooth check vinyl roof available in medium brown (shown) or black.

MERCURY COUGAR — Ford

Turn, Turn, Turn | 253

ACKNOWLEDGMENTS

Most of the imagery in this book came from vintage ads, brochures, and marketing materials. We are indebted to those professional and amateur archivists who have saved, cataloged, and scanned these materials and made them available. Although we had many originals in our collections or purchased them from online sellers, the ability to research large amounts of material online was invaluable. There were several resources we didn't directly use material from, but they really helped us in the hunt.

Most of the paper originals we scanned had been originally mass-produced with large dot screens, had become yellowed with age, were torn or slightly damaged, or otherwise were not the best for print reproduction. Rather than present these items in their current flawed state, we chose to present everything in the way they would have originally appeared in the most ideal situation. That meant hours of extensive retouching, descreening, and color correction, with the goal to present the past in the way it was intended when new—bright, crisp, richly colored, and full of glamour.

The task of discovering and then locating over 500 images—and the stories that go with them—was monumental. We couldn't have done it without some help, and special thanks go to the following:

Antique Automobile Association of America (AACA) Library, Hershey, PA—Mike Reilly, catalog librarian. The AACA Library is the premier automotive library in the world, housing nearly three million documents, ads, photographs, manuals, books, and more. The library is free and open to the general public six days a week. The AACA Library was formed in 1977 and merged with the Antique Automobile Club of America in January 2008. The AACA promotes the preservation and enjoyment of automotive history of all types and is a 501(C)(3) charitable organization. Visit AACALibrary.org for more information.

The Automotive Design Oral History Project, University of Michigan

Brett Barris

Central Electric Railfans' Association

The Detroit Public Library

Bobby Dezarov

Phil Fogel*

General Motors Research & Licensing, Archive and Special Collections—Larry Kinsel

Blaine Jenkins*

JEVPIC

Alden Jewell (flickr.com/people/autohistorian)

Gere Kavanaugh

Ross Klein

Daniel Lewandowski (dannylewandowski.com/paul-rand.html)

Chris Menrad

Motorcities.org

Museum of History and Industry (Seattle)

The Old Car Manual Project—Rusty Petrovic, webmaster (oldcarmanualproject.com, oldcarbrochures.com, oldcaradvertising.com)

The Online Imperial Club (imperialclub.com)

Brad Prescott, The Prescott Collection

Jim Secreto

Jim Shulman

Susan Skarsgard

And to our senior editors at Schiffer Publishing, **Cheryl Weber and Karla Rosenbusch.**

*deceased

◀ 1968 Oldsmobile brochure

NOTES

Chapter 2

1. Press release from the Museum of the City of New York, "Everything is Design: The Work of Paul Rand," on view at the Museum of the City of New York. (New York: Feb. 2015).

Chapter 3

1. Dr. Paul R. Woudenberg, *Lincoln and Continental: The Postwar Years* (Osceola, WI: Motorbooks International, 1980).

Chapter 6

1. C. Gayle Warnock, *The Edsel Affair* (Paradise Valley, AZ: Pro West, 1980).

Chapter 8

1. Mary Norris, *Detroit News* (March 6, 1949).
2. Helene Rother, Society of Automotive Engineers (Nov. 15, 1948).
3. 1954 La Comtesse Concept Car, Imperialclub.com.
4. Sue Vanderbilt, Midwest College Placement Association (April 22, 1986).

Chapter 9

1. Dye transfer print, Moma.org.

Chapter 10

1. Blaine Jenkins, author conversation (2012).
2. Dr. Paul R. Woudenberg, *Lincoln and Continental: The Postwar Years* (Osceola, WI: Motorbooks International, 1980).
3. *The Mustang Story,* Ford press release (Sept. 17, 2013).
4. Gail D. Brown, *Mlive.com* (Dec. 7, 2013).
5. Ibid.
6. "George Barris Sonny & Cher's Mustangs: We Got Two Babe," Ford performance vehicles press release (August 9, 2018).
7. "The Mustang Story," Ford Press Release (Sept. 17, 2013).

Chapter 11

1. Ross Klein, author conversation (2015).

Chapter 12

1. Mary Wells Lawrence, *A Big Life (in Advertising)*, (New York: Touchstone, 2002).
2. Ibid.

BIBLIOGRAPHY

Books and Publications

Art Directors Club of New York, The. *32nd Annual Annual of Advertising and Editorial Art.* New York: Visual Arts Books, 1953.

Arts & Architecture Magazine. Artsandarchitecture.com.

Berghoff, Bruce. *The GM Motorama Dream Cars of the Fifties.* Osceola, WI: Motorbooks International, 1995.

"Bernice Fitz-Gibbon, 87, Dies; Retail Advertising Specialist." *New York Times*, Feb. 25, 1982.

Chrysler *Events*, Feb.-March 1956.

Dammann, George H., and James K. Wagner. *The Cars of Lincoln-Mercury.* Sarasota, FL: Crestline, 1987.

"Front Matter." *Michigan Historical Review 44*, no. 2. 2018. Jstor.org.

Girard, A. H., and W. D. Laurie Jr., eds. *An Exhibition for Modern Living.* Exhibition catalog. Detroit: Detroit Institute of Arts, 1949.

Krevsky, Margery. *Sirens of Chrome: The Enduring Allure of Auto Show Models.* Momentum Books, 2008.

Langworth, Richard M. "Carleton Spencer: Kaiser's King of Color." *Collectible Automobile*, Oct. 2009.

Langworth, Richard M. *Kaiser-Frazer: The Last Onslaught on Detroit.* Princeton, NJ: Princeton, 1975.

Moloney, James H. *Studebaker Cars.* Osceola, WI: Motorbooks International, 1994.

"Only in the U.S.A." *House and Garden Magazine*, July 1949. Condé Nast.

Semuels, Alana. "The Role of Highways in American Poverty." *The Atlantic*, March 18, 2016.

Skarsgard, Susan. *Where Today Meets Tomorrow: Eero Saarinen and the General Motors Technical Center.* New York: Princeton Architectural Press, 2019.

Smith, Constance A. *Damsels in Design: Women Pioneers in the Automobile Industry, 1939–1959.* Atglen, PA: Schiffer, 2018.

Spivack, Emily. "Stocking Series, Part 1: Wartime Rationing and Nylon Riots." *Smithsonian Magazine*, Sept. 4, 2012.

Strohl, Daniel. "Fact Check: Did a GM president really tell Congress 'What's good for GM is good for America?'" *Hemmings*, Sept. 5, 2019.

Stuever, Hank. "They Always Said Cher (and Cockroaches) Could Survive the End of the World. Lately, She's Not So Sure about That." *Washington Post*, Nov. 27, 2018.

Vogue magazine. Conde Nast, Jan. 1, 1959 and Jan. 15, 1960.

White, Constance C.R. "Celebrating Claire McCardell." *New York Times*, Nov. 17, 1998.

Wilcox, Claire. *The Golden Age of Couture: Paris and London, 1947–1957.* London: Victoria and Albert Museum, 2009.

Williams, Jim. *Boulevard Photographic: The Art of Automobile Advertising.* Osceola, WI: Motorbooks International, 1997.

Young, Steve, and Sport Murphy. *Everything's Coming Up Profits: The Golden Age of Industrial Musicals.* New York: Blast Books, 2013.

Websites, Forums, and Online Archives

"1935 Super Eight Vacuum Brakes." Antique Automobile Club of America forum. Forums.aaca.org.

"1950s Overview." Media.volvocars.com.

"1954 Desoto Coronado Info?" Antique Automobile Club of America forum. Forums.aaca.org.

"1954 Pasadena Tournament of Roses Review." Online Imperial Club. Imperialclub.com.

"1959 DeSoto Firesweep Seville Spring Special colors." The Forward Look forum. Forwardlook.net.

American Advertising Federation Hall of Fame. Wikipedia.

Auto/Truck/Fleet Paint Cross Reference. Paintref.com.

Bellis, Mary. "The History of Color Television." Thoughtco.com.

Bernice Fitz-Gibbon. Wikipedia.

Bigman, Alex. "Tripping Out: The History of Psychedelic Design." 2015. 99designs.com.

Bowen Field House, Eastern Michigan Athletics. emueagles.com.

"City of Tomorrow." City of Lakewood, 2004 and 2014. Lakewoodcity.org.

Curious Cumulus Productions. "Patti Page: Riding the Oldsmobile Publicity Machine." Goneautos.com.

DLM Group and the Cadillac & LaSalle Club Museum and Research Center. Newcadillacdatabase.org.

Dye Transfer Print. Moma.org.

Early Television Museum. Earlytelevision.org.

Edmunds forum. "The Mink Test." Forums.edmunds.com.

Esaak, Shelley. "Overview of the Op Art Movement." ThoughtCo.com.

Fiocchi, Carl L., Jr. "A Sustainable Design for the AmericanCommercial Strip Mall." Master's thesis, Graduate School of theUniversity of Massachusetts Amherst, May 2010. Scholarworks.umass.edu.

Fone, Martin. "I Predict a Riot—Part Ten." June 27, 2016. Windowthroughtime.wordpress.com.

Freeman, Tyson. "The 1950s: Post-war America Hitches Up and Heads for the 'burbs." Sept. 30, 1999. Nreionline.com.

G.I. Bill. Great Depression History. History.com.

General Motors Technical Center. Michiganmodern.org.

Gordon, Grace. "We Reveal Exactly What Made Dior's 'New Look' So Revolutionary." Jan. 21, 2019. Savoirflair.com.

Hansen, Jan Olaf. Hometownbuick.com.

Hedgbeth, Llewellyn. "Cadillac in the 'Madmen' Era: Advertising Mid-century Luxury." Secondchancegarage.com.

"International Harvester ... Refrigerators? Femineered!" Phil-are-go.blogspot.com.

Khatam, Ryan. Flickr.com/people/timetravelnow.

Klos, Anna. "Psychedelic Style in Graphic Design." April 21, 2016. Retroavangarda.com.

Lakewood Center photo archive. Lakewood-ca.smugmug.com.

Lehto, Steve. "General Motors Has Had Major Problems with Recalls for at Least 60 Years." June 5, 2015. Jalopnik.com.

"List of Chrysler Transmissions." Wikipedia.

"Lost Show & Concept Cars of GM." Lost-show-cars.blogspot.com.

"Mechanical Power Brakes." Pierce-Arrow Society forum. Dec. 2009. Pierce-arrow.org.

Olito, Frank, and Erin McDowell. "The Oldest Mall in Every State." Businessinsider.com.

Op Art Movement Overview and Analysis. Pop Art Movement Overview and Analysis. TheArtStory.org.

Patti Page Biography. Imdb.com.

"Power Brake Conversion for a 1952?" Cadillac LaSalle Club forum. Forums.cadillaclasalleclub.org.

Pruitt, Sarah. "The Post World War II Boom: How America Got into Gear." History.com.

"Refrigerator Capital of the World." Industrialchicnewsnatterings.blogspot.com.

Rosenberg, Diego. "Wild Muscle Car Paint Colors of the 1960s–1970s: You Won't Believe Who Did It First." Jan. 31, 2019. Hotrod.com.

"See the USA in Your Chevrolet." Wikipedia.

Tafoya, Renée C. "Psychedelia and the Psychedelic Movement, 1960–1975." Visualartsdepartment.wordpress.com.

"The Big Record." Wikipedia.

The Dinah Shore Chevy Show. Wayback Machine Internet Archive. Web.archive.org.

"The First Hasselblad Consumer Camera." Hasselblad.com.

"The Rise of Suburbs." Americanyawp.com.

"These Advertisements Prove Florence Henderson Could Sell You Anything." Metv.com.

Tomes, Jan. "The New Look: How Christian Dior Revolutionized Fashion 70 Years Ago." Dw.com.

TV History. Tvhistory.tv.

Weaver, Scott. "A Look Back at the History of Power-Assisted Brakes." July 16, 2012. Tirereview.com.

Weingroff, Richard F. "Federal-Aid Highway Act of 1956, Creating the Interstate System." *Public Roads*, Summer 1996. Federal Highway Administration. Fhwa.dot.gov.

"World War II Mobilization, 1939–1943." Encyclopedia.com.

Znaimer, Moses. "Philco Predicta." MZTV Museum of Television. Mztv.oncell.com.

Other Media

Bill Hayes and Florence Henderson—This Is OLDSmobility. (LP). Discogs.com.

Did You Buy Your Bond Today? (video). Youtube.com.

Dinah Shore Sings "See the U.S.A in Your Chevrolet". (video). Aaaa.org.

Florence Henderson for Oldsmobile (video). Vimeo.com.

Good News About Olds (Oldsmobile's 1959 Announcement Show). (LP) Discogs.com.

Inside U.S.A. with Chevrolet. (TV show). Imdb.com.

McGuire, Bill. *Video: GM's Last Motorama, 1961. Video: Patti Page Pitches the 1958 Oldsmobile. Video: The Sensational 1953 GM Motorama.* Macsmotorcitygarage.com.

The Patti Page Oldsmobile Show (TV show). Imdb.com.

The Solid Gold Cadillac (Broadway play). Ibdb.com.

Bibliography | 255

Virgil Exner, director of styling for Chrysler Corporation, 1953. This photo was part of an elaborate, large-scale brochure that promoted the styling department and Exner's role there since 1949. Photo by Vogue fashion photographer John Rawlings.

256 | GLAMOUR ROAD

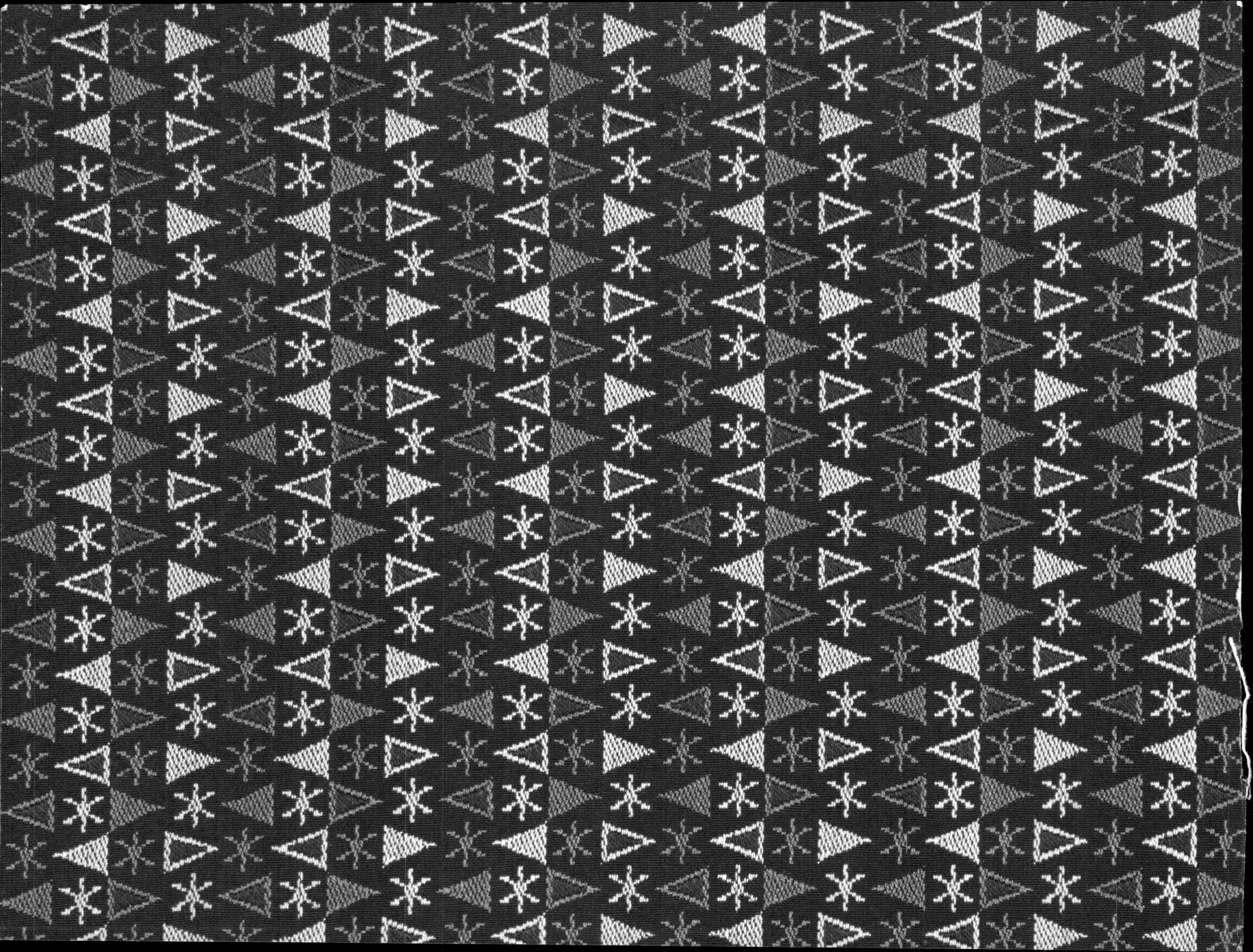